CHiCKEN WiNGS

BY MICHAEL AND STEFAN STRASSER

To Cynthia!
Enjoy our
"Fowl" jokes!

CHICKEN WINGS 3 – THINK BIG
AVIATION COMICS AND CARTOONS BY MICHAEL AND STEFAN STRASSER

Copyright © 2008 by Michael and Stefan Strasser

ISBN 978-1-60702-858-1

Published by Michael and Stefan Strasser
www.chickenwingscomics.com
info@roost-air.com

Printed in china through LASERWAVE INC.
Published November 2008

To Connie and Heidi

Authors' note

We want to take this opportunity to thank you, our readers! We received so much positive feedback after our second book. Interestingly enough, about 90% of it was something along the lines of "Where is the new book?" and "I already read the second one twenty times, where is number three?" or "How much longer until the next book?" and "Yada yada yada!" So, here it is! We hope it will quench your insatiable appetite for flying chickens until number four comes out!

COME ON! MOVE!! I'M AT FULL THROTTLE ALREADY WHY WON'T YOU MOVE?!?
FINALLY!!
HOP
WHOA, SOMEBODY SHOULD REALLY FIX THAT CRACK IN THE TAXIWAY. IT'S GOTTA BE HUGE!
YEAH, I'M SURE THAT'S WHAT IT WAS.
© Michael and Stefan Strasser - 238
www.chickenwingscomics.com

© Michael and Stefan Strasser - 232
www.chickenwingscomics.com
OKAY, FOR THE LAST TIME: I AM SORRY FOR SCRATCHING THE WINGTIP ON THE HANGAR DOOR FIVE WEEKS AGO!!

HANS, YOUR ACCOUNTANT WANTS TO KNOW WHY YOU CHARGED CHOCOLATE CAKE TO YOUR EXPENSES.
TELL HIM TO FILE IT UNDER "MEALS AND ENTERTAINMENT".
© Michael and Stefan Strasser - 294
MHM... OH, AHA! YES, I SEE.
www.chickenwingscomics.com
HE SAYS THAT'S NOT THE POINT. HE SAYS YOU ARE GOOD ON DEDUCTIONS THIS YEAR. WHAT YOU NEED IS ***INCOME!***

WHAT ARE YOU DOING?
I JUST HAD AN IDEA HOW TO MAKE OUR PLANES FLY BETTER AND SAFER.
© Michael and Stefan Strasser - 220
OH! SO... ARE YOU LOOKING FOR A BETTER ENGINE?
NO.
A STORM RADAR?
NOT EXACTLY.
www.chickenwingscomics.com
HEY! WAIT JUST A SECOND! YOU ARE READING THE PILOT CLASSIFIEDS!!

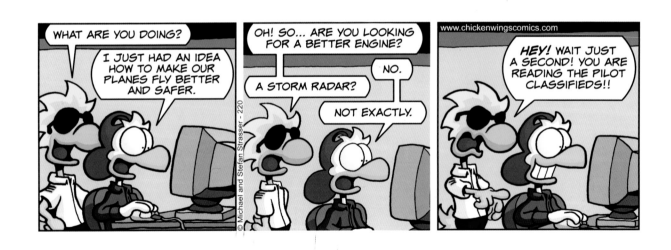

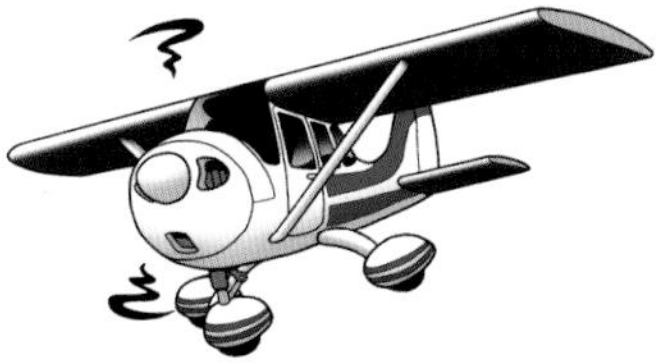

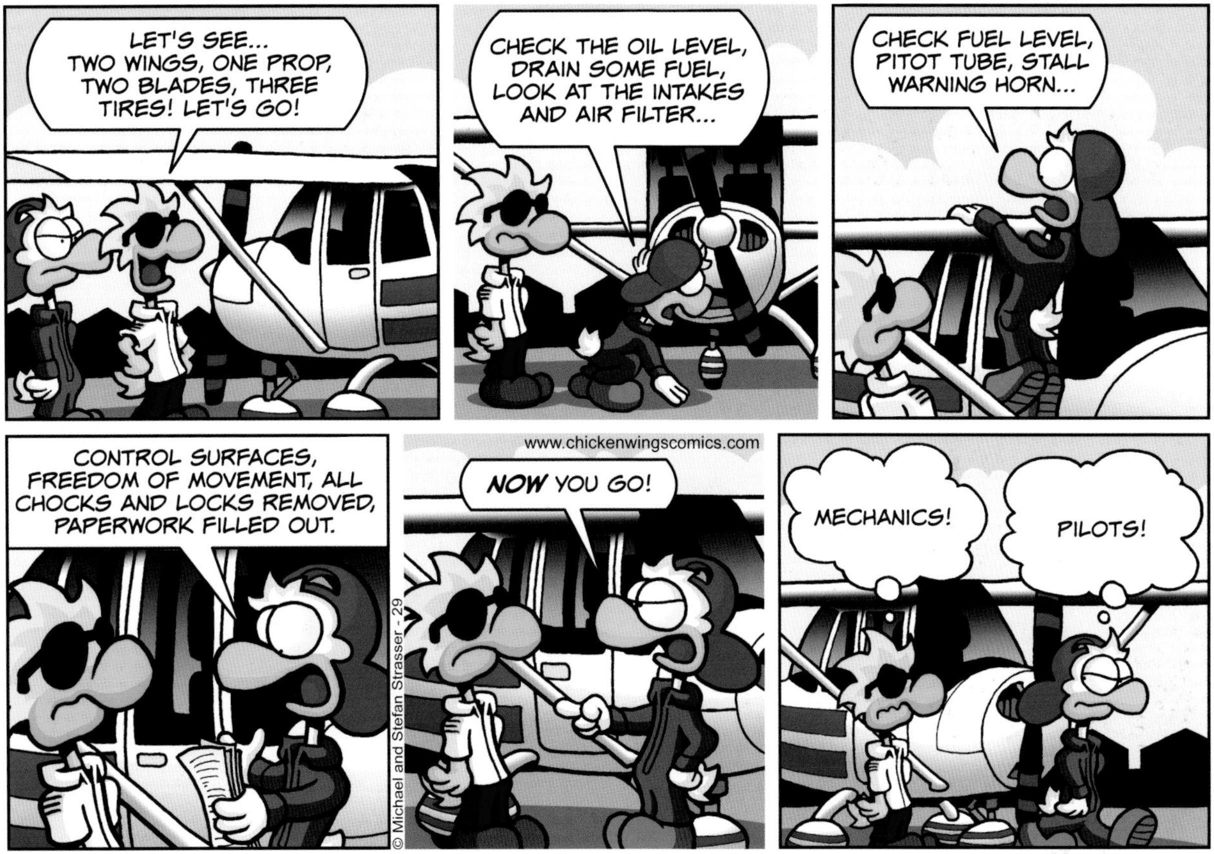
LET'S SEE... TWO WINGS, ONE PROP, TWO BLADES, THREE TIRES! LET'S GO!
CHECK THE OIL LEVEL, DRAIN SOME FUEL, LOOK AT THE INTAKES AND AIR FILTER...
CHECK FUEL LEVEL, PITOT TUBE, STALL WARNING HORN...
CONTROL SURFACES, FREEDOM OF MOVEMENT, ALL CHOCKS AND LOCKS REMOVED, PAPERWORK FILLED OUT.
© Michael and Stefan Strasser - 29
www.chickenwingscomics.com
NOW YOU GO!
MECHANICS!
PILOTS!

THIS HANGAR IS FULL OF USELESS TRASH! IT'S IMPOSSIBE TO WORK HERE!
© Michael and Stefan Strasser - 334
WORRY NOT, MATE! I'LL HELP YOU CLEAN UP!
WHICH PIECE OF JUNK SHALL GO FIRST?
www.chickenwingscomics.com
WHY ARE YOU LOOKING AT ME LIKE THAT?

WHAT'S WRONG? I CAN HEAR YOU CURSING ALL OVER THE AIRPORT!
HNGH!! I CAN'T GET THE STUPID VACUUM PUMP OFF.
CAN I HELP YOU?
NO.
AWW, COME ON! LET ME MAKE YOUR DAY!
© Michael and Stefan Strasser - 222
OKAY... PLEASE TAKE THIS WRENCH AND SLAM IT ON YOUR FOREHEAD.
WHAT? HOW IS THIS GOING TO FIX THE PUMP?!
www.chickenwingscomics.com
IT WON'T FIX THE PUMP... BUT IT WOULD SURELY MAKE MY DAY!

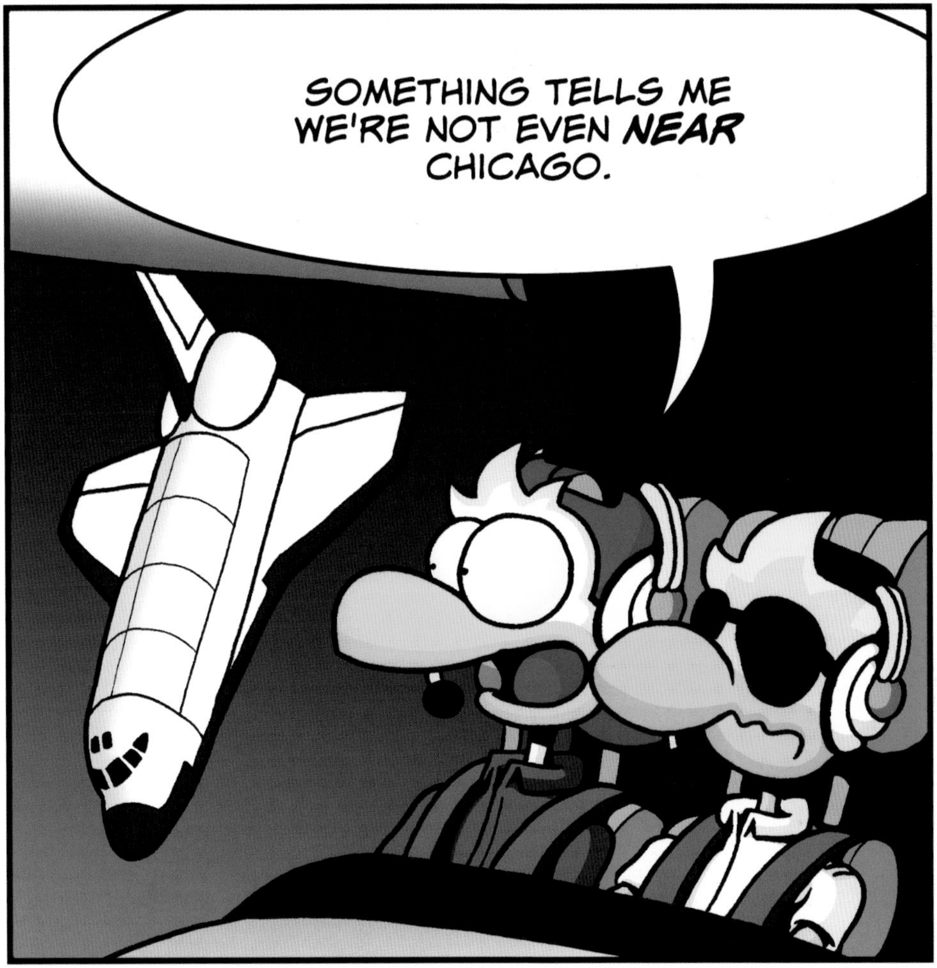
SOMETHING TELLS ME WE'RE NOT EVEN *NEAR* CHICAGO.

HELLO, MY NAME IS NOBUTADA YAKITORI! I'M THE NEW PILOT FROM NEXT DOOR.
NICE TO MEET YOU! I AM CHUCK!
© Michael and Stefan Strasser - 223
www.chickenwingscomics.com
OH! YOU'RE THE FAMOUS CHUCK? I ALREADY HEARD A LOT ABOUT YOU!
HEHE, DON'T BELIEVE A WORD!
DON'T WORRY!
AFTER ALL YOU WOULD HAVE LONG LOST YOUR PILOT LICENSE IF YOU REALLY WERE ***THAT*** STUPID, RIGHT?

HELLO, I'M NOBU!
HE'S THE NEW PILOT FROM NEXT DOOR.
HI!
© Michael and Stefan Strasser - 224
AND NOBU IS SHORT FOR?
YAKITORI NOBUTADA.
NAKAMORI NOBUNAGA? IS THAT JAPANESE?
IT IS, BUT IT'S YA-KI-TO-RI.
WA-KI...
YA-KI.
YA-KI-MO-RI.
TO-RI.
www.chickenwingscomics.com
SO... ***NOBU***, NICE TO MEET YOU!

SO, NOBU, IF YOU'RE FROM JAPAN, DO YOU HAVE ANY PROBLEMS WITH THE LANGUAGE HERE?
WELL, SOMETIMES IT'S A BIT HARD, ESPECIALLY ON THE RADIO.
© Michael and Stefan Strasser - 225
WELL, ISN'T THAT GOOD NEWS FOR YOU, CHUCK?
HUH? WHY?
www.chickenwingscomics.com
IT MEANS THAT YOU'RE NOT THE ONLY ONE ON THIS AIRPORT TO WHOM THE RADIO TALK SOUNDS LIKE A FOREIGN LANGUAGE!

HEY, LET'S GO FOR LUNCH, NOBU. HOW ABOUT SOME SUSHI?
© Michael and Stefan Strasser - 226
YOU HAVE TO BE CAREFUL WITH YOUR STEREOTYPES, CHUCK! JUST BECAUSE I'M JAPANESE DOESN'T MEAN I LIKE SUSHI!
OH, SORRY! YOU DON'T LIKE IT?
www.chickenwingscomics.com
WHAT? NO, I ***LOVE*** SUSHI! C'MON, LET'S TAKE A PICTURE WITH MY DIGITAL CAMERA!

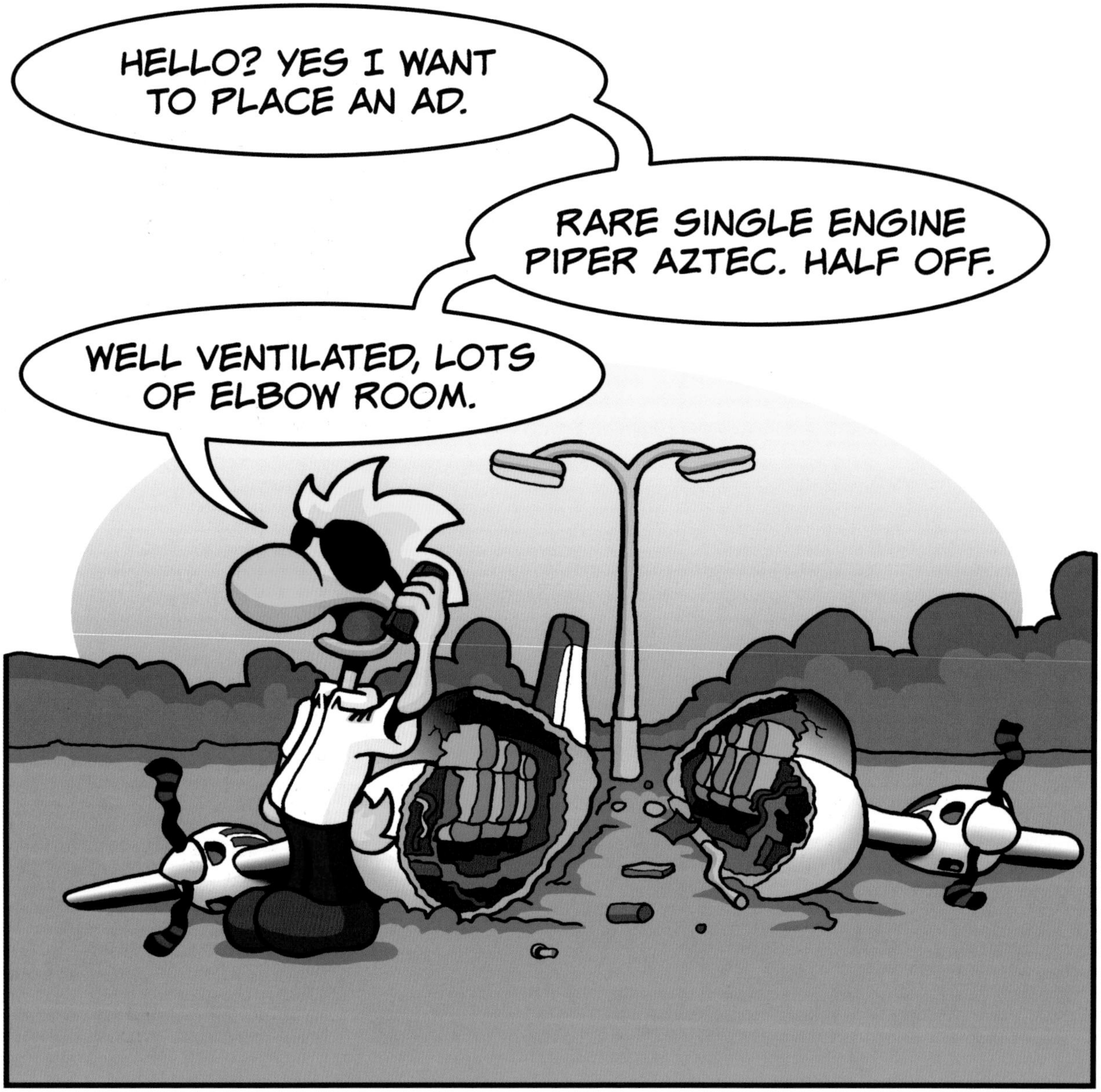
HELLO? YES I WANT TO PLACE AN AD.
RARE SINGLE ENGINE PIPER AZTEC. HALF OFF.
WELL VENTILATED, LOTS OF ELBOW ROOM.

WHEN YOU TAKE OFF WITH THE HELICOPTER, THE FIRST THING YOU DO IS TO TURN THE NOSE INTO THE WIND.
I SEE.
© Michael and Stefan Strasser - 227
www.chickenwingscomics.com
I WAS TALKING ABOUT THE NOSE OF THE HELICOPTER.
A-HA!

HEY CHUCK, CAN YOU HAVE A TIRE BLOW OUT DURING LANDING?
IN THEORY YES, BUT...
REALLY? SO WHAT DO YOU DO THEN?
© Michael and Stefan Strasser - 342
SEE, RIGHT NOW WE...
DOES THE PLANE RUN OFF THE RUNWAY?
JASON!
WILL IT FLIP OVER?
JASON!
www.chickenwingscomics.com
WHAT?
DON'T PANIC! WE'RE FLYING THE HELICOPTER TODAY, REMEMBER?
OH, RIGHT...

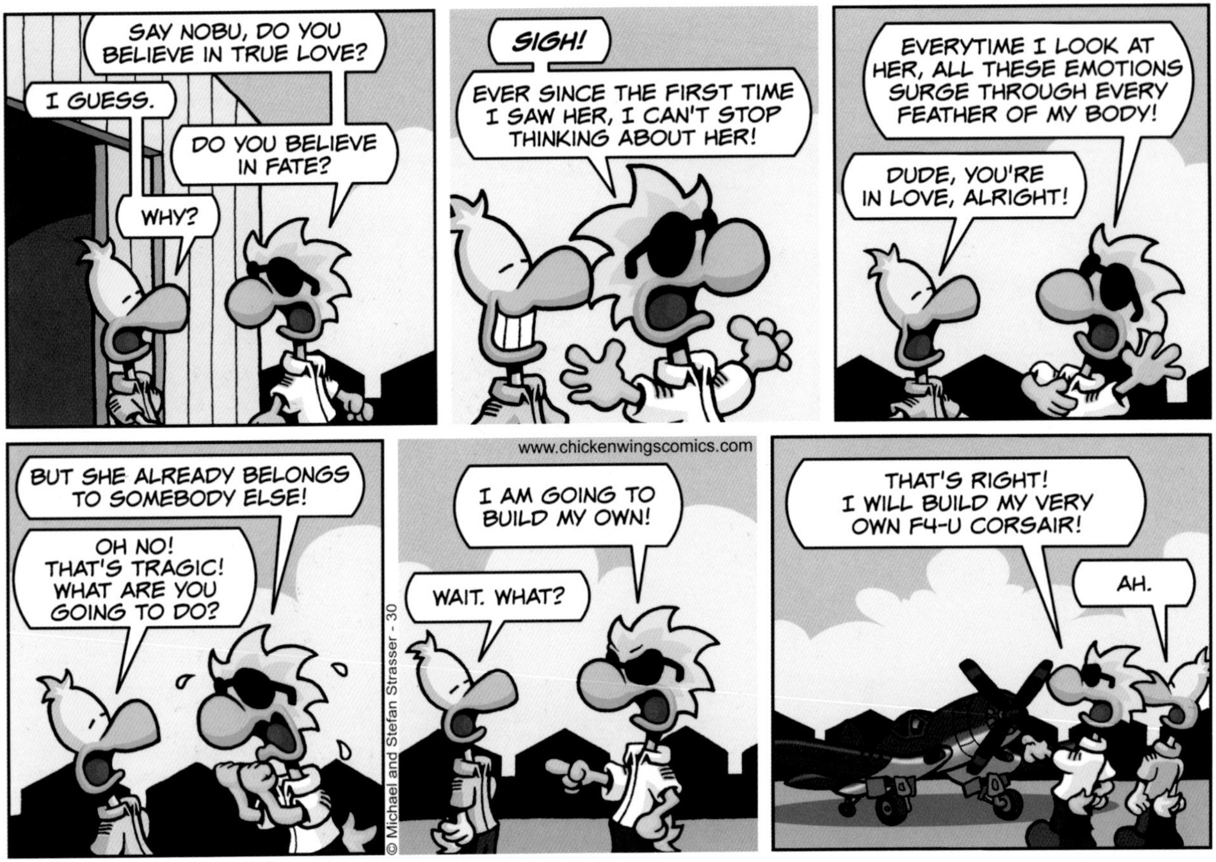
SAY NOBU, DO YOU BELIEVE IN TRUE LOVE?
I GUESS.
WHY?
DO YOU BELIEVE IN FATE?
SIGH!
EVER SINCE THE FIRST TIME I SAW HER, I CAN'T STOP THINKING ABOUT HER!
EVERYTIME I LOOK AT HER, ALL THESE EMOTIONS SURGE THROUGH EVERY FEATHER OF MY BODY!
DUDE, YOU'RE IN LOVE, ALRIGHT!
BUT SHE ALREADY BELONGS TO SOMEBODY ELSE!
OH NO! THAT'S TRAGIC! WHAT ARE YOU GOING TO DO?
© Michael and Stefan Strasser - 30
www.chickenwingscomics.com
I AM GOING TO BUILD MY OWN!
WAIT. WHAT?
THAT'S RIGHT! I WILL BUILD MY VERY OWN F4-U CORSAIR!
AH.

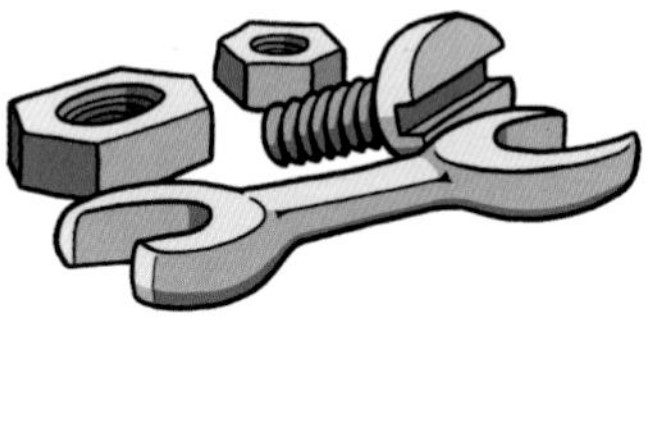

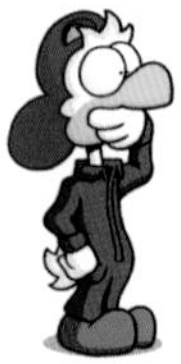

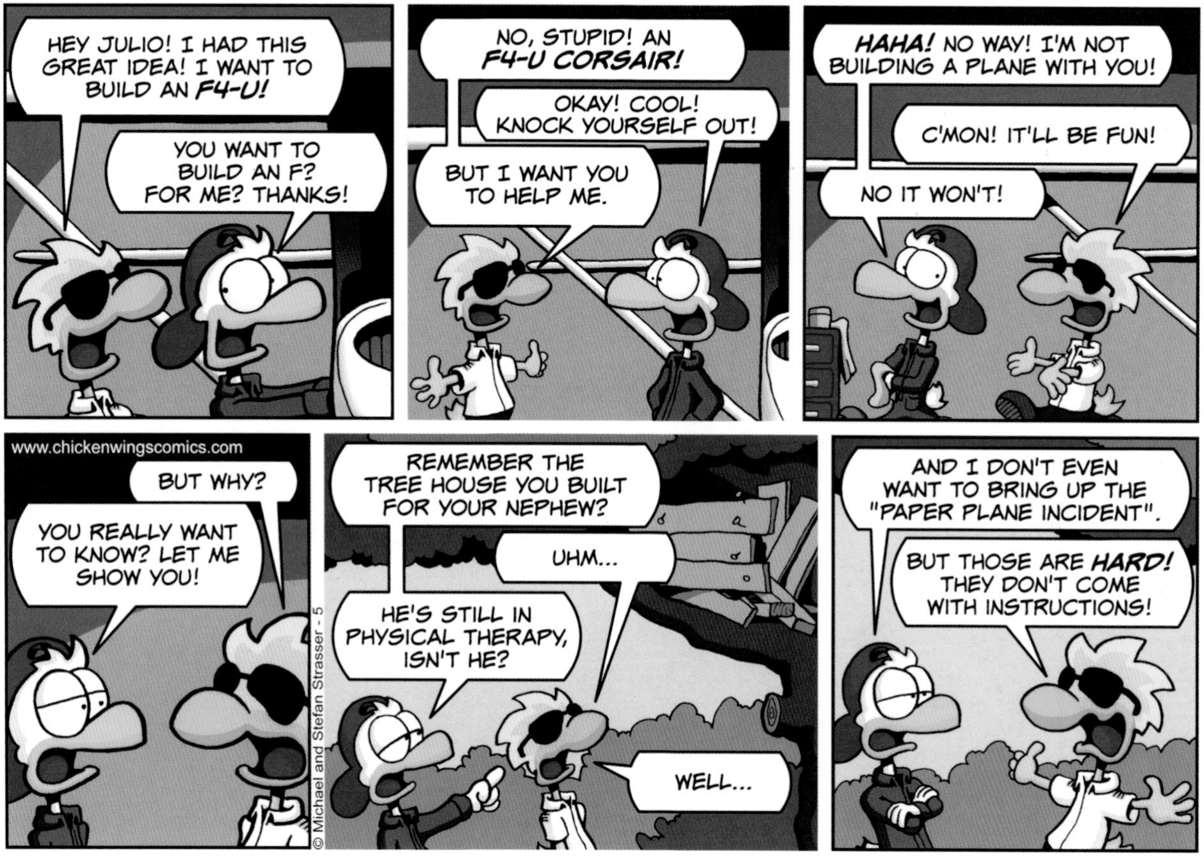
HEY JULIO! I HAD THIS GREAT IDEA! I WANT TO BUILD AN F4-U!
YOU WANT TO BUILD AN F? FOR ME? THANKS!
NO, STUPID! AN F4-U CORSAIR!
OKAY! COOL! KNOCK YOURSELF OUT!
BUT I WANT YOU TO HELP ME.
HAHA! NO WAY! I'M NOT BUILDING A PLANE WITH YOU!
C'MON! IT'LL BE FUN!
NO IT WON'T!
www.chickenwingscomics.com
BUT WHY?
YOU REALLY WANT TO KNOW? LET ME SHOW YOU!
© Michael and Stefan Strasser - 5
REMEMBER THE TREE HOUSE YOU BUILT FOR YOUR NEPHEW?
UHM...
HE'S STILL IN PHYSICAL THERAPY, ISN'T HE?
WELL...
AND I DON'T EVEN WANT TO BRING UP THE "PAPER PLANE INCIDENT".
BUT THOSE ARE HARD! THEY DON'T COME WITH INSTRUCTIONS!

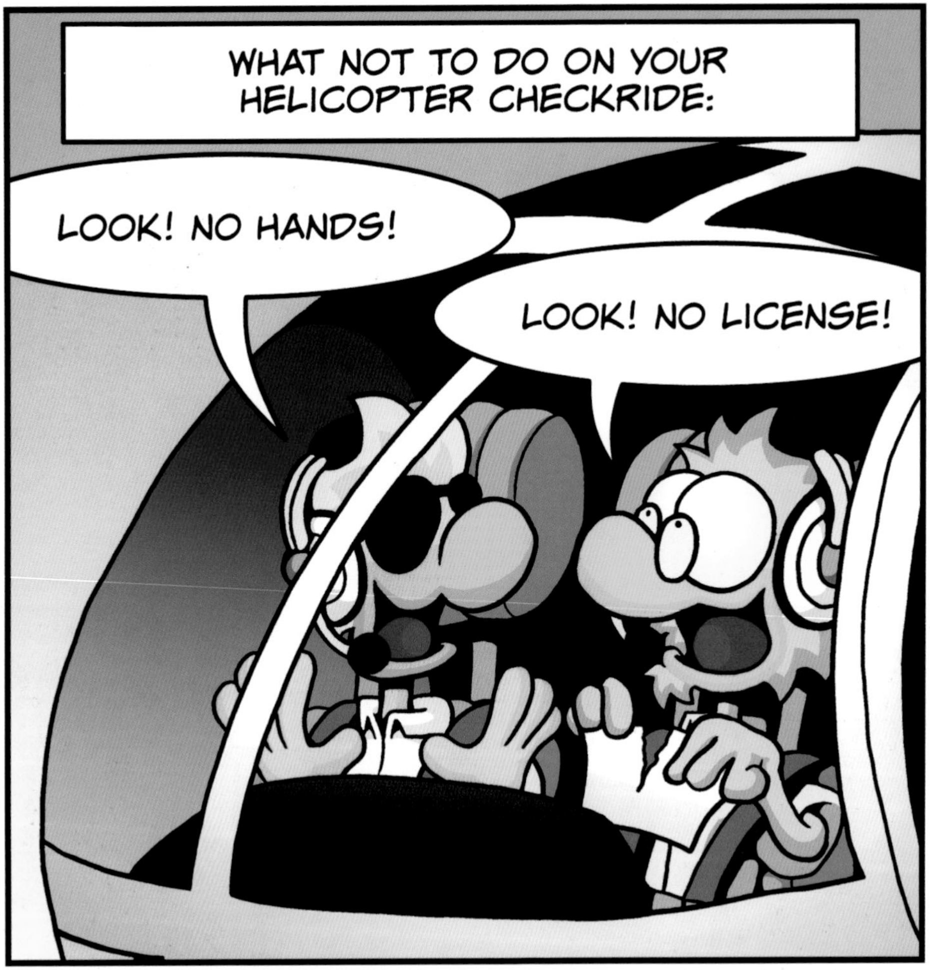
WHAT NOT TO DO ON YOUR HELICOPTER CHECKRIDE:
LOOK! NO HANDS!
LOOK! NO LICENSE!

WHEN THE SAFETY INSPECTOR COMES TODAY, I WANT YOU TO SHOW HIM EVERYTHING IN ITS BEST LIGHT, OKAY JULIO?
SURE, I CAN DO THAT!
© Michael and Stefan Strasser - 242
TELL HIM THAT WE ONLY USE THE VERY BEST TOOLS AND MATERIALS.
NO PROBLEM!
AND THAT WE SPARE NEITHER COST NOR EFFORT TO KEEP OUR AIRCRAFT TOP NOTCH AND 110% SAFE.
PIECE OF CAKE!
www.chickenwingscomics.com
AND TRY TO KEEP A STRAIGHT FACE!
OOH!

SO, DON'T YOU THINK WE SHOULD TURN EASTBOUND NOW?
HANG ON A SECOND!
© Michael and Stefan Strasser - 243
www.chickenwingscomics.com
AHA! SO THE BROWN AREAS ARE LAND AND THE BLUE ONES ARE WATER, RIGHT?
GULP!

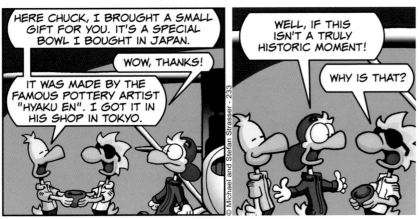

HERE CHUCK, I BROUGHT A SMALL GIFT FOR YOU. IT'S A SPECIAL BOWL I BOUGHT IN JAPAN.
WOW, THANKS!
IT WAS MADE BY THE FAMOUS POTTERY ARTIST "HYAKU EN". I GOT IT IN HIS SHOP IN TOKYO.
© Michael and Stefan Strasser - 233
WELL, IF THIS ISN'T A TRULY HISTORIC MOMENT!
WHY IS THAT?
www.chickenwingscomics.com
THIS IS THE FIRST TIME I COULD ACTUALLY CALL YOU A "GIFTED" PILOT! HEHEHE!

CLANG!
JINGLE
OH NO!
OH NO!
© Michael and Stefan Strasser - 234
OKAY, WHAT DID YOU BREAK THIS TIME?
I DROPPED THE JAPANESE BOWL NOBU GAVE ME.
SEEMS YOU SHOULD HAVE PAID BETTER ATTENTION TO THE SAFETY POSTER!
HUH? WHICH POSTER?
www.chickenwingscomics.com
AVOID F.O.D
"AVOID FOREIGN OBJECT DAMAGE"!
FUNNY, HAHA.

AFTER THE WINGNUT INCIDENT LAST WEEK I DECIDED TO INVEST IN SOME STATE-OF-THE-ART FOREIGN OBJECT SCANNING AND REMOVAL DEVICE FOR THE HANGAR.
SWEET!
© Michael and Stefan Strasser - 236
SOUNDS LIKE SOME NIFTY PIECE OF EQUIPMENT! CAN I TRY IT FIRST?
NO! LET ME TRY IT FIRST! PLEASE!!
www.chickenwingscomics.com
HERE YOU GO! IF I HAD KOWN YOU'D BE SO EAGER, I WOULD HAVE BOUGHT TWO OF THEM.

CHUCK AT THE OSHKOSH AIRVENTURE...
CLICK
CLICK
WOW! COOL!
CHECK THIS OUT! SWEET!
CLICKEDICLICK
CLICK
CLICK
© Michael and Stefan Strasser - 212
www.chickenwingscomics.com
AWWWESOME!!
CLICK
CLICK
CLICK
UMPH... MAN! I REALLY NEED TO GET A DIGITAL CAMERA!

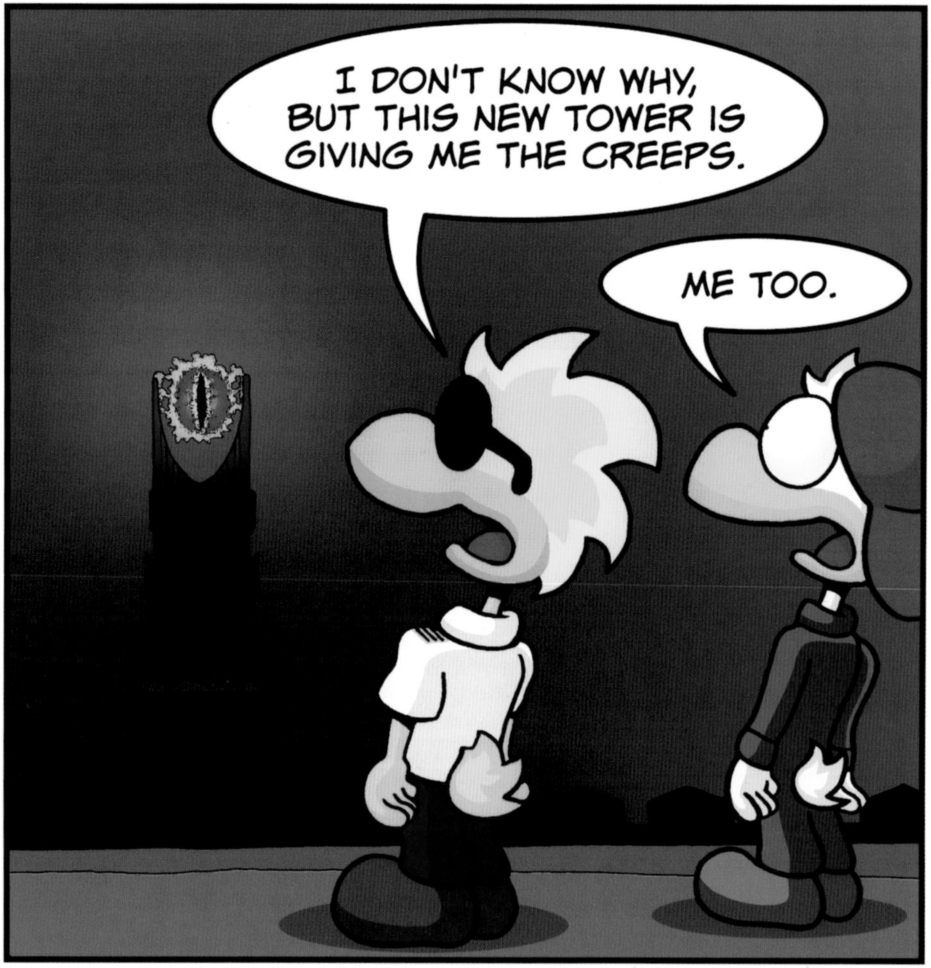
I DON'T KNOW WHY, BUT THIS NEW TOWER IS GIVING ME THE CREEPS.
ME TOO.

AS A PILOT, IT IS VERY IMPORTANT THAT YOU ARE ABLE TO CONCENTRATE AND FOCUS!
I SEE!
© Michael and Stefan Strasser - 213
WOW, LOOK! A CORVETTE STINGRAY!
I'M HUNGRY!
www.chickenwingscomics.com
WHAT TIME IS IT?
I DON'T KNOW... WHAT WERE WE JUST TALKING ABOUT?

HEY JULIO, DO YOU SEE THE EROSION ON THE ROTOR BLADES?
EVERY DAY, MY MAN, EVERY DAY.
© Michael and Stefan Strasser - 332
HOW COME ONE BLADE HAS MORE PAINT MISSING THAN THE OTHERS?
THAT'S BECAUSE IT'S THE "MASTER BLADE". WHEN THE ROTOR TURNS, IT IS THE FIRST ONE TO HIT THE AIR, SO IT GETS MORE ERODED.
REALLY? WOW!
www.chickenwingscomics.com
BOY, HE IS SO GONNA FAIL HIS HELICOPTER CHECKRIDE.
YES, BUT HE IS LEARNING A VALUABLE LESSON FOR HIS AVIATION CAREER.
LIKE WHAT?
DON'T BUG YOUR MECHANIC!

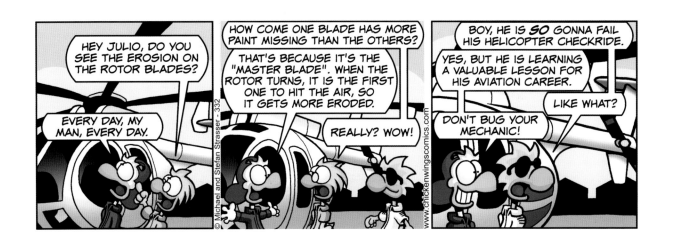

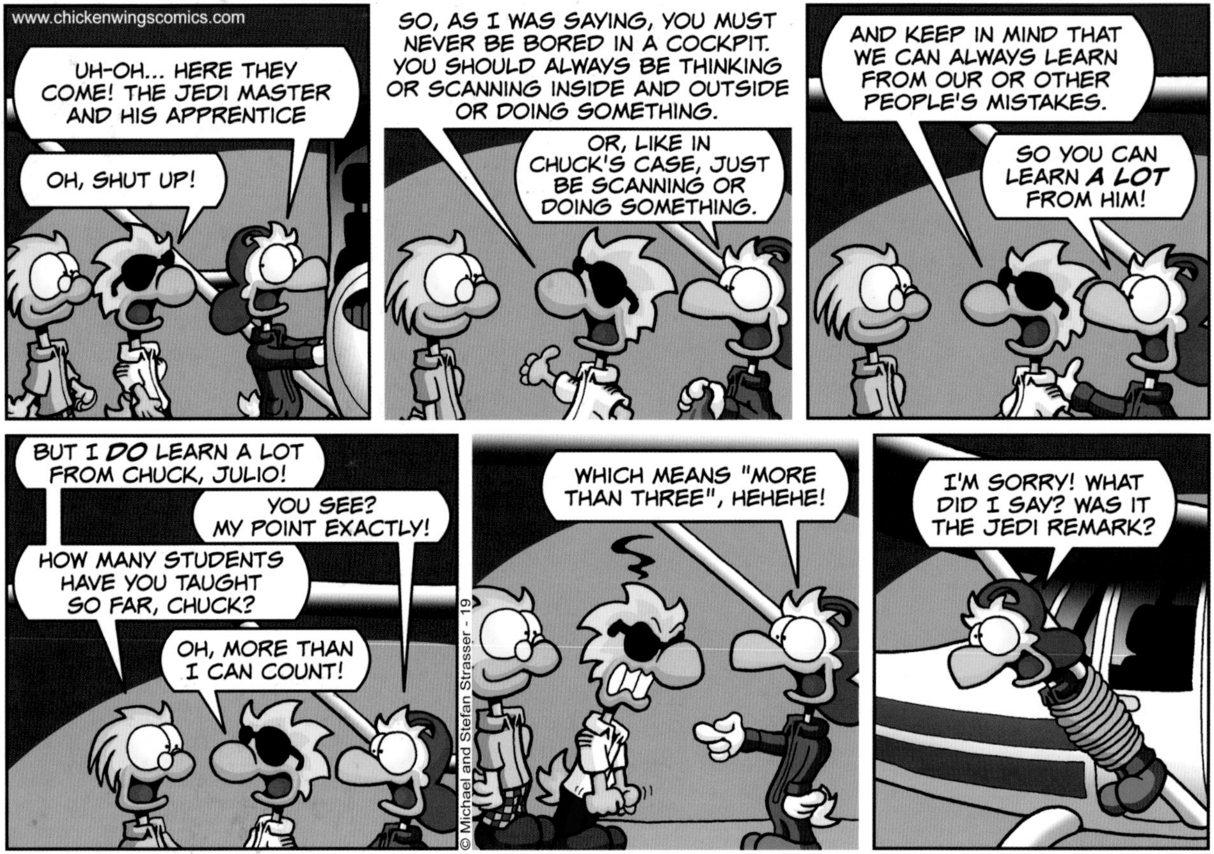
www.chickenwingscomics.com
UH-OH... HERE THEY COME! THE JEDI MASTER AND HIS APPRENTICE
OH, SHUT UP!
SO, AS I WAS SAYING, YOU MUST NEVER BE BORED IN A COCKPIT. YOU SHOULD ALWAYS BE THINKING OR SCANNING INSIDE AND OUTSIDE OR DOING SOMETHING.
OR, LIKE IN CHUCK'S CASE, JUST BE SCANNING OR DOING SOMETHING.
AND KEEP IN MIND THAT WE CAN ALWAYS LEARN FROM OUR OR OTHER PEOPLE'S MISTAKES.
SO YOU CAN LEARN **A LOT** FROM HIM!
BUT I **DO** LEARN A LOT FROM CHUCK, JULIO!
YOU SEE? MY POINT EXACTLY!
HOW MANY STUDENTS HAVE YOU TAUGHT SO FAR, CHUCK?
OH, MORE THAN I CAN COUNT!
© Michael and Stefan Strasser - 19
WHICH MEANS "MORE THAN THREE", HEHEHE!
I'M SORRY! WHAT DID I SAY? WAS IT THE JEDI REMARK?

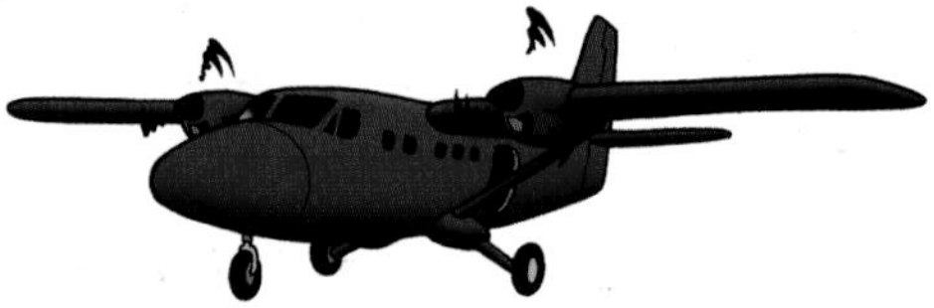

HEY SALLY! TELL JULIO THE POI FROM THE FAA SAID THE VOR/DME ON THE 172 IS INOP.
© Michael and Stefan Strasser - 214
WHY DON'T *YOU* TELL HIM? I'M NOT YOUR SLAVE, YOU KNOW?
UHM... OKAY! SORRY!
www.chickenwingscomics.com
PHEW! THAT WAS CLOSE! I HAD NO IDEA WHAT ANY OF THAT JUST MEANT!

MOVE IT!! SOME OF US ACTUALLY WANT TO GO FLYING ***TODAY!***
© Michael and Stefan Strasser - 215
WHAT IS THIS GUY DOING? HE'S TAXIING REALLY SLOW AND ERRATIC.
HERE, TAKE A CLOSER LOOK!
www.chickenwingscomics.com
OH, OF COURSE... GUESS WHO IT IS, FRANK!

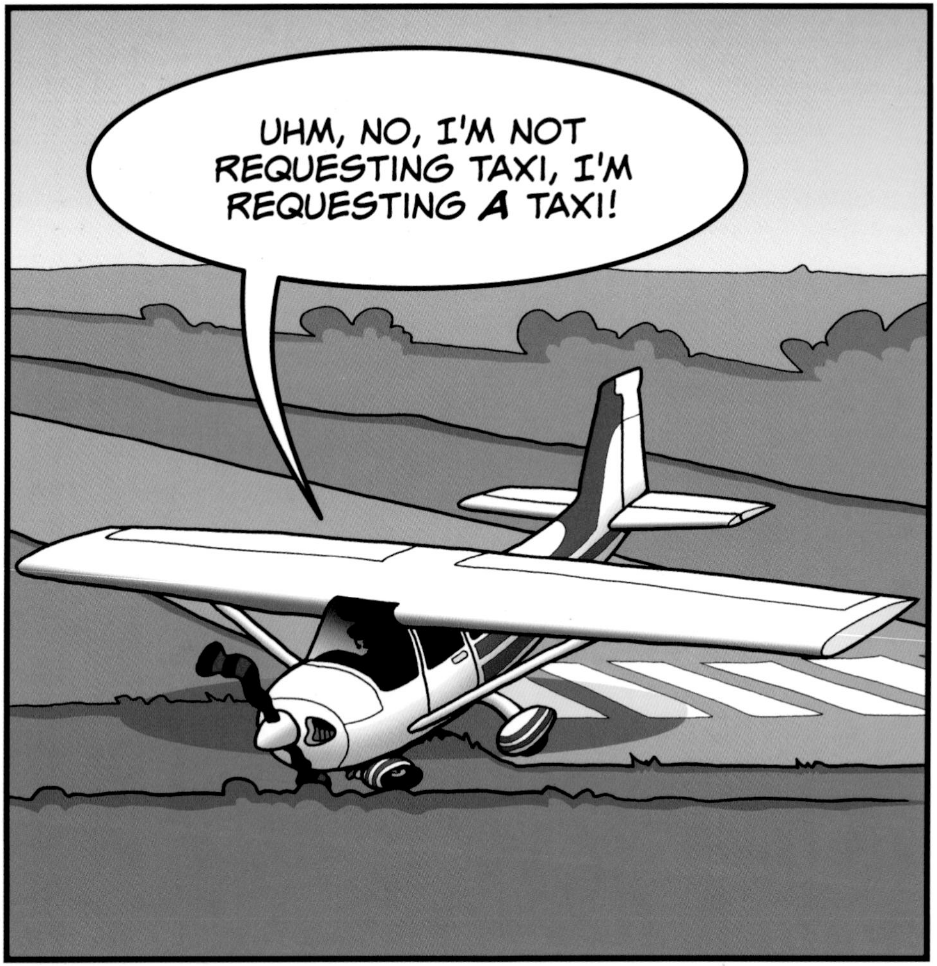
UHM, NO, I'M NOT REQUESTING TAXI, I'M REQUESTING A TAXI!

GOOD MORNING!
GOOD MORNING?! HOW CAN THIS POSSIBLY BE A GOOD MORNING?!
WHAT'S WRONG WITH HIM?
HE JUST FOUND OUT THE NAVY RETIRED THE F-14.
AND HE'S CRYING ABOUT THAT?! THAT'S RIDICULOUS HOW IMMATURE!
© Michael and Stefan Strasser - 216
www.chickenwingscomics.com
BOOHOO!! NOW I'LL NEVER BE A TOP GUN PILOT!!

I DON'T GET IT! WHAT'S SO SAD ABOUT THE F-14 BEING RETIRED?
BUHAA!
© Michael and Stefan Strasser - 217
IT'S LIKE THE F-14 IS THE LAST CHOCOLATE CAKE OF FIGHTER JETS! AND FROM NOW ON IT'S NOTHING BUT BROCCOLI AND CARROTS!
OH NO! BUT THAT'S TERRIBLE!
www.chickenwingscomics.com
GROUP HUG!
SNIFF SO SAD!
SOB BROCCOLI!
BUT THEY DIDN'T RETIRE TOM CRUISE YET, DID THEY?

HEY SALLY, I JUST RAN INTO HANS' WIFE OUTSIDE AND SHE BROUGHT THIS ALMOST COMPLETE CAKE FOR HIM.
THANKS! I'LL TAKE CARE OF IT!
JULIO, HANS' WIFE BROUGHT HALF A CAKE FOR HIM.
OOH! GIVE ME! I'LL TAKE IT TO HIM!
© Michael and Stefan Strasser - 326
CHUCK, COULD YOU GIVE THIS CAKE TO HANS? HIS WIFE JUST DROPPED IT OFF.
PIECE OF CAKE! HEHE!
www.chickenwingscomics.com
UHM, HANS? YOUR WIFE SAYS HI!
THANKS!

THAT'S FUNNY! WHEN LOOKING AT OUR FINANCIAL HISTORY, YOU CAN SEE THAT OUR PROFITS TOOK A NOSEDIVE EXACTLY SEVEN YEARS AGO, AND I CAN'T FIGURE OUT WHY!
© Michael and Stefan Strasser - 231
www.chickenwingscomics.com
WAIT, HOW LONG HAVE YOU BEEN WORKING FOR THIS COMPANY?
HA! I KNEW YOU WERE GOING TO ASK THAT! BUT IT'S SEVEN AND A HALF YEARS!

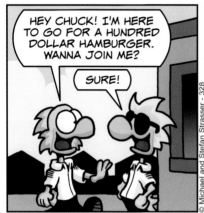

HEY CHUCK! I'M HERE TO GO FOR A HUNDRED DOLLAR HAMBURGER. WANNA JOIN ME?
SURE!
© Michael and Stefan Strasser - 328
OKAY, THE RESTAURANT IS THIS WAY, RIGHT?
HUH? AREN'T WE GOING TO *FLY* ANYWHERE?
www.chickenwingscomics.com
ARE YOU KIDDING? WITH AN SUV LIKE MINE AND TODAY'S GASPRICES, IT ALREADY COST ME A HUNDRED BUCKS JUST TO COME *HERE!*

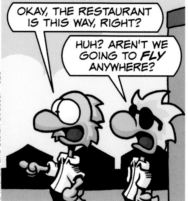

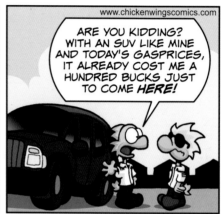

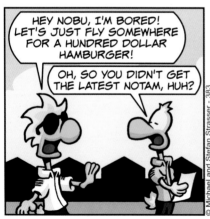

HEY NOBU, I'M BORED! LET'S JUST FLY SOMEWHERE FOR A HUNDRED DOLLAR HAMBURGER!
OH, SO YOU DIDN'T GET THE LATEST NOTAM, HUH?
© Michael and Stefan Strasser - 383
NOTAM? WHAT NOTAM?
DUE TO CURRENT GAS PRICE LEVELS, THE TERM "$100 HAMBURGER" IS TO BE REPLACED BY "$200 HAMBURGER", STARTING JUNE 2008.
www.chickenwingscomics.com
UHM, LET'S JUST GO FOR PIZZA THEN.
OR SUSHI!

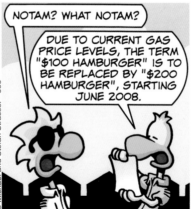

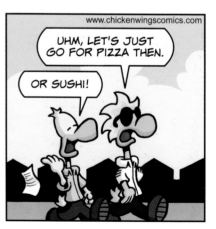

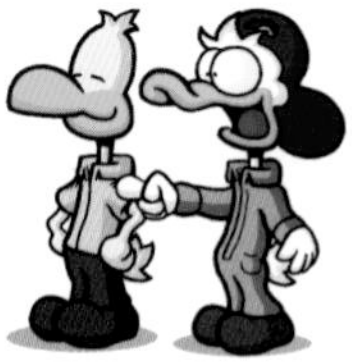

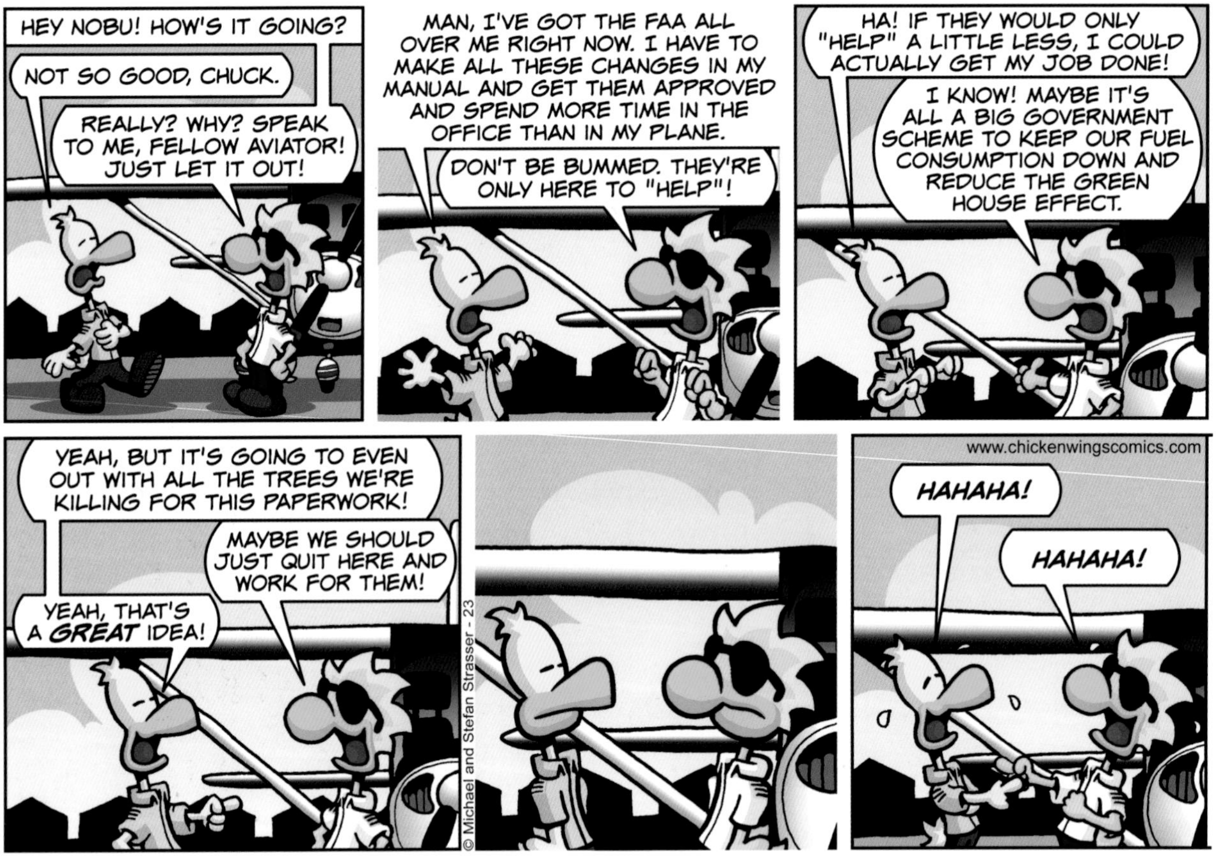
HEY NOBU! HOW'S IT GOING?
NOT SO GOOD, CHUCK.
REALLY? WHY? SPEAK TO ME, FELLOW AVIATOR! JUST LET IT OUT!
MAN, I'VE GOT THE FAA ALL OVER ME RIGHT NOW. I HAVE TO MAKE ALL THESE CHANGES IN MY MANUAL AND GET THEM APPROVED AND SPEND MORE TIME IN THE OFFICE THAN IN MY PLANE.
DON'T BE BUMMED. THEY'RE ONLY HERE TO "HELP"!
HA! IF THEY WOULD ONLY "HELP" A LITTLE LESS, I COULD ACTUALLY GET MY JOB DONE!
I KNOW! MAYBE IT'S ALL A BIG GOVERNMENT SCHEME TO KEEP OUR FUEL CONSUMPTION DOWN AND REDUCE THE GREEN HOUSE EFFECT.
YEAH, BUT IT'S GOING TO EVEN OUT WITH ALL THE TREES WE'RE KILLING FOR THIS PAPERWORK!
MAYBE WE SHOULD JUST QUIT HERE AND WORK FOR THEM!
YEAH, THAT'S A ***GREAT*** IDEA!
© Michael and Stefan Strasser - 23
www.chickenwingscomics.com
HAHAHA!
HAHAHA!

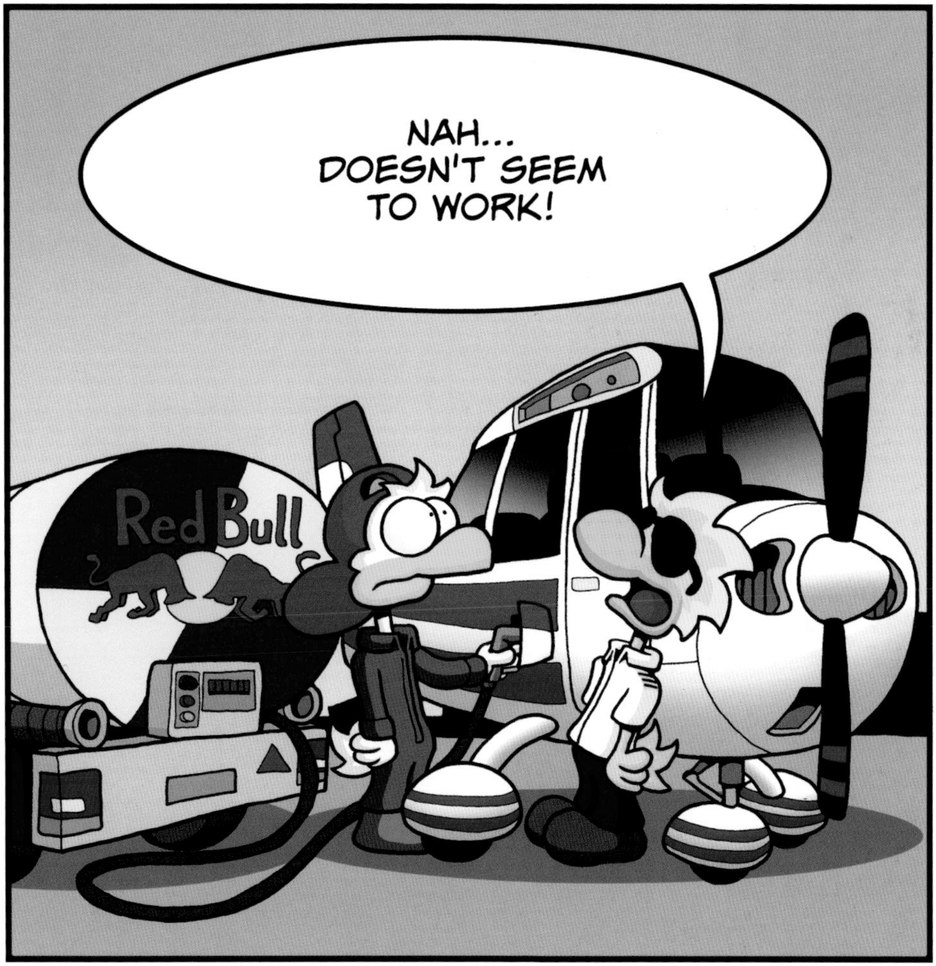
NAH...
DOESN'T SEEM
TO WORK!
Red Bull

SO, WHAT IS THE POINT OF FLYING GLIDERS?
IT'S FUN!
HOW CAN IT BE FUN, IF YOU DON'T HAVE A TURBOCHARGER, ENGINE NOISE OR A TACHGAGE?
© Michael and Stefan Strasser - 244
WELL, THAT'S THE WHOLE POINT! WE DON'T NEED A TACHGAGE TO HAVE FUN!
REALLY?
www.chickenwingscomics.com
BUT... WITHOUT A TACHGAGE... HOW DO YOU MEASURE HOW MUCH FUN YOU ARE HAVING?

THE REAL CHARM OF FLYING A GLIDER IS THE PEACE AND QUIET YOU CAN ENJOY UP THERE!
PEACE AND QUIET, HUH?
WELL, BUT YOU STILL HEAR THE RADIO AND THE WIND, RIGHT?
© Michael and Stefan Strasser - 245
www.chickenwingscomics.com
AND ISN'T IT SCARY NOT TO HEAR THE COMFORTING SOUND OF AN ENGINE? OH, AND CAN YOU HEAR THE SPAR BENDING AT HIGH LOADS? DO YOU HEAR THE TOW PLANE ON THE WAY UP?
ARE GLIDERS SINGLE SEATERS?
MOST OF THEM.
I'M BEGINNING TO SEE THE ATTRACTION!
WHAT? HUH? I DON'T! CAN YOU TELL ME?

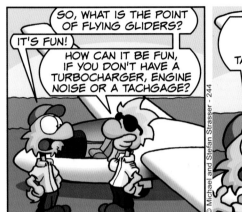

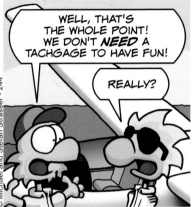

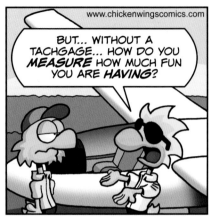

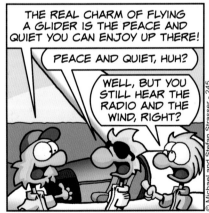

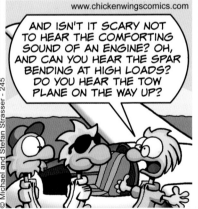

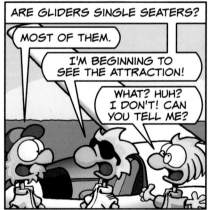

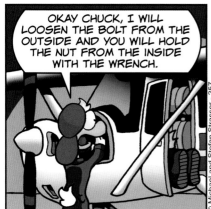

OKAY CHUCK, I WILL LOOSEN THE BOLT FROM THE OUTSIDE AND YOU WILL HOLD THE NUT FROM THE INSIDE WITH THE WRENCH.
© Michael and Stefan Strasser - 257
THERE IS ALMOST NO WAY TO GET DOWN THERE IF YOU MESS THIS UP. SO WHATEVER YOU DO, MAKE SURE YOU DON'T DROP THE...
CLANG
CLING
CLONK!
UH-OH.
www.chickenwingscomics.com
UHM... YOU WEREN'T GONNA SAY "WRENCH", WERE YOU?

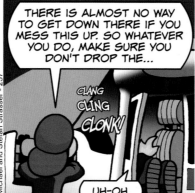

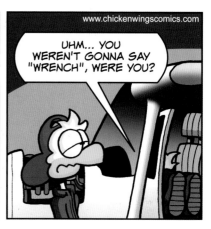

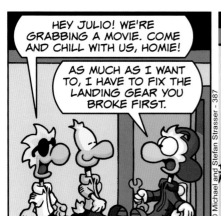

HEY JULIO! WE'RE GRABBING A MOVIE. COME AND CHILL WITH US, HOMIE!
AS MUCH AS I WANT TO, I HAVE TO FIX THE LANDING GEAR YOU BROKE FIRST.
© Michael and Stefan Strasser - 387
www.chickenwingscomics.com
AND *THEN* I HAVE TO DO AN INSPECTION ON THE PIPER AND *THEN* I HAVE TO CLEAN THE HANGAR!
WELL, TO EACH HIS OWN, I GUESS.
MECHANICS. THEY JUST DON'T KNOW HOW TO RELAX.

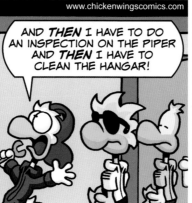

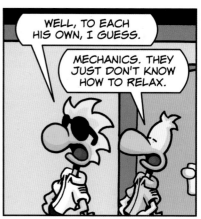

HEY JULIO! THANKS FOR FIXING THE ENGINE! THERE IS NO MORE MORE OIL DRIPPING NOW.
YOU'RE WELCOME!
© Michael and Stefan Strasser - 318
www.chickenwingscomics.com
ABOUT TIME TO ADD SOME OIL AGAIN, HUH?
I'LL SAY!

...SO MINE GOT ALL MAD AT ME AND DIDN'T TALK TO ME ALL DAY.
SHEESH, THEY CAN BE SO MOODY! MINE EXPECTS ME TO JUST DROP EVERYTHING AND FIX WHATEVER THE LATEST EMERGENCY IS.
THEY ARE SO SELFISH, HUH?
© Michael and Stefan Strasser - 354
www.chickenwingscomics.com
MOODY AND SELFISH!
AND ALWAYS CONCERNED ABOUT THEIR LOOKS!
NOW WAIT A MINUTE! NOT ALL WOMEN ARE LIKE THAT!
WOMEN?
WE'RE TALKING ABOUT OUR **PILOTS**.
OH!

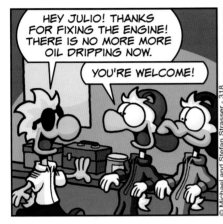

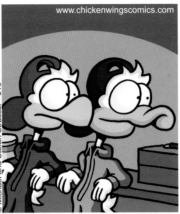

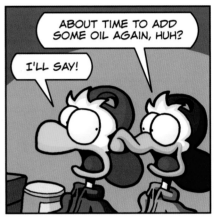

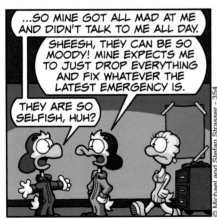

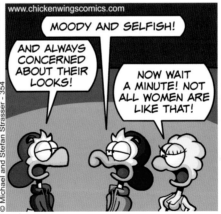

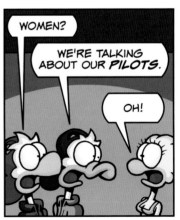

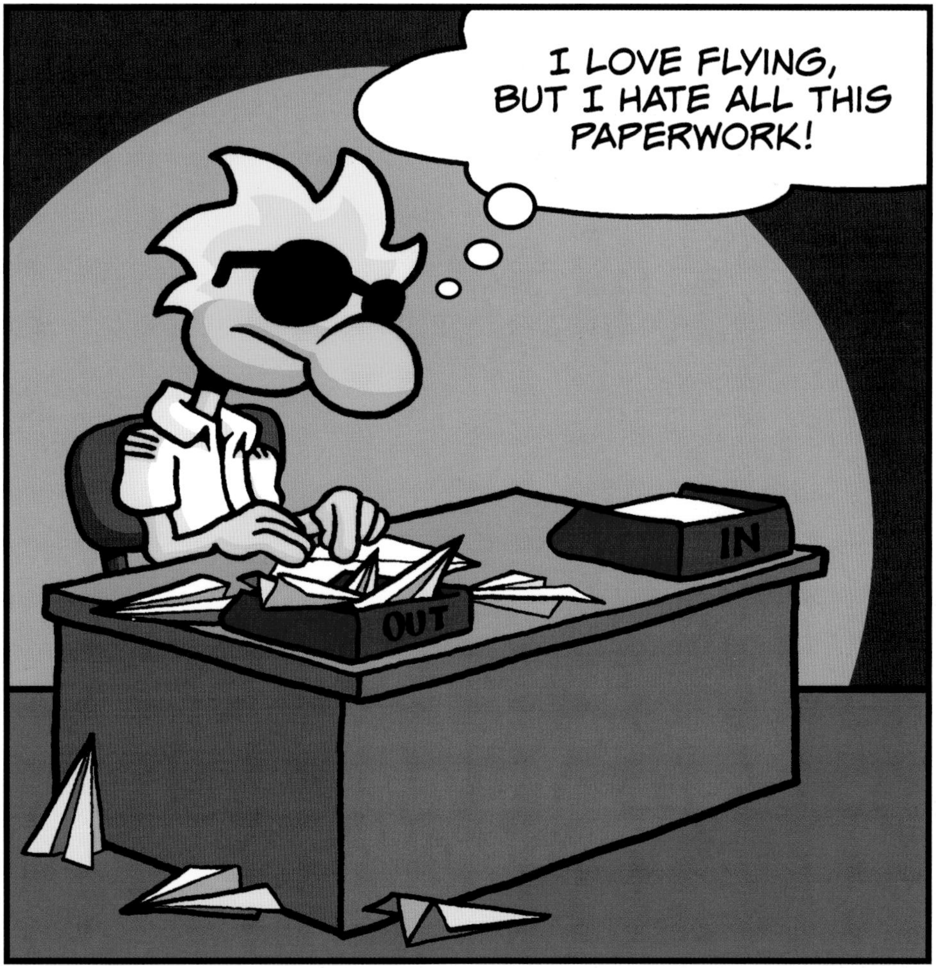
I LOVE FLYING, BUT I HATE ALL THIS PAPERWORK!
IN
OUT

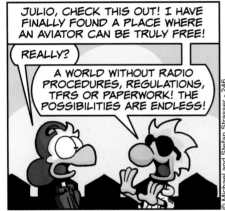

JULIO, CHECK THIS OUT! I HAVE FINALLY FOUND A PLACE WHERE AN AVIATOR CAN BE TRULY FREE!
REALLY?
A WORLD WITHOUT RADIO PROCEDURES, REGULATIONS, TFRS OR PAPERWORK! THE POSSIBILITIES ARE ENDLESS!
© Michael and Stefan Strasser - 246
www.chickenwingscomics.com
ARE YOU GOING TO MOVE TO SOME BACKWATER COUNTRY SOMEWHERE?
WHAT?! NO!
I GOT MYSELF AN AEROBATIX 200 XL! WITH A SIXTEEN CHANNEL REMOTE CONTROL!
WOW, COOL! IT'S GONNA MAKE "OUR" WORLD SUCH A SAFER PLACE IN THE MEANTIME!

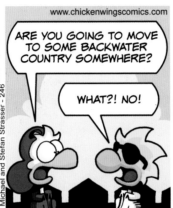

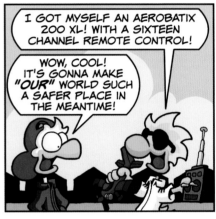

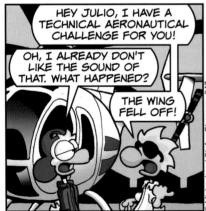

HEY JULIO, I HAVE A TECHNICAL AERONAUTICAL CHALLENGE FOR YOU!
OH, I ALREADY DON'T LIKE THE SOUND OF THAT. WHAT HAPPENED?
THE WING FELL OFF!
© Michael and Stefan Strasser - 247
THE WHAT?! DID WHAT?!?! ...HOW?
IT HIT THE HANGAR.
BUT, BUT...
RELAX! IT'S JUST A WING!
SEE? I NEED SOME GLUE OR SOMETHING, RIGHT?
DON'T YOU EVER DO THIS AGAIN, YOU HEAR? YOU JUST SHORTENED MY LIFE SPAN BY FIVE YEARS!
WHAT?
www.chickenwingscomics.com

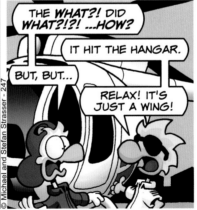

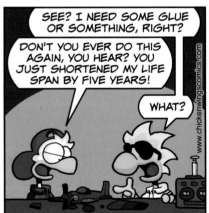

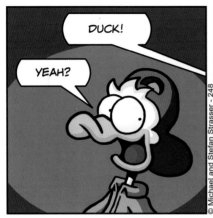

DUCK!
YEAH?
© Michael and Stefan Strasser - 248
VROOOM
AARGH!
www.chickenwingscomics.com
I SAID DUCK!

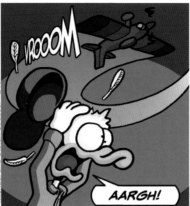

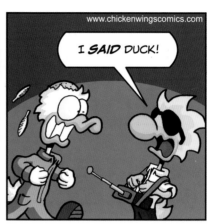

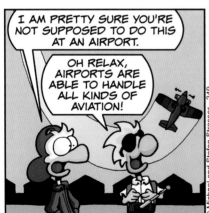

I AM PRETTY SURE YOU'RE NOT SUPPOSED TO DO THIS AT AN AIRPORT.
OH RELAX, AIRPORTS ARE ABLE TO HANDLE ALL KINDS OF AVIATION!
© Michael and Stefan Strasser - 249
www.chickenwingscomics.com
WHAT IF YOUR MODEL GETS SUCKED INTO A PROPELLER OR SOMETHING?
JEEZ, MR. NEGATIVE! I JUST CHECKED, AND THERE ARE NO PLANES FLYING LOW HERE!
NO, BUT HELICOPTERS...

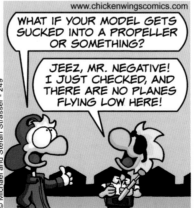

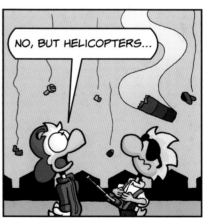

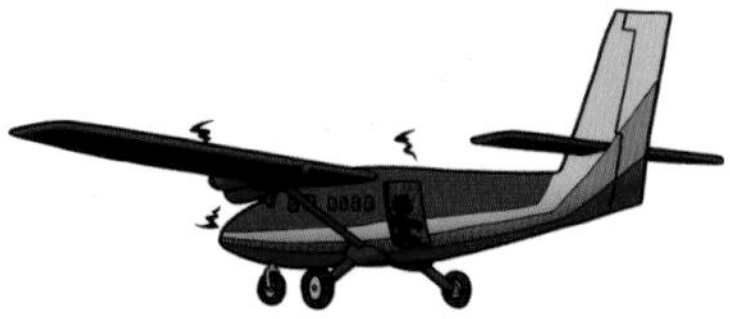

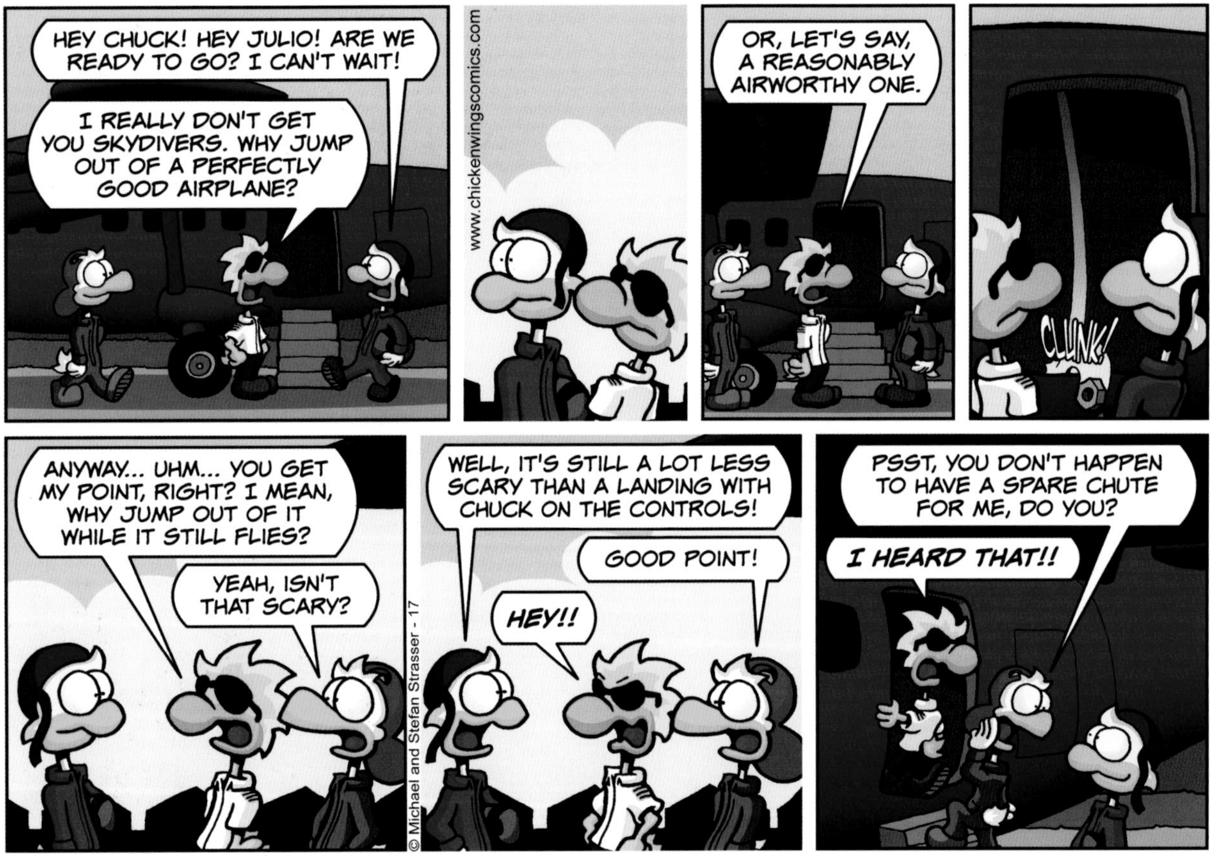
HEY CHUCK! HEY JULIO! ARE WE READY TO GO? I CAN'T WAIT!
I REALLY DON'T GET YOU SKYDIVERS. WHY JUMP OUT OF A PERFECTLY GOOD AIRPLANE?
www.chickenwingscomics.com
OR, LET'S SAY, A REASONABLY AIRWORTHY ONE.
CLUNK!
ANYWAY... UHM... YOU GET MY POINT, RIGHT? I MEAN, WHY JUMP OUT OF IT WHILE IT STILL FLIES?
YEAH, ISN'T THAT SCARY?
© Michael and Stefan Strasser - 17
WELL, IT'S STILL A LOT LESS SCARY THAN A LANDING WITH CHUCK ON THE CONTROLS!
GOOD POINT!
HEY!!
PSST, YOU DON'T HAPPEN TO HAVE A SPARE CHUTE FOR ME, DO YOU?
I HEARD THAT!!

www.chickenwingscomics.com

SALLY, HAVE YOU SEEN MY LUCKY WRENCH SOMEWHERE?

YOU HAVE A LUCKY WRENCH? I THOUGHT YOU WEREN'T SUPERSTICIOUS!

AH, HERE IT IS! THIS VERY IMPORTANT TOOL PROTECTS ME FROM THE EVIL WRAITH THAT HAUNTS THIS HANGAR!

I DIDN'T KNOW THERE WAS ONE! HOW DOES IT WORK?

© Michael and Stefan Strasser - 311

BEGONE, FOUL SPIRIT!!

OUCH!

I SEE! CAN I HAVE ONE TOO FOR THE BIG EVIL SPIRIT IN THE OFFICE?

WHACK!

www.chickenwingscomics.com

OH NO! I TOTALLY SPACED IT WAS HALLOWEEN AGAIN AND THE PARTY IS TODAY! I HAVE NO COSTUME!

© Michael and Stefan Strasser - 312

THAT'S OKAY! YOU CAN BORROW ONE OF MINE.

REALLY? YOU'RE THE BEST!

WOAHAHAHAHAHA HAHAHAHAHAHAHA.....

WHEEZE...

MAN! IRONIC DOESN'T EVEN *BEGIN* TO DESCRIBE IT!

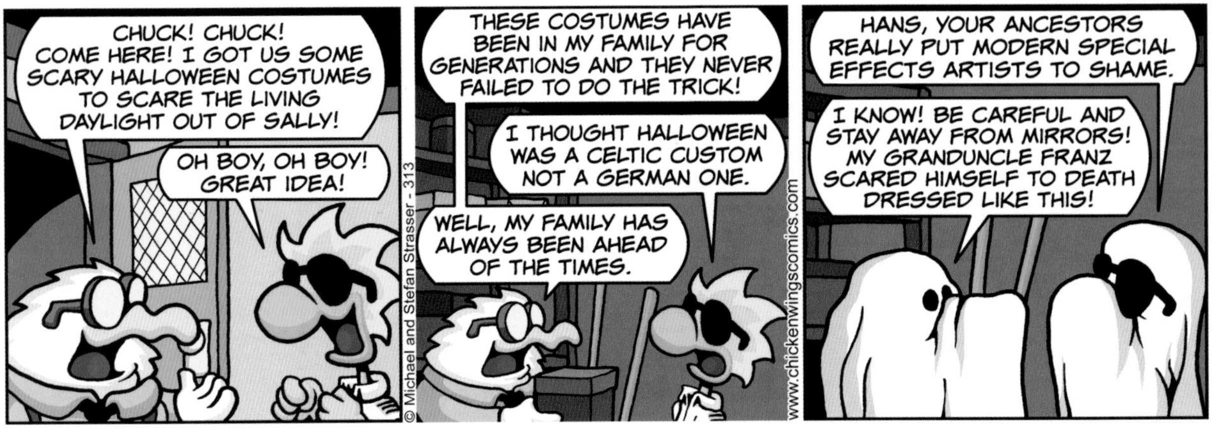
CHUCK! CHUCK! COME HERE! I GOT US SOME SCARY HALLOWEEN COSTUMES TO SCARE THE LIVING DAYLIGHT OUT OF SALLY!
OH BOY, OH BOY! GREAT IDEA!
© Michael and Stefan Strasser - 313
THESE COSTUMES HAVE BEEN IN MY FAMILY FOR GENERATIONS AND THEY NEVER FAILED TO DO THE TRICK!
I THOUGHT HALLOWEEN WAS A CELTIC CUSTOM NOT A GERMAN ONE.
WELL, MY FAMILY HAS ALWAYS BEEN AHEAD OF THE TIMES.
www.chickenwingscomics.com
HANS, YOUR ANCESTORS REALLY PUT MODERN SPECIAL EFFECTS ARTISTS TO SHAME.
I KNOW! BE CAREFUL AND STAY AWAY FROM MIRRORS! MY GRANDUNCLE FRANZ SCARED HIMSELF TO DEATH DRESSED LIKE THIS!

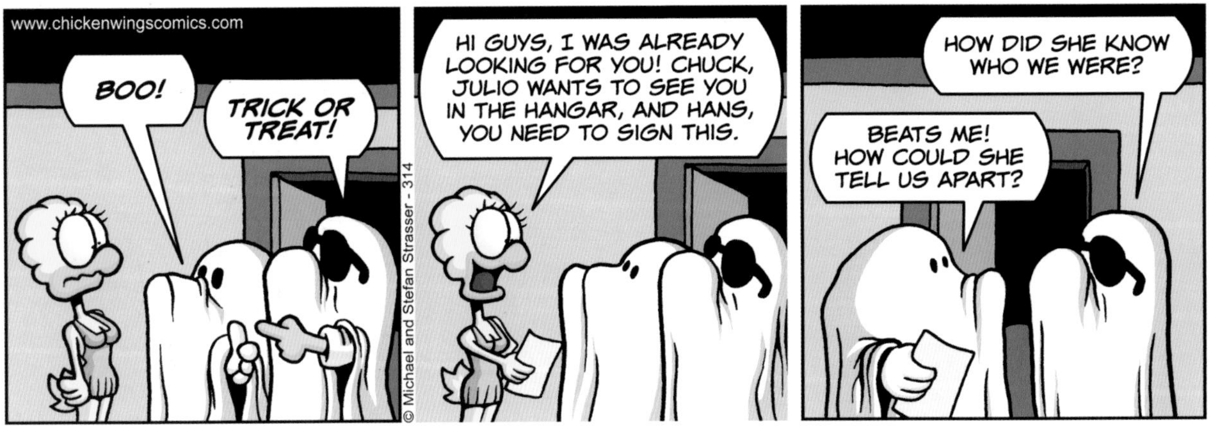
www.chickenwingscomics.com
BOO!
TRICK OR TREAT!
© Michael and Stefan Strasser - 314
HI GUYS, I WAS ALREADY LOOKING FOR YOU! CHUCK, JULIO WANTS TO SEE YOU IN THE HANGAR, AND HANS, YOU NEED TO SIGN THIS.
HOW DID SHE KNOW WHO WE WERE?
BEATS ME! HOW COULD SHE TELL US APART?

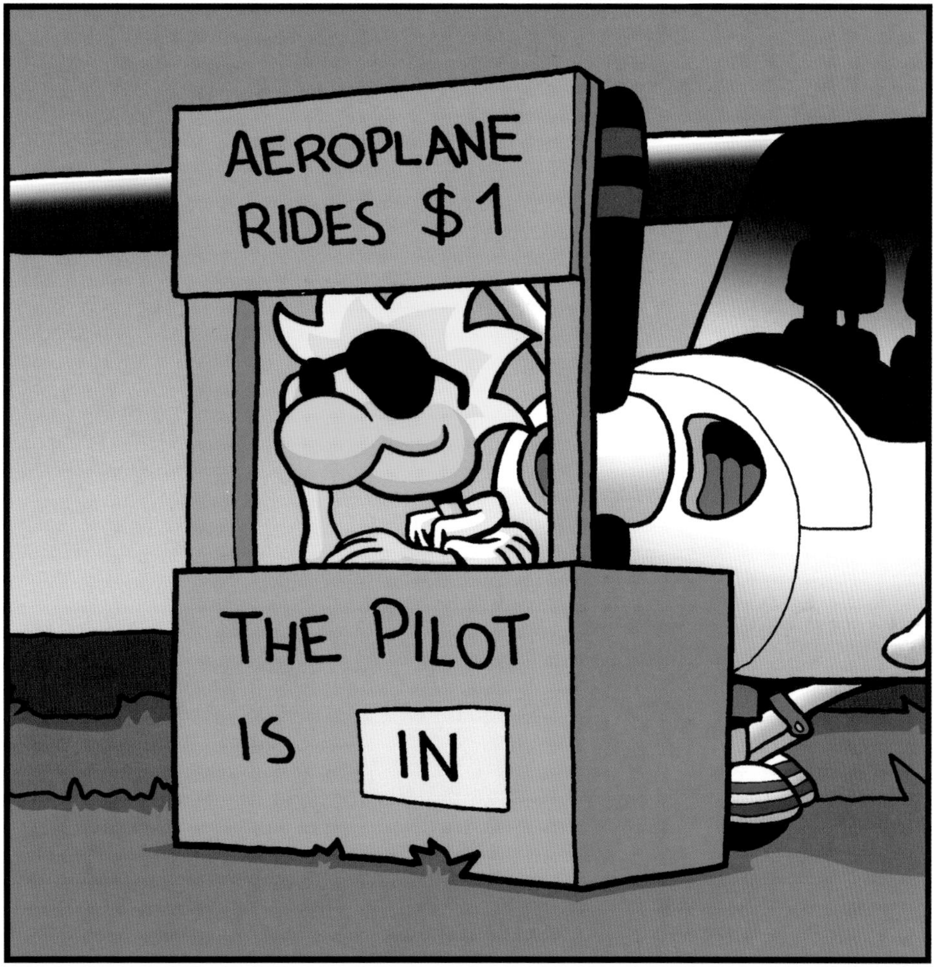
AEROPLANE RIDES $1
THE PILOT IS IN

WOW! IT SURE IS FOGGY!

YEAH... DIDN'T THE WEATHER FORECAST SAY IT WAS GOING TO BE SUNNY TODAY?

© Michael and Stefan Strasser - 329

THOSE CLOWNS AT THE WEATHER SERVICE NEVER GET IT RIGHT!

TRUE.

OH.

UHM... IT LOOKS LIKE IT'S CLEARING UP.

www.chickenwingscomics.com

SALLY, IS THE PLANE READY?

WHICH ONE? THE ONE THAT SMELLS LIKE OLD CHEESE?

THE ONE THAT HAS THE HIGHEST PROFIT MARGIN.

THE ONE THE ROCK STAR THREW UP IN?

© Michael and Stefan Strasser - 266

NO, THE ONE THAT COSTS THE MOST INSURANCE!

THE ONE WITH THE FAN ON TOP?

STOP IT, YOU GUYS!! I CAN'T TAKE IT ANYMORE!!

www.chickenwingscomics.com

THE "PIPER" IS READY.

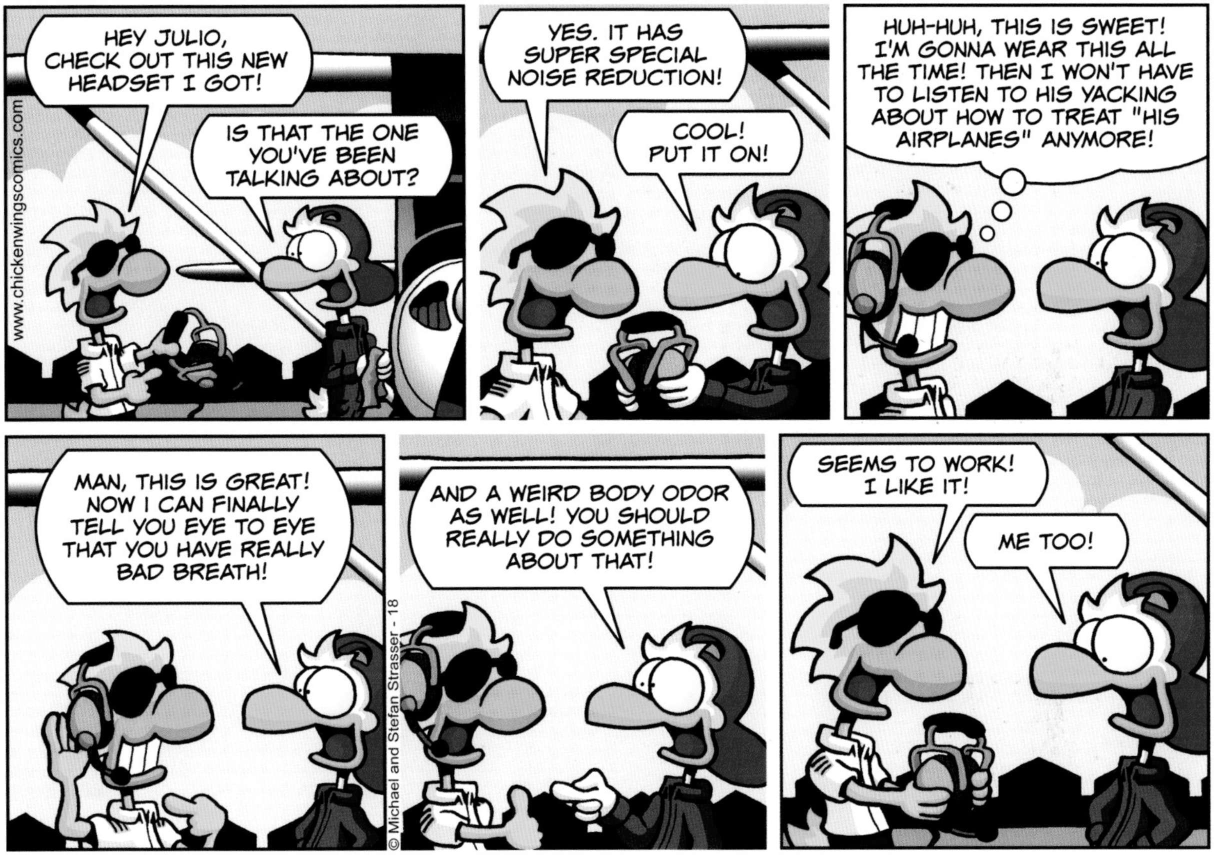
HEY JULIO, CHECK OUT THIS NEW HEADSET I GOT!
IS THAT THE ONE YOU'VE BEEN TALKING ABOUT?
www.chickenwingscomics.com
YES. IT HAS SUPER SPECIAL NOISE REDUCTION!
COOL! PUT IT ON!
HUH-HUH, THIS IS SWEET! I'M GONNA WEAR THIS ALL THE TIME! THEN I WON'T HAVE TO LISTEN TO HIS YACKING ABOUT HOW TO TREAT "HIS AIRPLANES" ANYMORE!
MAN, THIS IS GREAT! NOW I CAN FINALLY TELL YOU EYE TO EYE THAT YOU HAVE REALLY BAD BREATH!
© Michael and Stefan Strasser - 18
AND A WEIRD BODY ODOR AS WELL! YOU SHOULD REALLY DO SOMETHING ABOUT THAT!
SEEMS TO WORK! I LIKE IT!
ME TOO!

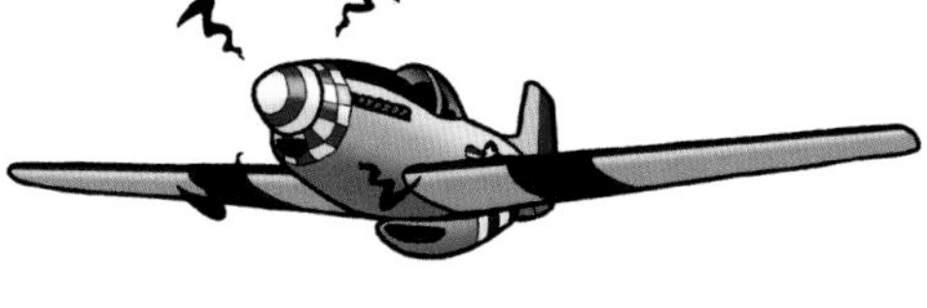

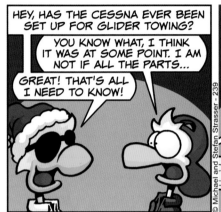

HEY, HAS THE CESSNA EVER BEEN SET UP FOR GLIDER TOWING?
YOU KNOW WHAT, I THINK IT WAS AT SOME POINT. I AM NOT IF ALL THE PARTS...
GREAT! THAT'S ALL I NEED TO KNOW!
© Michael and Stefan Strasser - 239
WAIT A MINUTE! YOU'RE NOT PLANNING ANYTHING FUNNY WITH A GLIDER, ARE YOU?
NO, I'M NOT PLANNING ANYTHING FUNNY **WITH A GLIDER!**
OKAY, NOW I'LL JUST HAVE TO DO A WEIGHT AND BALANCE ON THIS THING...
www.chickenwingscomics.com

www.chickenwingscomics.com
HEY GUYS! CHECK OUT OUR NEW CHRISTMAS TREE!
© Michael and Stefan Strasser - 240
ISN'T IT GRAND? LITTLE ANGELS IN AIRPLANES, SPARKPLUGS FOR CANDLES AND A LITTLE HELICOPTER ON THE TOP. THIS YEAR I REALLY THOUGHT OF **EVERY LITTLE DETAIL!**
DID YOU ALSO THINK ABOUT HOW WE ARE GOING TO GET OUR AIRCRAFT IN AND OUT OF THE HANGAR NOW?
WELL, UHM... SO MAYBE NOT **EVERY** LITTLE DETAIL!

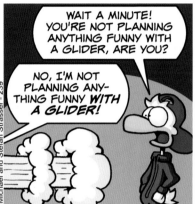

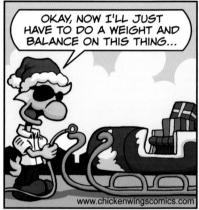

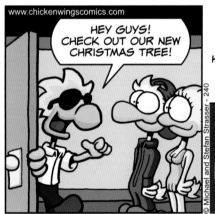

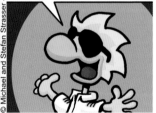

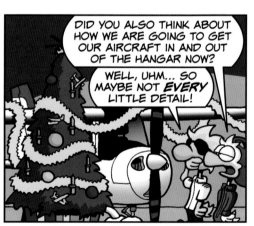

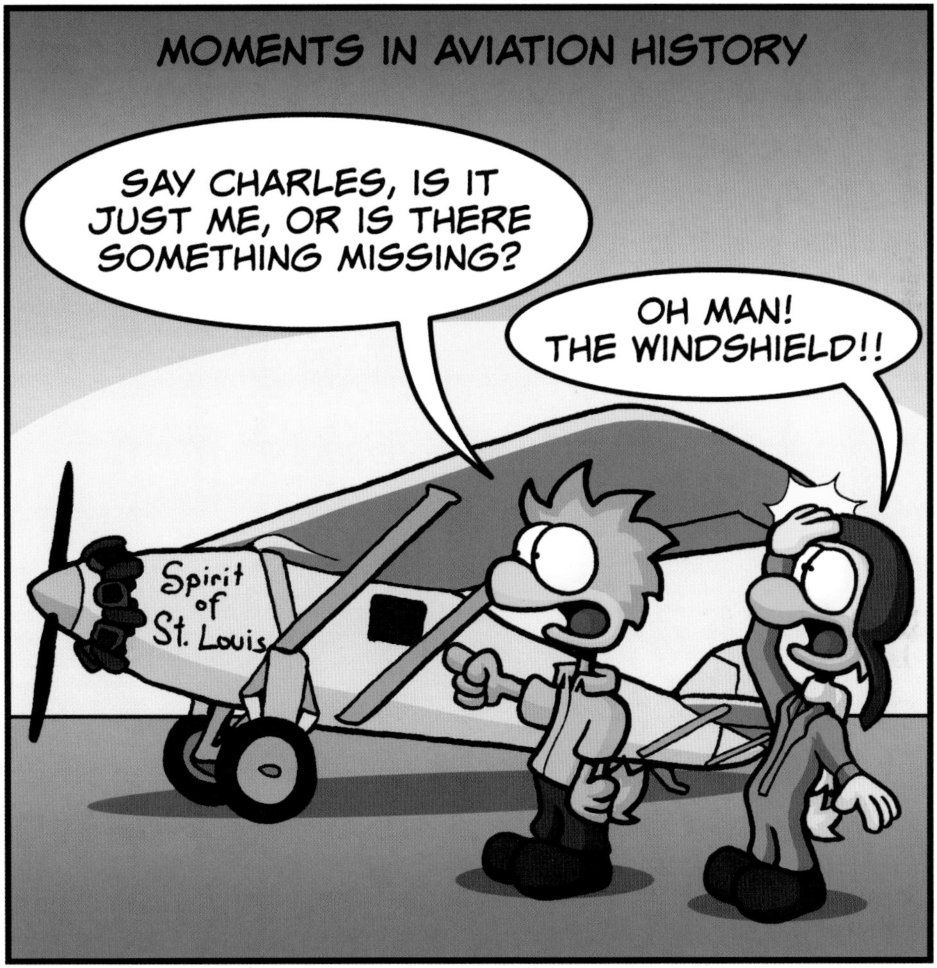
MOMENTS IN AVIATION HISTORY
SAY CHARLES, IS IT JUST ME, OR IS THERE SOMETHING MISSING?
OH MAN! THE WINDSHIELD!!
Spirit of St. Louis

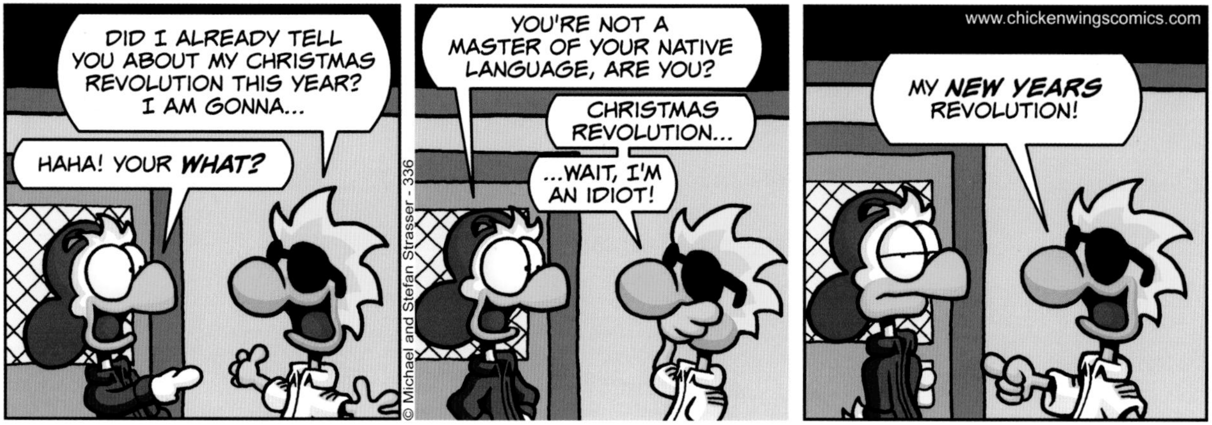
www.chickenwingscomics.com
DID I ALREADY TELL YOU ABOUT MY CHRISTMAS REVOLUTION THIS YEAR? I AM GONNA...
HAHA! YOUR WHAT?
YOU'RE NOT A MASTER OF YOUR NATIVE LANGUAGE, ARE YOU?
CHRISTMAS REVOLUTION...
...WAIT, I'M AN IDIOT!
MY NEW YEARS REVOLUTION!
© Michael and Stefan Strasser - 336

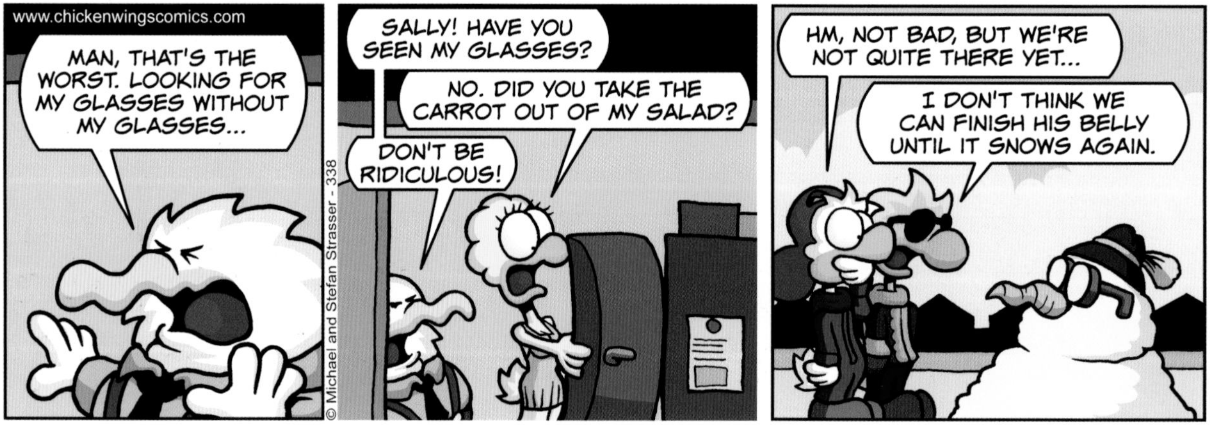
www.chickenwingscomics.com
MAN, THAT'S THE WORST. LOOKING FOR MY GLASSES WITHOUT MY GLASSES...
SALLY! HAVE YOU SEEN MY GLASSES?
NO. DID YOU TAKE THE CARROT OUT OF MY SALAD?
DON'T BE RIDICULOUS!
HM, NOT BAD, BUT WE'RE NOT QUITE THERE YET...
I DON'T THINK WE CAN FINISH HIS BELLY UNTIL IT SNOWS AGAIN.
© Michael and Stefan Strasser - 338

THIS NEW SNOWBLOWER IS AWESOME! IT'S LIKE CUTTING THROUGH BUTTER!
IT'S GONNA SAVE US SO MUCH TIME!
© Michael and Stefan Strasser - 335
OUR PLANES WILL BE IN THE AIR IN NO TIME, JUST WATCH!
www.chickenwingscomics.com

MAN, THIS WEATHER SUCKS! WE NEED A BIGGER ENGINE!
WHY?
SO WE CAN FLY FASTER.
© Michael and Stefan Strasser - 341
THEN AT LEAST WE COULD BE JUST LIKE EVERYBODY ELSE AND BUILD UP ICE ON THE WINGS...
www.chickenwingscomics.com
INSTEAD OF SNOW!

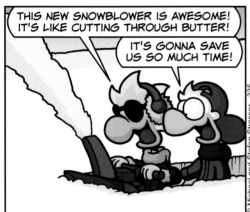

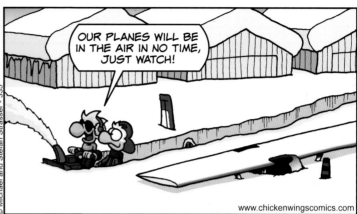

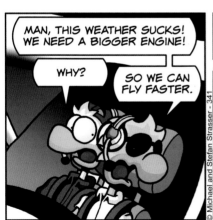

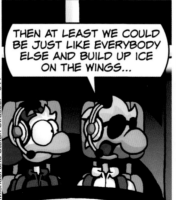

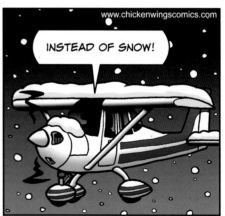

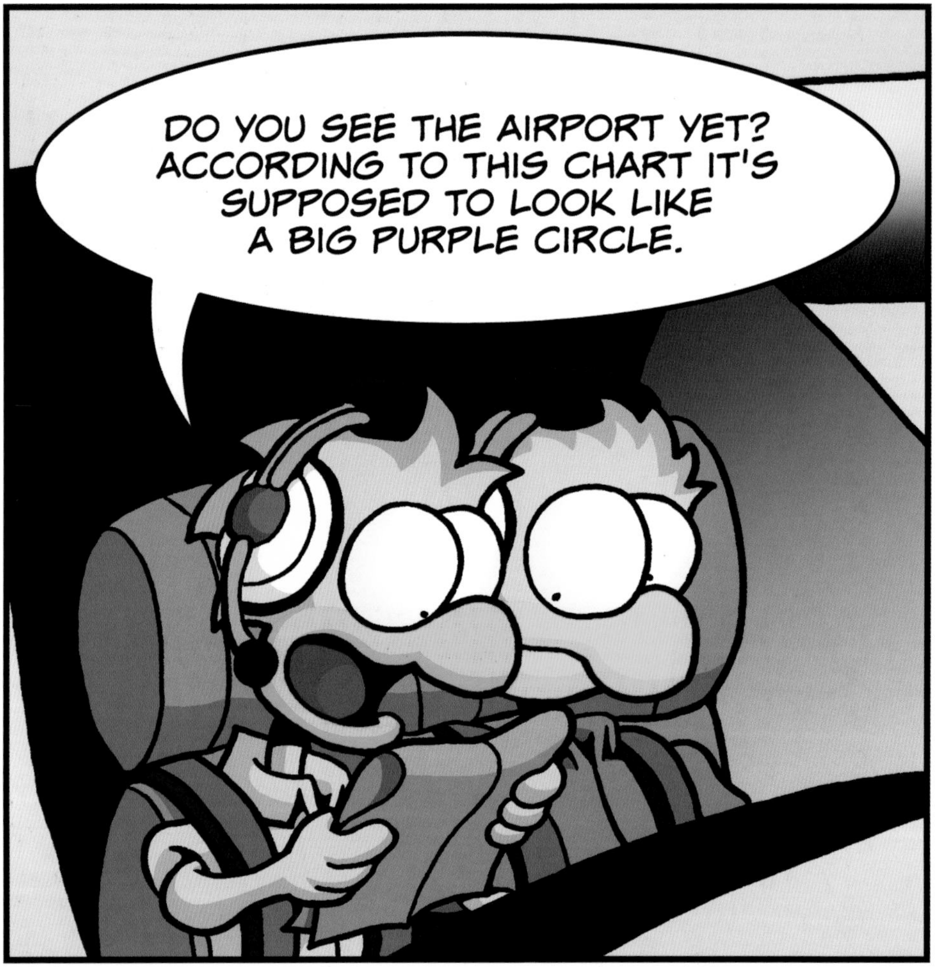
DO YOU SEE THE AIRPORT YET? ACCORDING TO THIS CHART IT'S SUPPOSED TO LOOK LIKE A BIG PURPLE CIRCLE.

WHAT'S WITH THAT PILE OF DIRT?
WE'RE BUILDING THE BIGGEST SNOWMAN IN TOWN!
YOU GUYS CHOSE THE WORST POSSIBLE TIME FOR THAT. THERE'S HARDLY ANY SNOW!
© Michael and Stefan Strasser - 331
ARE YOU KIDDING? IT'S THE PERFECT TIME!
IT IS PROBABLY THE ONLY SNOWMAN AROUND, THUS AUTOMATICALLY MAKING IT THE BIGGEST ONE!
THAT MAKES SENSE.
www.chickenwingscomics.com
WOW, THAT SURE IS HARDER WORK THAN I EXPECTED!
YES, BUT AT LEAST IT'S NOT REAL WORK!
TRUE!

www.chickenwingscomics.com
© Michael and Stefan Strasser - 263
YOU KNOW THAT ON A "PHOTOFLIGHT" THEY USUALLY TAKE PHOTOS OF SOMETHING ON THE GROUND FROM THE HELICOPTER, AND NOT PHOTOS OF THE PILOT, RIGHT?
UH, OF COURSE!

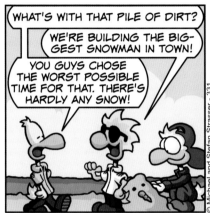

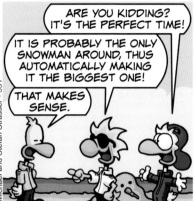

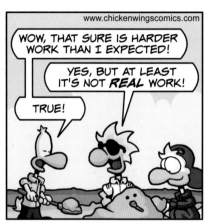

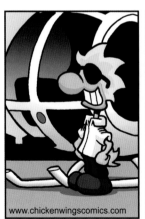

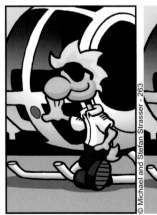

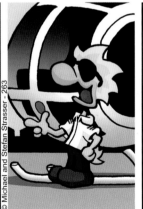

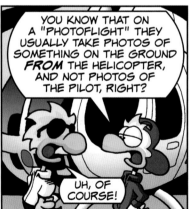

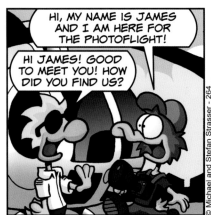

HI, MY NAME IS JAMES AND I AM HERE FOR THE PHOTOFLIGHT!
HI JAMES! GOOD TO MEET YOU! HOW DID YOU FIND US?
WELL, I HAVE TO HAVE THIS FLIGHT DONE TODAY FOR MY ENDANGERED BIRD PROJECT. SO I JUST WENT TO THE AIRPORT AND ASKED FOR THE BEST PILOT ON THE FIELD.
WOW! REALLY?
YEAH, BUT IT TURNED OUT THEY WERE ALL BOOKED ALREADY. CAN YOU BELIEVE IT?
© Michael and Stefan Strasser - 264
www.chickenwingscomics.com

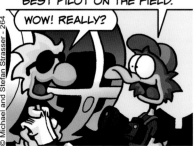

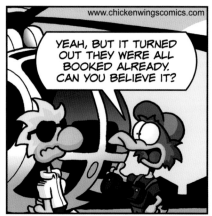

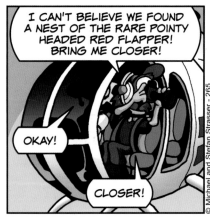

I CAN'T BELIEVE WE FOUND A NEST OF THE RARE POINTY HEADED RED FLAPPER! BRING ME CLOSER!
OKAY!
CLOSER!
WOOSH!
THAT'S FUNNY, DID WE PASS IT? I CAN'T SEE IT ANYMORE!
© Michael and Stefan Strasser - 265
www.chickenwingscomics.com

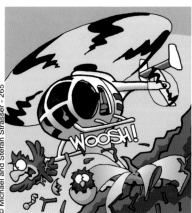

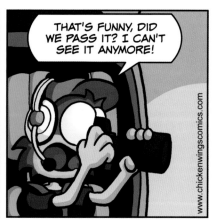

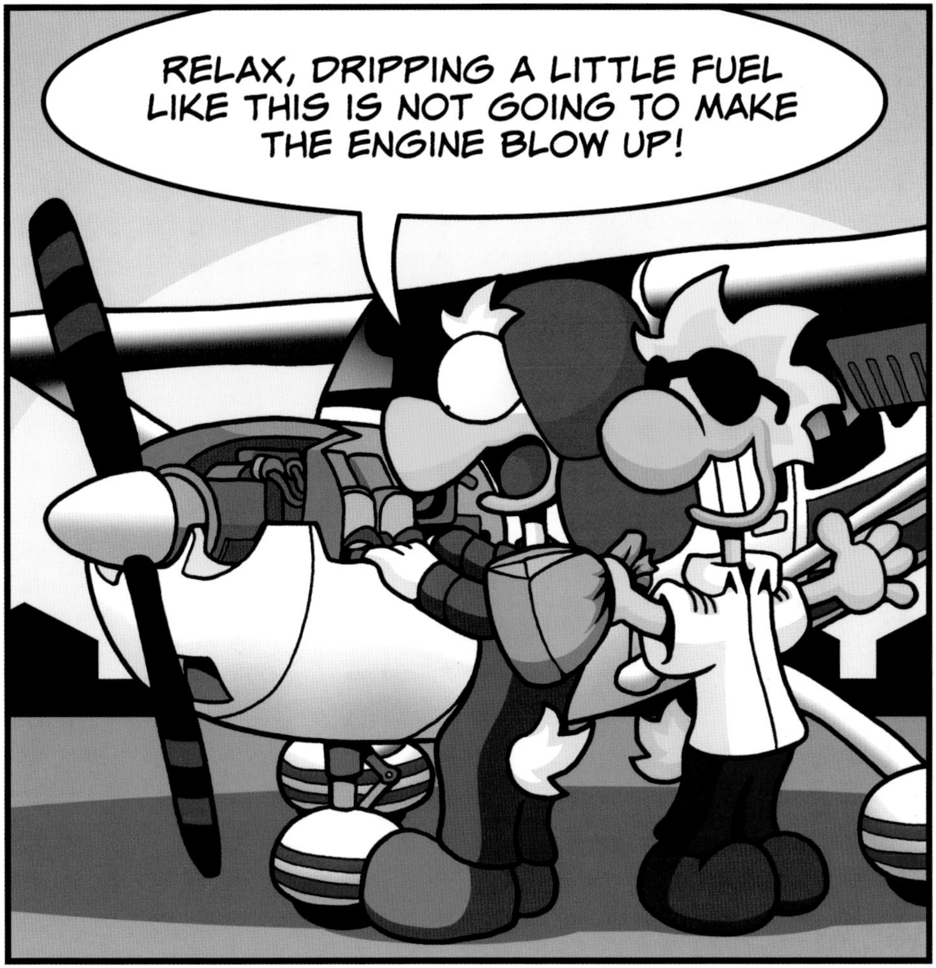
RELAX, DRIPPING A LITTLE FUEL LIKE THIS IS NOT GOING TO MAKE THE ENGINE BLOW UP!

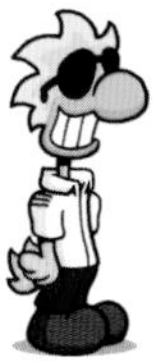

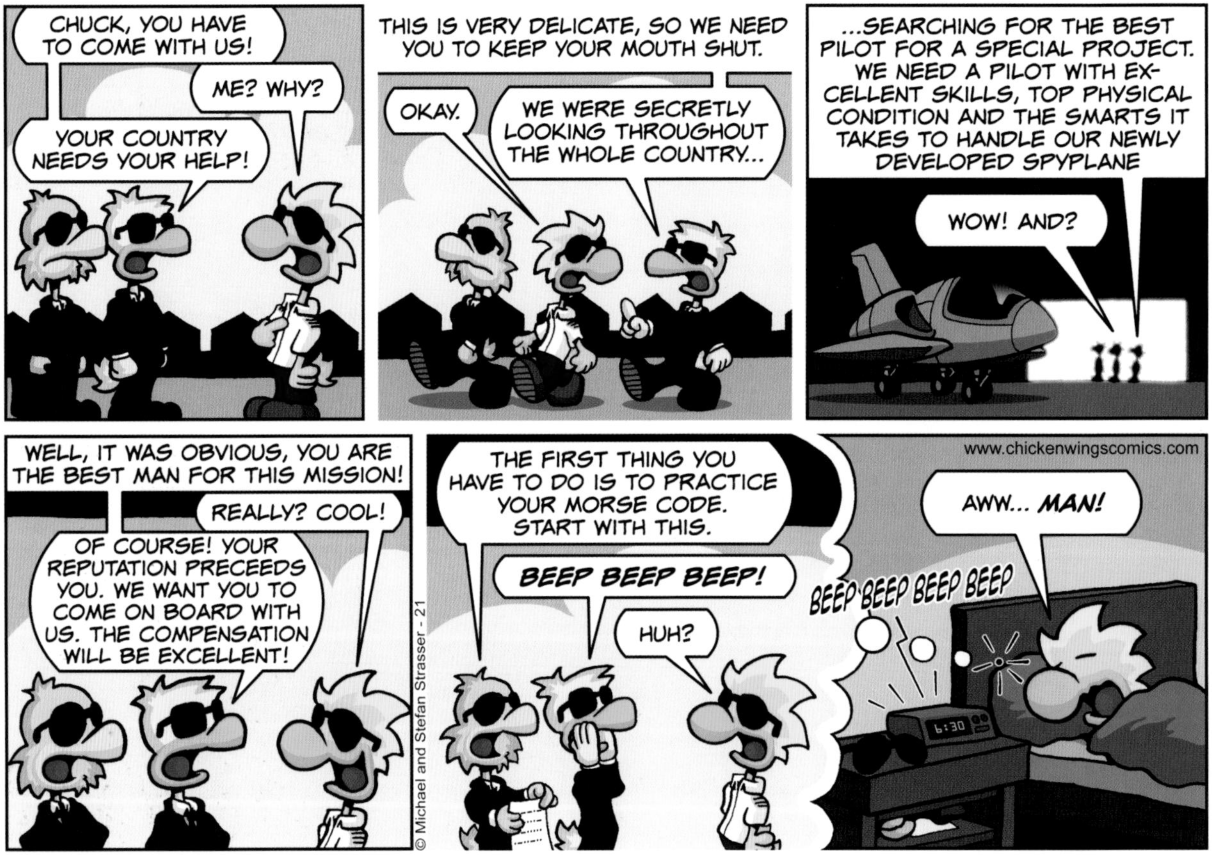
CHUCK, YOU HAVE TO COME WITH US!
ME? WHY?
YOUR COUNTRY NEEDS YOUR HELP!
THIS IS VERY DELICATE, SO WE NEED YOU TO KEEP YOUR MOUTH SHUT.
OKAY.
WE WERE SECRETLY LOOKING THROUGHOUT THE WHOLE COUNTRY...
...SEARCHING FOR THE BEST PILOT FOR A SPECIAL PROJECT. WE NEED A PILOT WITH EX-CELLENT SKILLS, TOP PHYSICAL CONDITION AND THE SMARTS IT TAKES TO HANDLE OUR NEWLY DEVELOPED SPYPLANE
WOW! AND?
WELL, IT WAS OBVIOUS, YOU ARE THE BEST MAN FOR THIS MISSION!
REALLY? COOL!
OF COURSE! YOUR REPUTATION PRECEEDS YOU. WE WANT YOU TO COME ON BOARD WITH US. THE COMPENSATION WILL BE EXCELLENT!
© Michael and Stefan Strasser - 21
THE FIRST THING YOU HAVE TO DO IS TO PRACTICE YOUR MORSE CODE. START WITH THIS.
BEEP BEEP BEEP!
HUH?
www.chickenwingscomics.com
AWW... MAN!
BEEP BEEP BEEP BEEP
6:30

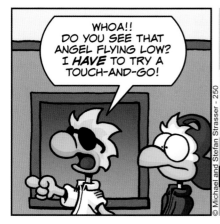

WHOA!! DO YOU SEE THAT ANGEL FLYING LOW? I *HAVE* TO TRY A TOUCH-AND-GO!
© Michael and Stefan Strasser - 250
OH, HER? THAT'S ALEX. SHE KNOWS KARATE! IT WOULD END AS A "TOUCH-AND-WAKE-UP-IN-HOSPITAL", HEHEHE...
www.chickenwingscomics.com
REALLY? HMM... IN THAT CASE I'LL JUST TRY A QUICK FLY-BY.

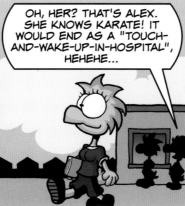

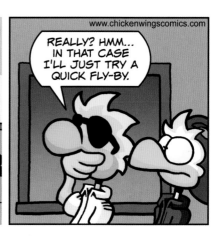

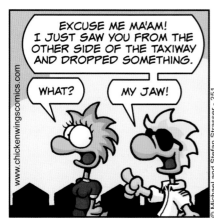

www.chickenwingscomics.com
EXCUSE ME MA'AM! I JUST SAW YOU FROM THE OTHER SIDE OF THE TAXIWAY AND DROPPED SOMETHING.
WHAT?
MY JAW!
© Michael and Stefan Strasser - 251
HOW ORIGINAL! NOW MOVE ALONG CREEPY CREATURE!
SHOO!
HAHA! MISSED APPROACH!
SHUT UP, THE APPROACH WAS FINE! THE AIRPORT JUST WASN'T ACCEPTING ANY LANDINGS.

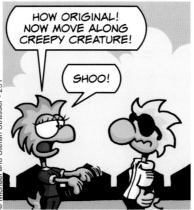

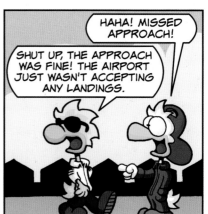

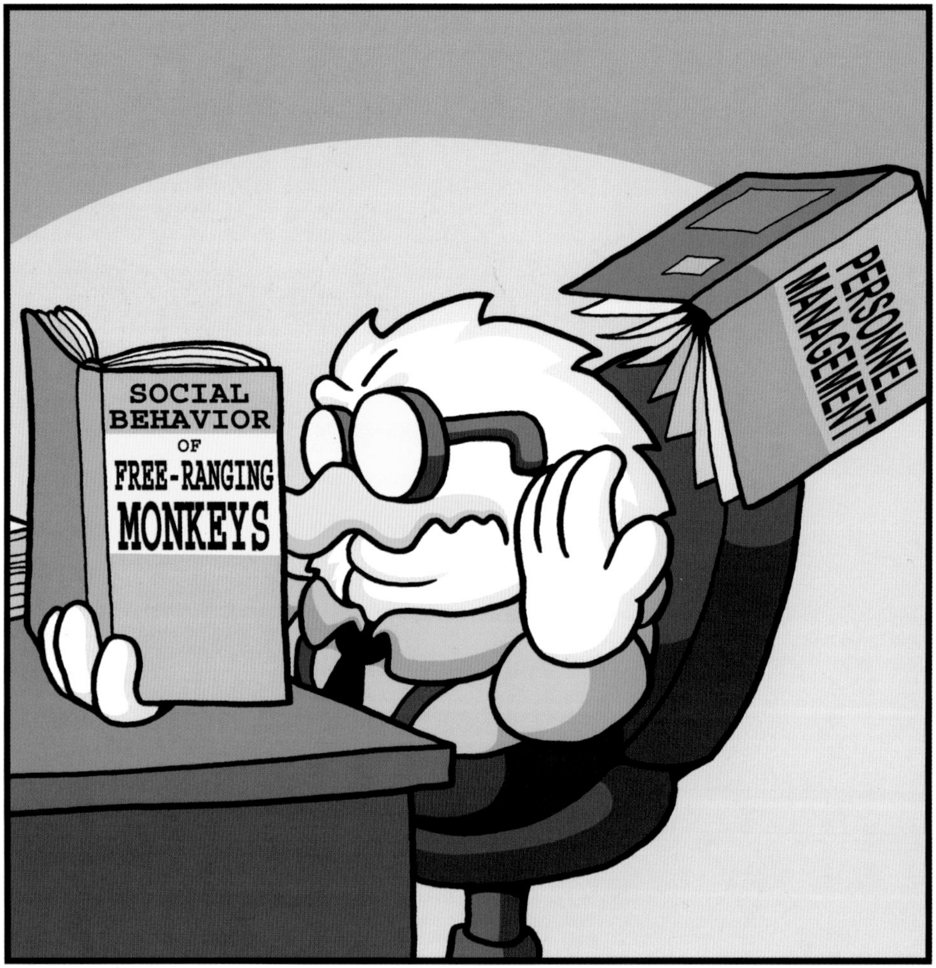
SOCIAL BEHAVIOR OF FREE-RANGING MONKEYS
PERSONNEL MANAGEMENT

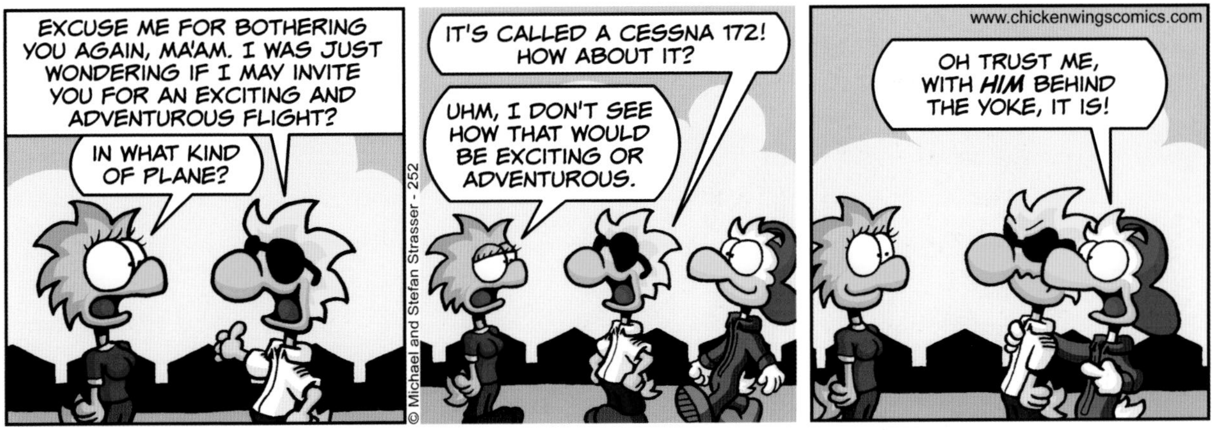
EXCUSE ME FOR BOTHERING YOU AGAIN, MA'AM. I WAS JUST WONDERING IF I MAY INVITE YOU FOR AN EXCITING AND ADVENTUROUS FLIGHT?
IN WHAT KIND OF PLANE?
© Michael and Stefan Strasser - 252
IT'S CALLED A CESSNA 172! HOW ABOUT IT?
UHM, I DON'T SEE HOW THAT WOULD BE EXCITING OR ADVENTUROUS.
www.chickenwingscomics.com
OH TRUST ME, WITH ***HIM*** BEHIND THE YOKE, IT IS!

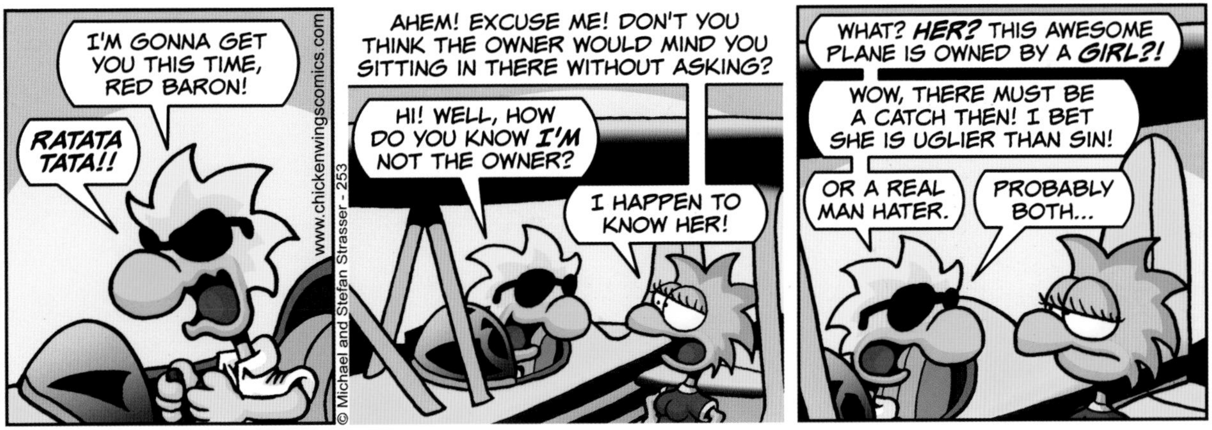
I'M GONNA GET YOU THIS TIME, RED BARON!
RATATA TATA!!
www.chickenwingscomics.com
© Michael and Stefan Strasser - 253
AHEM! EXCUSE ME! DON'T YOU THINK THE OWNER WOULD MIND YOU SITTING IN THERE WITHOUT ASKING?
HI! WELL, HOW DO YOU KNOW ***I'M*** NOT THE OWNER?
I HAPPEN TO KNOW HER!
WHAT? ***HER?*** THIS AWESOME PLANE IS OWNED BY A ***GIRL?!***
WOW, THERE MUST BE A CATCH THEN! I BET SHE IS UGLIER THAN SIN!
OR A REAL MAN HATER.
PROBABLY BOTH...

HEY, HOW COME YOU'RE ALLOWED TO SIT IN IT?
CHECK THIS OUT, I AM EVEN GONNA FLY THIS BABY!
© Michael and Stefan Strasser - 254
WOW! YOU MUST BE REALLY CLOSE WITH THE OWNER!
SURE! SOME PEOPLE SAY WE LOOK LIKE THE SAME PERSON!
BOY! WHAT ARE THE ODDS OF TWO PRETTY GIRLS FLYING THIS COOL PLANE?!
www.chickenwingscomics.com
UH... YOU'RE NOT THE SHARPEST TOOL IN THE SHED, ARE YOU?
NO. WAIT! SHED? HUH?

SAY JULIO, CAN I ASK YOU A QUESTION?
© Michael and Stefan Strasser - 306
SURE YOU CAN! AFTER ALL, WE LIVE IN A FREE COUNTRY AND YOU HAVE THE FREEDOM OF SPEECH!
YOU'RE RIGHT!
www.chickenwingscomics.com
AND I HAVE THE FREEDOM NOT TO LISTEN!

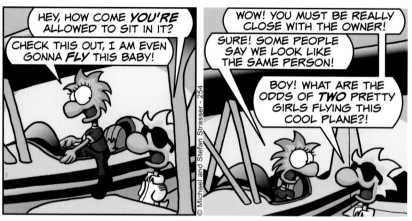

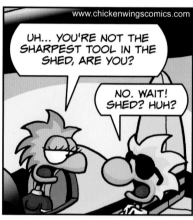

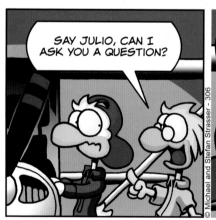

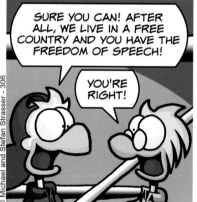

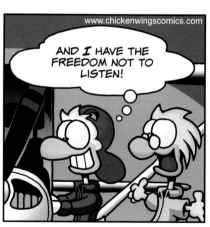

OH NO! I CAN'T FLY THE APPROACH! THE CG... IT'S TOO FAR AFT... SHE'S GONNA STALL!
QUICK! FLIGHT ATTENDANT! TELL THE PASSENGER IN 24B TO PUT HIS SEAT BACK UP!
THE REAL REASON WHY WE HAVE TO PUT OUR SEATS IN THE "UPRIGHT POSITION" FOR LANDING.

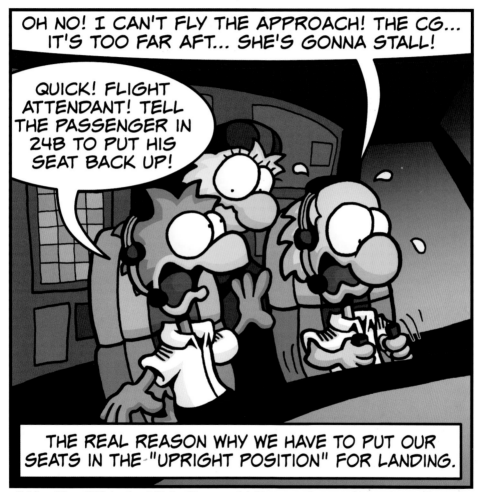

SO, IS THERE A WAY TO MAKE THIS AIRPLANE FASTER?
WHAT? EVEN FASTER THAN IT ALREADY IS? YOU'D BE MESSING WITH THE SPEED OF SOUND!
REALLY?
www.chickenwingscomics.com
© Michael and Stefan Strasser - 307
COULD YOU, LIKE, PUT IN AN ENGINE WITH TWICE THE HORSEPOWER?
WELL, I GUESS THEORETICALLY...
AND A BIGGER PROP?
JASON, DID YOU KNOW THAT, THEORETICALLY, FREEDOM OF SPEECH ALSO MEANS YOU ARE FREE NOT TO SPEAK?
SURE, WHY ARE YOU ASKING?
JUST MAKING SURE YOU KNOW.

www.chickenwingscomics.com
HEY JULIO, CAN I HELP YOU WITH ANYTHING ON THAT ENGINE?
HAHA! GOOD ONE!
© Michael and Stefan Strasser - 270
NO! I AM SERIOUS! HOW COME YOU NEVER LET ME HELP YOU?
DON'T GET ME WRONG, BUT YOU'RE NOT NECESSARILY KNOWN FOR YOUR "MOTOR SKILLS".
HAHA, VERY FUNNY! WELL THEN I MIGHT JUST SEND JASON IN HERE. HE SAID HE HAS A FEW QUESTIONS FOR YOU!
WHAT? NO!! UHM... WAIT... HERE... UH, HELP ME HOLD THIS WRENCH!

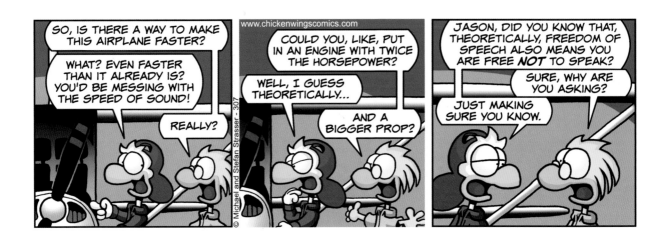

www.chickenwingscomics.com
© Michael and Stefan Strasser - 271
THIS IS COOL! I ALMOST FEEL LIKE A MECHANIC!
NOT BAD, HUH?
UHM... ARE YOU GONNA NEED THE WRENCH ANYTIME SOON?
NO, BUT IT'S COMFORTING TO KNOW THAT I HAVE IT RIGHT THE SECOND I NEED IT!

www.chickenwingscomics.com
© Michael and Stefan Strasser - 272
HOW ABOUT NOW? DO YOU NEED THE WRENCH NOW?
NOT QUITE.
I AM STARTING TO WONDER WHAT I AM DOING HERE.
DUH! YOU'RE HELPING!
AWW... COME ON! I'VE BEEN STANDING HERE FOR TWO HOURS NOW!
DON'T START WITH ME! WHY DO YOU THINK THEY CALL IT A "100 HOUR INSPECTION"?

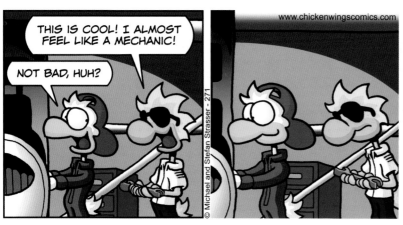

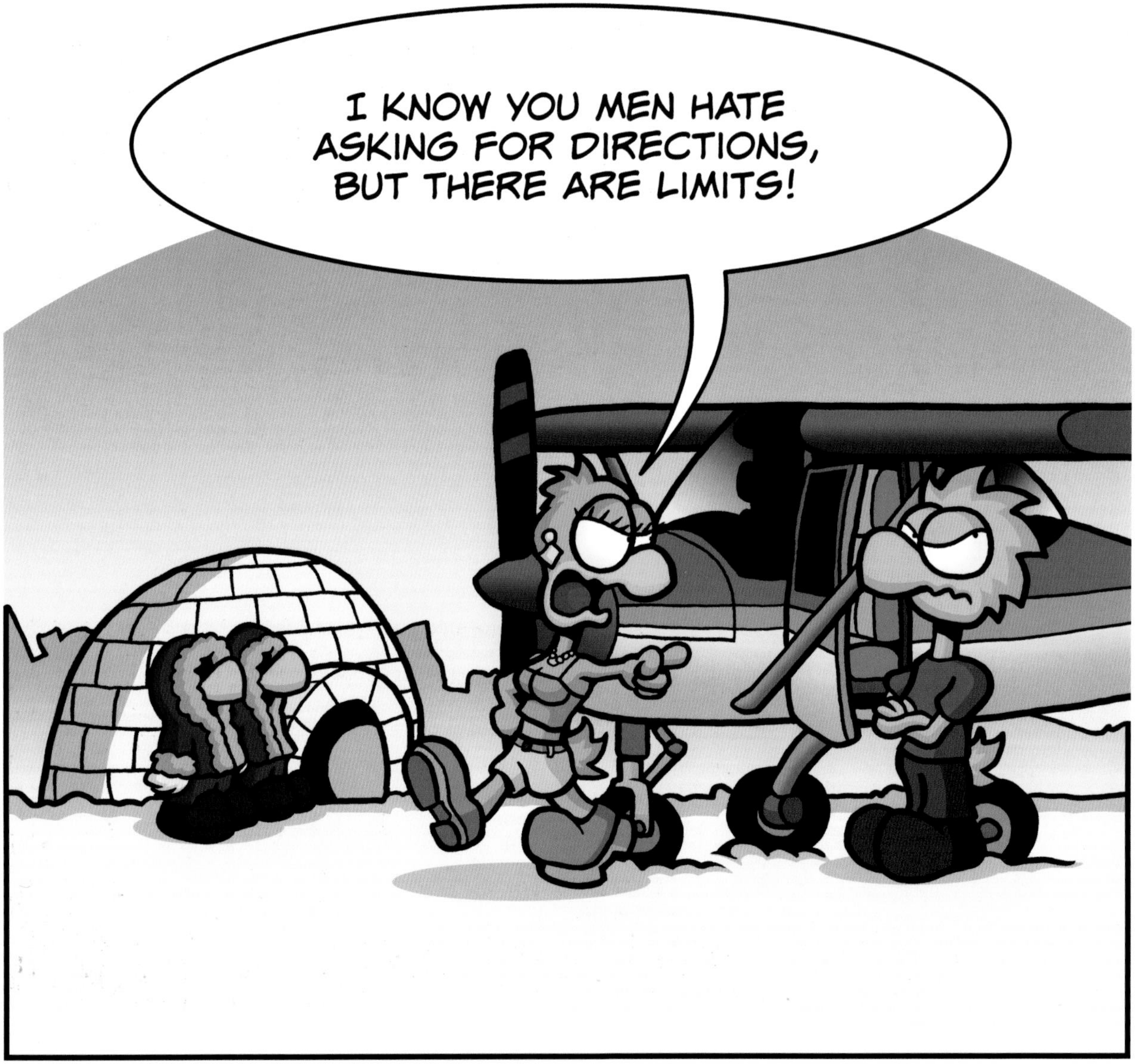
I KNOW YOU MEN HATE
ASKING FOR DIRECTIONS,
BUT THERE ARE LIMITS!

HI JULIO! SAY, CAN YOU DO AN OIL CHANGE ON MY PLANE?
HMM... I'VE HEARD RUMORS YOU'VE BEEN GIVING MY PILOT A HARD TIME.
© Michael and Stefan Strasser - 284
WHAT? THAT LITTLE GUY WITH THE SUNGLASSES AND THE BIG WATCH?
DID YOU OR DID YOU NOT MESS WITH HIM? BE HONEST!
OF COURSE I DID! HE WAS SO DUMB AND CLUMSY, I JUST COULDN'T RESIST!
www.chickenwingscomics.com
THAT'S NOT GONNA AFFECT MY OIL CHANGE, IS IT?
ARE YOU KIDDING? OF COURSE IT WILL! I WILL GIVE YOU A DISCOUNT!

SO THE GUY WITH THE BIG MOUTH AND THE BIG WATCH IS YOUR PILOT, HUH?
EASY THERE, MISSY! HE HAPPENS TO HAVE A SPOTLESS SAFETY RECORD AND IS PROBABLY THE BEST AND MOST RESPECTABLE PILOT I KNOW!
© Michael and Stefan Strasser - 285
www.chickenwingscomics.com
YOU CAN'T KNOW TOO MANY PILOTS THEN, HEHEHE!
HAHA! I TOTALLY JUST SAID "SPOTLESS SAFETY RECORD" WITH A STRAIGHT FACE!
HAHAHA!

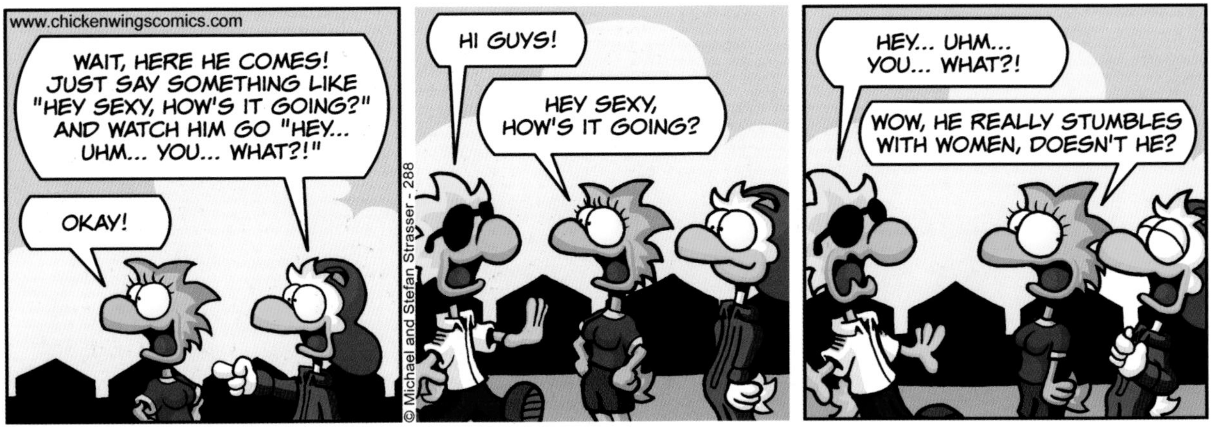
www.chickenwingscomics.com
WAIT, HERE HE COMES! JUST SAY SOMETHING LIKE "HEY SEXY, HOW'S IT GOING?" AND WATCH HIM GO "HEY... UHM... YOU... WHAT?!"
OKAY!
© Michael and Stefan Strasser - 288
HI GUYS!
HEY SEXY, HOW'S IT GOING?
HEY... UHM... YOU... WHAT?!
WOW, HE REALLY STUMBLES WITH WOMEN, DOESN'T HE?

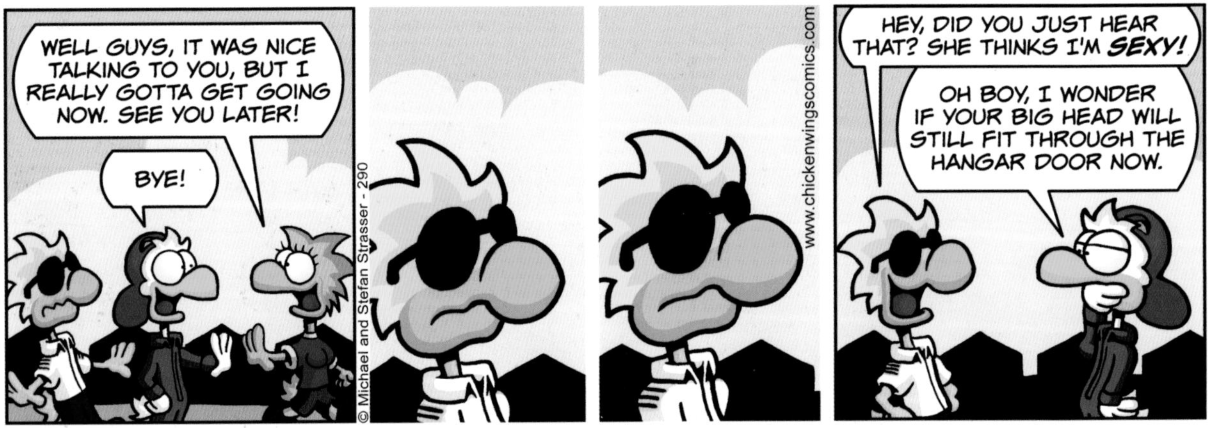
WELL GUYS, IT WAS NICE TALKING TO YOU, BUT I REALLY GOTTA GET GOING NOW. SEE YOU LATER!
BYE!
© Michael and Stefan Strasser - 290
www.chickenwingscomics.com
HEY, DID YOU JUST HEAR THAT? SHE THINKS I'M ***SEXY!***
OH BOY, I WONDER IF YOUR BIG HEAD WILL STILL FIT THROUGH THE HANGAR DOOR NOW.

DID YOU HEAR WHAT SHE CALLED ME?
SHE CALLED ME "SEXY"!
YES.
I SAID I HEARD HER.
SEXY!
© Michael and Stefan Strasser - 291
YOU KNOW WHAT? DON'T LET IT GET TO YOUR HEAD, BECAUSE I TOLD HER SO.
WHAT? YOU THINK I'M SEXY? GROSS!
NO, STUPID, I TOLD HER TO TELL YOU!
www.chickenwingscomics.com
HMM... SO SHE THINKS I'M SEXY BUT WAS TOO SHY TO JUST COME AND TELL ME?
YEP, DEFINITELY NOT GOING TO FIT THROUGH THE HANGAR DOOR.

www.chickenwingscomics.com
IS IT TRUE THAT YOU ARE RELIGIOUS, JULIO?
QUITE!
© Michael and Stefan Strasser - 219
HOW COME?
WELL...
HEY SPARKS! I NEED YOU TO GO ON A MAINTENANCE FLIGHT WITH ME!
AH, I THINK I KNOW WHY!

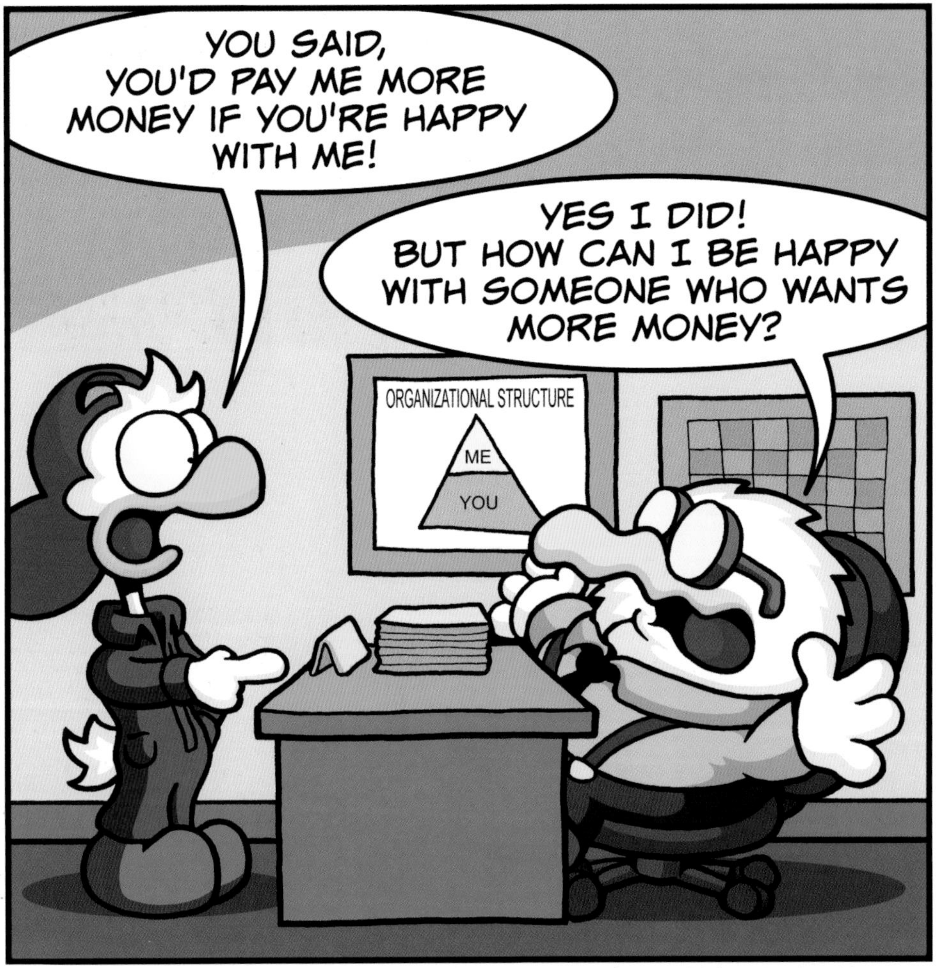
YOU SAID, YOU'D PAY ME MORE MONEY IF YOU'RE HAPPY WITH ME!
YES I DID! BUT HOW CAN I BE HAPPY WITH SOMEONE WHO WANTS MORE MONEY?
ORGANIZATIONAL STRUCTURE
ME
YOU

SALLY, CAN YOU HELP ME? I HAD TO FILE AN INSPECTION PANEL, BUT NOW I CAN'T SEEM TO FIND IT ANYMORE.
WHERE DID YOU LOOK SO FAR?
© Michael and Stefan Strasser - 241
I ALREADY LOOKED ALL OVER THE HANGAR.
WELL, MAYBE YOU SHOULD LOOK IN THE OFFICE!
WHY SHOULD I DO THAT?
www.chickenwingscomics.com
WELL, DUH! IF YOU FILED IT CORRECTLY, IT MUST BE IN THE FILING CABINET, RIGHT?
UHM... RIGHT. OF COURSE!

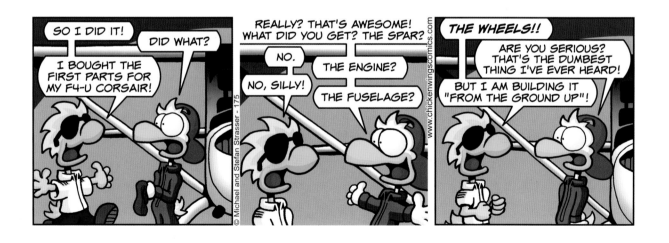

SO I DID IT!
DID WHAT?
I BOUGHT THE FIRST PARTS FOR MY F4-U CORSAIR!
© Michael and Stefan Strasser - 175
REALLY? THAT'S AWESOME! WHAT DID YOU GET? THE SPAR?
NO.
THE ENGINE?
NO, SILLY!
THE FUSELAGE?
www.chickenwingscomics.com
THE WHEELS!!
ARE YOU SERIOUS? THAT'S THE DUMBEST THING I'VE EVER HEARD!
BUT I AM BUILDING IT "FROM THE GROUND UP"!

WOW! IS THAT YOUR NEW CAR? CAN I DRIVE IT?
DRIVE IT? SURE! ANYTHING BUT WASH IT!
WHAT? WHY NOT WASH IT?
I WOULDN'T REALLY TRUST YOU WITH IT.
© Michael and Stefan Strasser - 229
www.chickenwingscomics.com
COME ON! PUH-LEASE! YOU CAN TRUST ME!! LET ME SHOW YOU!
HM, OKAY. BUT BE EXTRA CAREFUL, OKAY?
ALRIGHT!
WOW, THAT WAS EASIER THAN I THOUGHT!
HEY! BUT KEEP THAT SPONGE OFF THE CESSNA!
QUICK THINKING THERE!

COME ON UNCLE ED, LET ME SHOW YOU MY PROJECT IN THE HANGAR!
COOL! I CAN'T WAIT TO SEE IT! YOU'VE BEEN WORKING ON IT FOR QUITE SOME TIME NOW.
www.chickenwingscomics.com
© Michael and Stefan Strasser - 183
SO, WHAT DO YOU THINK?
UHM... WHAT IS THAT?
ARE YOU KIDDING? YOU CAN'T TELL?!
IT'S AN F4-U CORSAIR IN THE MAKING! ISN'T SHE A BEAUTY?
UHM... YEAH... OH YES! I SEE IT CLEARLY NOW!
PRETTY!

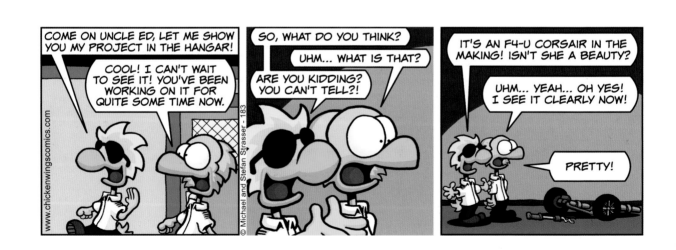

www.chickenwingscomics.com
© Michael and Stefan Strasser - 301
WHERE ARE ALL MY PLANES?
OH, I PUSHED ALL THE OTHER PLANES OUTSIDE!
WHEN YOU SAY OTHER PLANES, AREN'T YOU IMPLYING THERE IS A PLANE IN THE HANGAR RIGHT NOW?
DUH! IT IS! ARE YOU BLIND? IT'S MY PROJECT!
HOW ABOUT PUTTING THE "OTHER" PLANES BACK IN THE HANGAR, AS LONG AS YOUR PROJECT STILL FITS IN A DRAWER?

www.chickenwingscomics.com
© Michael and Stefan Strasser - 302
THERE'S NO WAY WE'RE LETTING MY PLANES SIT OUTSIDE WHILE YOU'RE FINISHING YOUR PROJECT!
C'MO-O-ON! IT'S ONLY TEMPORARY!
YOU CALL THE NEXT 20 YEARS TEMPORARY?
SO YOU WANT ME TO KEEP MY VINTAGE CLASSIC WARBIRD OUTSIDE AND THREATENED BY THE ELEMENTS?
NO, I WANT YOU TO KEEP IT IN A BOX UNTIL YOU CAN ACTUALLY PUT IT TOGETHER!
FINE!
BUT AT LEAST LET'S GET A REALLY COOL BOX!
OKAY.
AND LET ME KEEP IT IN THE HANGAR!

IT WAS DERRYLS FIRST TIME AS A VOLUNTEER AT THE AIR RACE.
NO, I TOLD YOU TO MARK THE COURSE WITH *PYLONS!*
AAH!

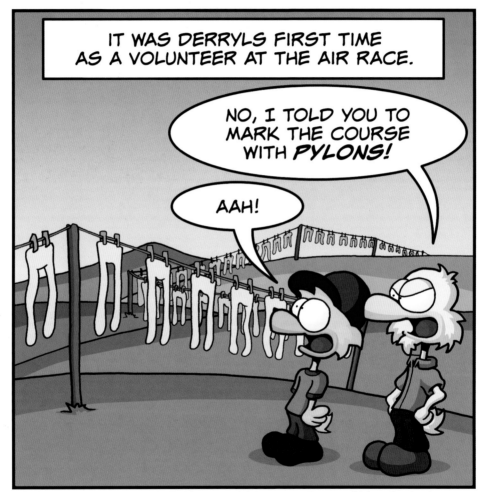

HEY JULIO, YOU KNOW WHAT I WANNA DO?!
BECOME A GOOD PILOT?
NO! WAIT... WHAT?
I WANT TO ENTER MY CORSAIR AT THE RENO AIR RACES!
ARE YOU SERIOUS?
OF COURSE! ALL I NEED IS A BIGGER ENGINE, BETTER PROPS AND LOTS AND LOTS OF TURBOCHARGERS!
© Michael and Stefan Strasser - 218
www.chickenwingscomics.com
WELL, THEN LET'S HOPE THEY STILL HAVE THE AIR RACES 30 YEARS FROM NOW!
UHM, YEAH...

RENO AIR RACES FRONT ROW! *YAY!*
© Michael and Stefan Strasser - 310
VROOM
WOW!!
www.chickenwingscomics.com
BRAZOOM
SWEET!!
SO, HOW CAN YOU THROW OUT YOUR NECK AT AN AIR RACE, FOR CRYING OUT LOUD?
WHAT? YES! VERY LOUD! BUT AWESOME!

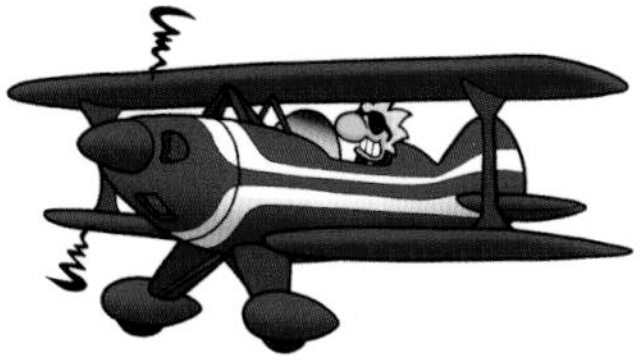

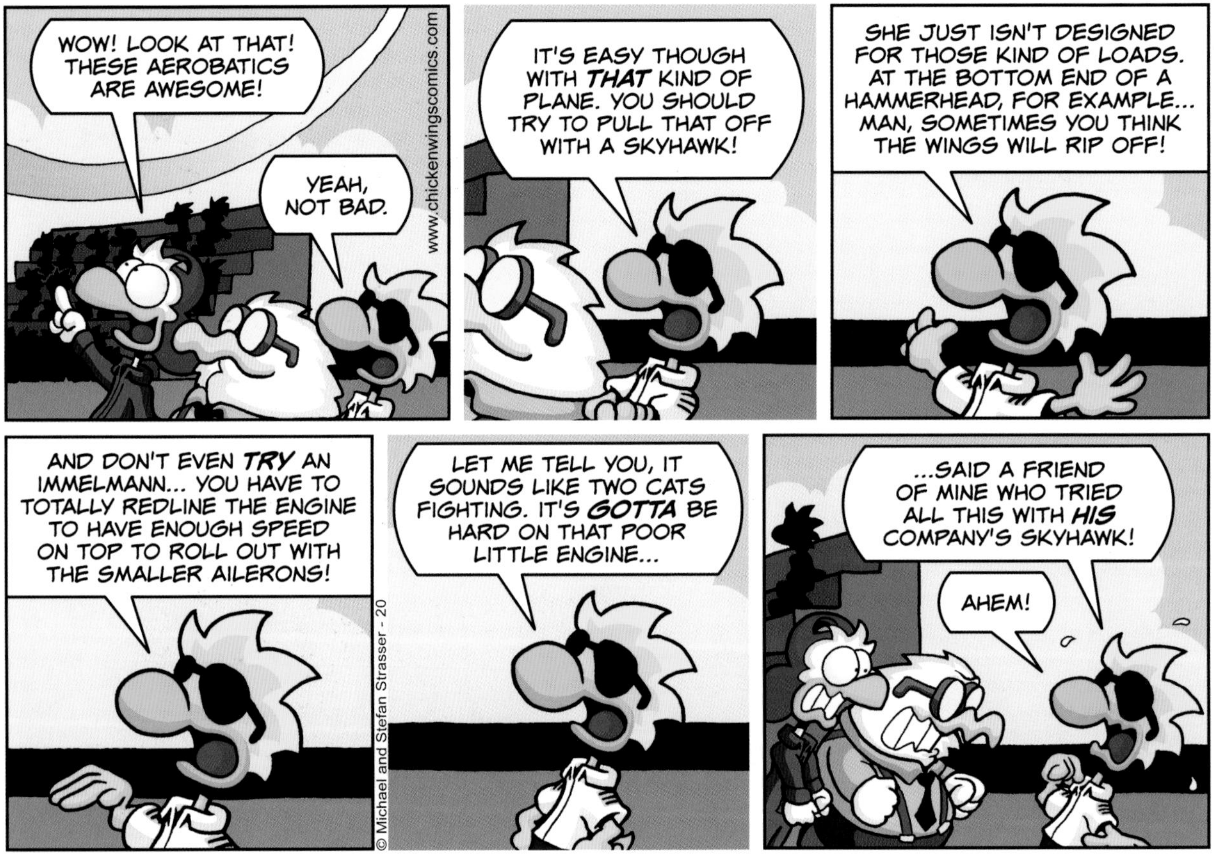
WOW! LOOK AT THAT! THESE AEROBATICS ARE AWESOME!
YEAH, NOT BAD.
www.chickenwingscomics.com
IT'S EASY THOUGH WITH THAT KIND OF PLANE. YOU SHOULD TRY TO PULL THAT OFF WITH A SKYHAWK!
SHE JUST ISN'T DESIGNED FOR THOSE KIND OF LOADS. AT THE BOTTOM END OF A HAMMERHEAD, FOR EXAMPLE... MAN, SOMETIMES YOU THINK THE WINGS WILL RIP OFF!
AND DON'T EVEN TRY AN IMMELMANN... YOU HAVE TO TOTALLY REDLINE THE ENGINE TO HAVE ENOUGH SPEED ON TOP TO ROLL OUT WITH THE SMALLER AILERONS!
© Michael and Stefan Strasser - 20
LET ME TELL YOU, IT SOUNDS LIKE TWO CATS FIGHTING. IT'S GOTTA BE HARD ON THAT POOR LITTLE ENGINE...
...SAID A FRIEND OF MINE WHO TRIED ALL THIS WITH HIS COMPANY'S SKYHAWK!
AHEM!

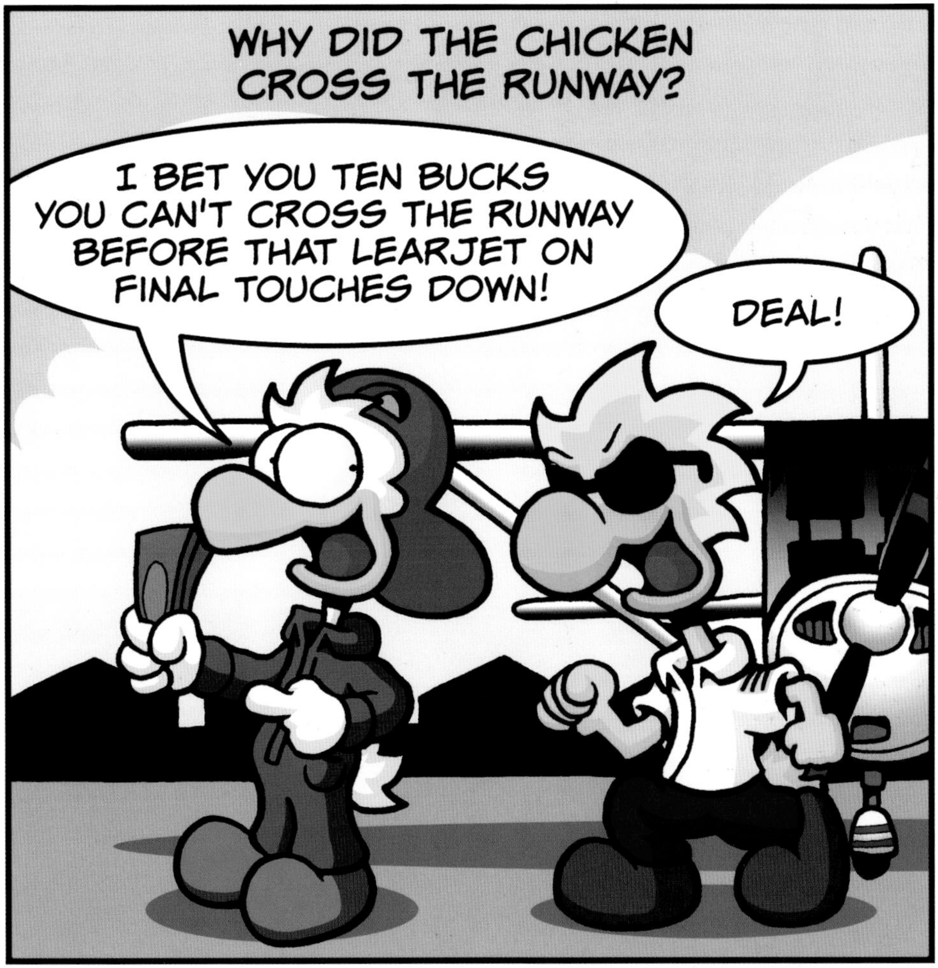
WHY DID THE CHICKEN CROSS THE RUNWAY?
I BET YOU TEN BUCKS YOU CAN'T CROSS THE RUNWAY BEFORE THAT LEARJET ON FINAL TOUCHES DOWN!
DEAL!

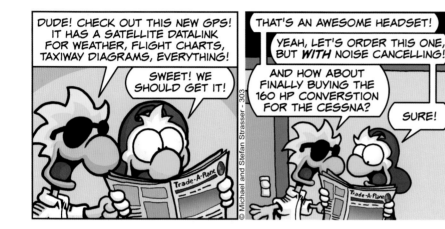

DUDE! CHECK OUT THIS NEW GPS! IT HAS A SATELLITE DATALINK FOR WEATHER, FLIGHT CHARTS, TAXIWAY DIAGRAMS, EVERYTHING!
SWEET! WE SHOULD GET IT!
Trade-A-Plane
© Michael and Stefan Strasser - 303
THAT'S AN AWESOME HEADSET!
YEAH, LET'S ORDER THIS ONE, BUT WITH NOISE CANCELLING!
AND HOW ABOUT FINALLY BUYING THE 160 HP CONVERSTION FOR THE CESSNA?
SURE!
Trade-A-Plane
www.chickenwingscomics.com
SO... WHAT ARE WE REALLY GETTING?
SOME COTTER PINS AND AN OIL FILTER.
Trade-A-Plane

WOOHOO! LIVIN' ON A PRAYER!
OH PUHLEEZE!! DO YOU HAVE TO SING THIS SONG ON EVERY FLIGHT?
© Michael and Stefan Strasser - 256
OF COURSE! DON'T YOU SEE? IN A SENSE WE ARE LIKE TOMMY AND GINA!
WHAT? WHY? YOU'RE NOT MAKING ANY SENSE AGAIN!
www.chickenwingscomics.com
LOOK AT THE GPS! WE'RE "HALFWAY THERE"!
OUCH.

www.chickenwingscomics.com
SIR, IT APPEARS THAT WITH YOUR SIZE, YOU MIGHT HAVE TO BUY TWO SEATS.
WAS? THAT'S OUTRAGEOUS! I WILL NOT PAY FOR THAT!
© Michael and Stefan Strasser - 262
BUT TRY TO LOOK ON THE BRIGHT SIDE. YOU WILL ALSO GET TWO INFLIGHT MEALS.
HMM... THOSE ARE USUALLY PRETTY SMALL...
AND TWO DESSERTS!
OKAY! TWO SEATS PLEASE!!

UH-OH... THIS LOOKS TRICKY. WHICH BUTTON SHOULD I PUSH? I HOPE I DON'T GET THE WRONG ONE!
© Michael and Stefan Strasser - 235
MAN, IF I SCREW THIS UP, IT IS GOING TO COST ME! I AM NOT EVEN PROPERLY CHECKED OUT ON THIS MACHINE!
www.chickenwingscomics.com
YAY! IT WORKED! I WAS AFRAID I'D GET THE DIET SODA...
SODA

FUNNY... DID YOU NOTICE THAT BUSINESS IS RUNNING REALLY SMOOTHLY RECENTLY?
YOU'RE RIGHT! NOW THAT YOU MENTION IT.
© Michael and Stefan Strasser - 237
NO PAPERWORK MESSED UP.
NO TWO JOBS SCHEDULED ON THE SAME DAY AND TOO CLOSE TO EACH OTHER.
AND THERE'S ALWAYS CHOCOLATE BARS IN THE VENDING MACHINE!
I WONDER WHY THAT IS!
www.chickenwingscomics.com
HEY EVERYONE! I'M BACK FROM VACATION! DID YOU GUYS MISS ME?

HEY JULIO, THE CESSNA REALLY NEEDS SOME EXTRA POWER!
WOW! WHAT A NEWSFLASH! AND I REALLY NEED A RAISE!
© Michael and Stefan Strasser - 221
BUT I AM SERIOUS! THE LACK OF POWER JUST GOT ME INTO A VERY INCONVENIENT SITUATION.
REALLY?
www.chickenwingscomics.com
YEAH, THE PLANE WOULDN'T START MOVING, EVEN AT FULL THROTTLE! I ACTUALLY HAD TO ***GET OUT AND REMOVE THE CHOCKS!*** CAN YOU BELIEVE IT?
OH, THE OUTRAGE!

AERONAUTICAL-CHART-FOLDING
RESEARCH LABORATORY
M.C. Escher
$S=\int L dt = -mc\int\left(c-\frac{v^2}{2c}+\frac{\Phi}{c}\right)dt$
$ds=\left(c-\frac{v^2}{2c}+\frac{\Phi}{c}\right)dt$
$g_{00}=1+\frac{2\Phi}{c^2}, \Phi=-\frac{MG}{r}$
ORI GAMI
WARPED SPACE-TIME

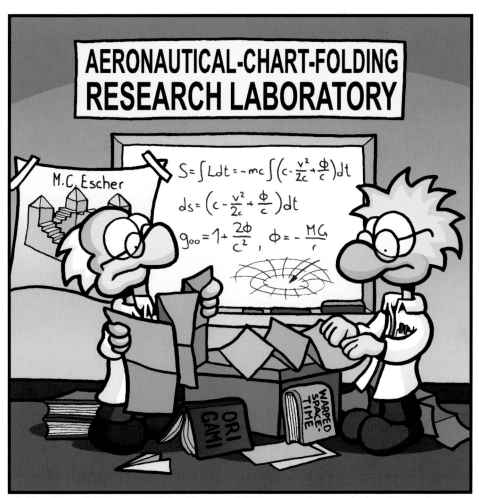

ARGH!! WHAT THE HELL HAVE YOU DONE TO MY PLANE?!

WELL, I THOUGHT I'D HELP YOU OUT. YOU DON'T WANT ME TO COME OVER AND BUG YOU WITH *EVERY LITTLE THING*, DO YOU?

© Michael and Stefan Strasser - 230

BUT... LITTLE THING... I MEAN...

YOU'RE NOT THE ONLY ONE HERE WHO KNOWS HOW TO TURN A SCREWDRIVER, YOU KNOW?

AND SO I WAS WATCHING "PIMP MY RIDE" LAST NIGHT AND I THOUGHT...

I BELIEVE YOU WERE WATCHING! I JUST DON'T BELIEVE YOU WERE *THINKING!*

www.chickenwingscomics.com

MAN, WHAT A DUMP! I THINK I WILL CLEAN UP THIS HANGAR!

GOOD CALL! I'M GONNA HELP YOU.

© Michael and Stefan Strasser - 258

THERE YOU ARE, YOU TWO LAZY BUMS! LOOK AT THIS MESS! I WANT YOU TO CLEAN THE HANGAR RIGHT NOW!

www.chickenwingscomics.com

SUDDENLY I DON'T FEEL LIKE IT ANYMORE.

FUNNY, ME NEITHER!

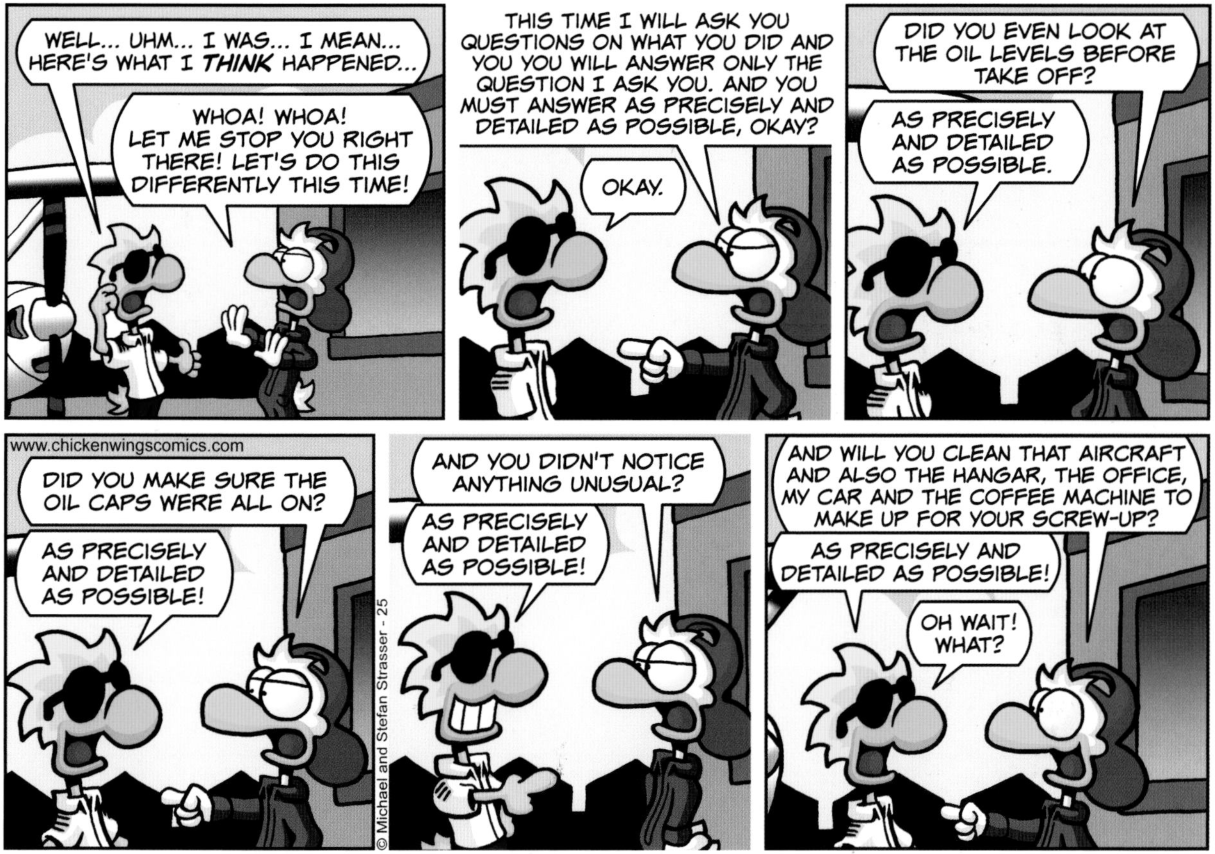
WELL... UHM... I WAS... I MEAN... HERE'S WHAT I ***THINK*** HAPPENED...
WHOA! WHOA! LET ME STOP YOU RIGHT THERE! LET'S DO THIS DIFFERENTLY THIS TIME!
THIS TIME I WILL ASK YOU QUESTIONS ON WHAT YOU DID AND YOU YOU WILL ANSWER ONLY THE QUESTION I ASK YOU. AND YOU MUST ANSWER AS PRECISELY AND DETAILED AS POSSIBLE, OKAY?
OKAY.
DID YOU EVEN LOOK AT THE OIL LEVELS BEFORE TAKE OFF?
AS PRECISELY AND DETAILED AS POSSIBLE.
www.chickenwingscomics.com
DID YOU MAKE SURE THE OIL CAPS WERE ALL ON?
AS PRECISELY AND DETAILED AS POSSIBLE!
© Michael and Stefan Strasser - 25
AND YOU DIDN'T NOTICE ANYTHING UNUSUAL?
AS PRECISELY AND DETAILED AS POSSIBLE!
AND WILL YOU CLEAN THAT AIRCRAFT AND ALSO THE HANGAR, THE OFFICE, MY CAR AND THE COFFEE MACHINE TO MAKE UP FOR YOUR SCREW-UP?
AS PRECISELY AND DETAILED AS POSSIBLE!
OH WAIT! WHAT?

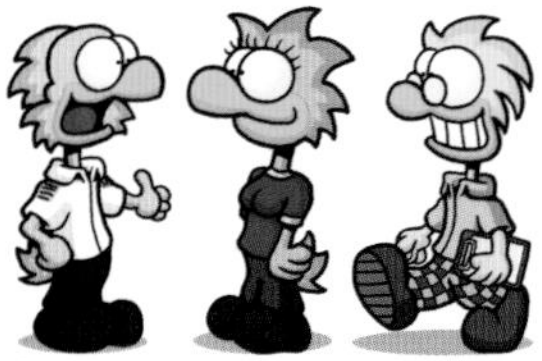

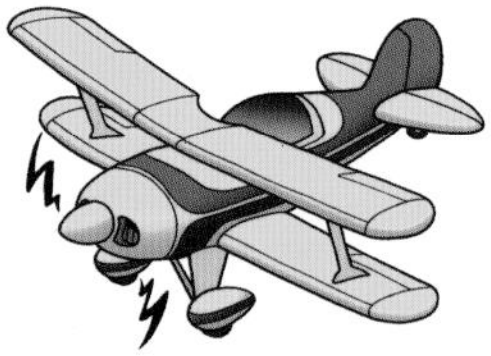

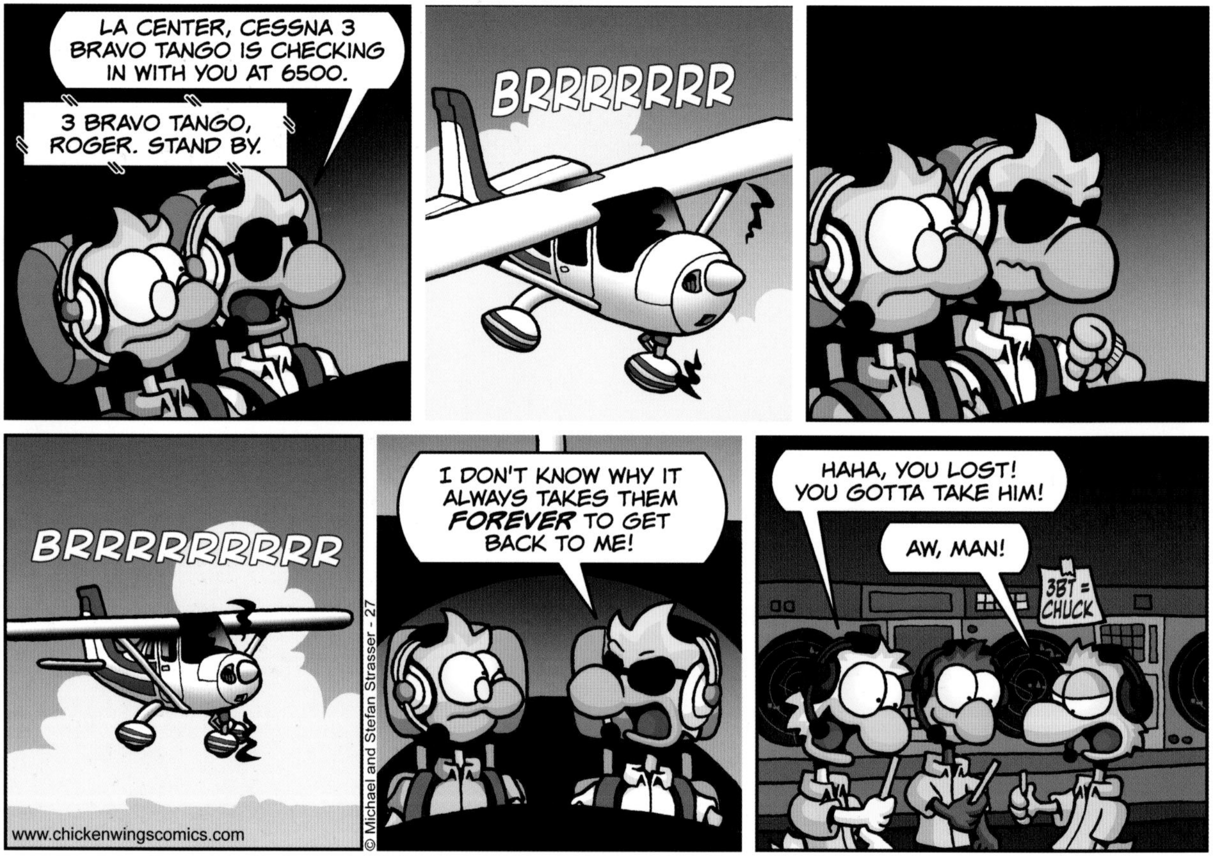

LA CENTER, CESSNA 3 BRAVO TANGO IS CHECKING IN WITH YOU AT 6500.
3 BRAVO TANGO, ROGER. STAND BY.
BRRRRRRR
BRRRRRRRRRR
www.chickenwingscomics.com
© Michael and Stefan Strasser - 27
I DON'T KNOW WHY IT ALWAYS TAKES THEM ***FOREVER*** TO GET BACK TO ME!
HAHA, YOU LOST! YOU GOTTA TAKE HIM!
AW, MAN!
3BT = CHUCK

AH, THE OLD CESSNA SKYMASTER!
THEY JUST DON'T BUILD 'EM LIKE THIS ANYMORE.
© Michael and Stefan Strasser - 275
NOPE, THEY SURE DON'T...
www.chickenwingscomics.com
THANK GOD!

POOR JULIO! HE'S GOT THE HICCUPS REALLY BAD!
FEAR NOT! I KNOW JUST THE THING!
HICK!
© Michael and Stefan Strasser - 255
HEY JULIO! HANS JUST TOLD ME HE'S GONNA ADD AN OLD, AIR-CONDITIONED CESSNA SKYMASTER TO THE FLEET.
WHAAAT?! THERE'S NO PARTS FOR THOSE! AND THE AIR CONDITION? WHAT A NIGHTMARE!
www.chickenwingscomics.com
ARE THE HICCUPS GONE?
YEAH, THANKS! YOU SCARED THE CRAP OUT OF ME!

HELI-SKIING:
WHY SHOULD
THE TOURISTS HAVE
ALL THE FUN?

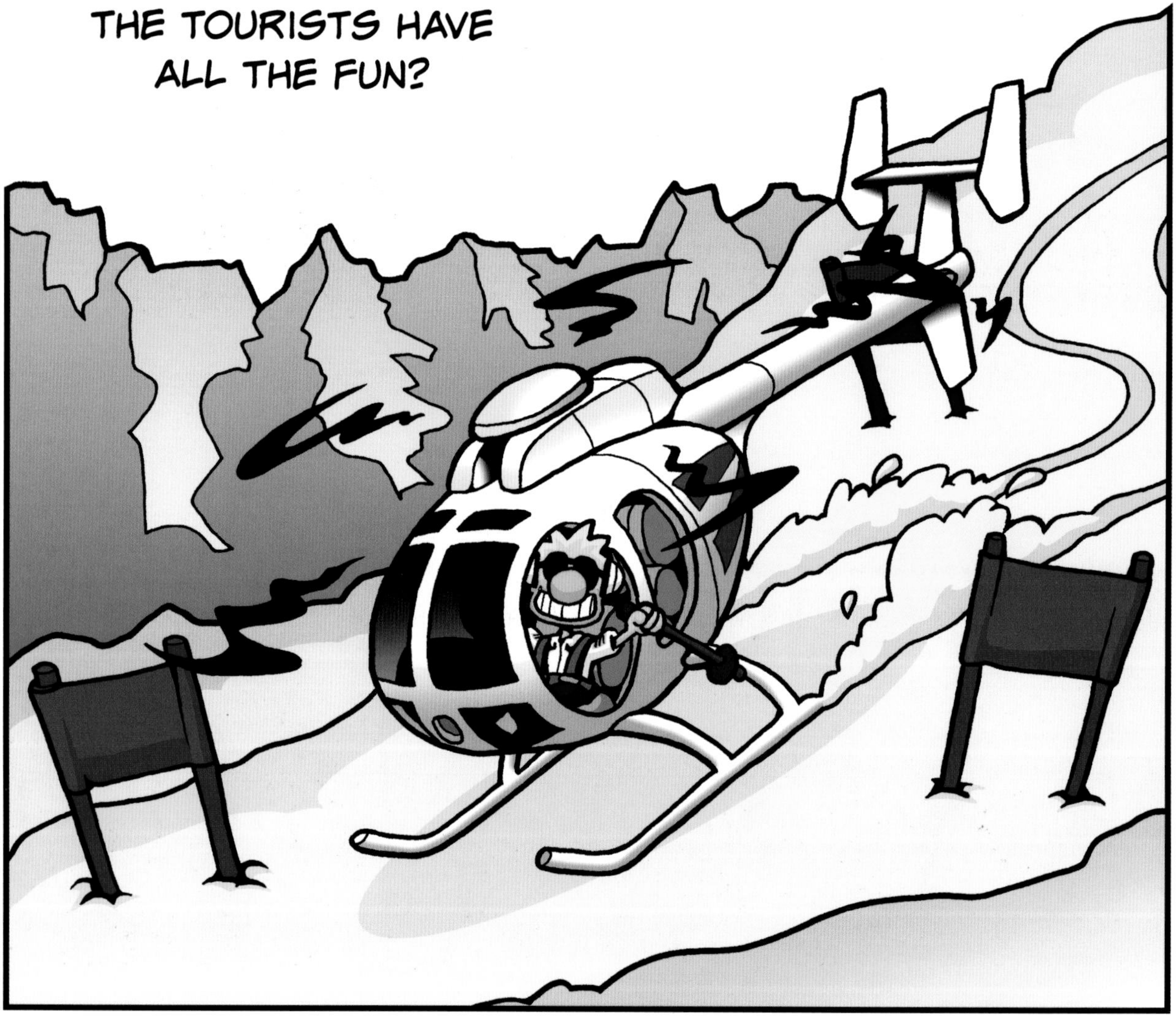

PFEW, THANKS MAN! THAT WAS A PRETTY TIGHT SPOT!

NO KIDDING!

www.chickenwingscomics.com

© Michael and Stefan Strasser - 259

GOOD AFTERNOON! IT SAYS HERE I HAVE BEEN RANDOMLY SELECTED FOR A DRUG TEST.

THAT'S RIGHT! WELCOME!

SO, WHICH DRUGS DO YOU WANT ME TO TEST? HOW MUCH WILL I GET PAID? LET ME CHECK OUT THE SAMPLES!

UH, NO SIR. YOU HAVE TO GIVE US A SAMPLE!

© Michael and Stefan Strasser - 260

www.chickenwingscomics.com

WHAT? BUT I DON'T HAVE ANY DRUGS!

BOY, HE'S LUCKY HE IS NOT HERE FOR AN IQ-TEST!

75

www.chickenwingscomics.com
AH, MAN! I STILL GOTTA CHANGE THAT VACUUM PUMP ON THE SKYHAWK.
AT LEAST YOU'RE INSIDE THE HANGAR! LOOK AT THE RAIN! I REALLY DON'T WANT TO FLY TODAY.
© Michael and Stefan Strasser - 261
SURE YOU'LL FLY! IT WILL BE ALRIGHT, BELIEVE ME!
AND YOU, JULIO, WHY DON'T YOU LET ALL THAT TIRESOME PLANE FIXING BE AND TAKE THE REST OF THE DAY OFF?
WHAT'S WRONG WITH YOU? DID YOU WIN THE LOTTERY OR SOMETHING?
SORT OF! I JUST GOT US A GREAT INSURANCE DEAL! IF ONE OF OUR PLANES CRASHES NOW, WE WILL GET MORE THAN IT IS ACTUALLY WORTH!
GULP!

HEY CHUCK! HOW'S IT GOING?
NOT SO GOOD. MY JAW HURTS!
© Michael and Stefan Strasser - 287
DID YOU DROP IT AGAIN?
WHAT? NO, I JUST GOT BACK FROM THE DENTIST AND I HAVE A HARD TIME KEEPING MY MOUTH OPEN THAT LONG.
www.chickenwingscomics.com
REALLY? NOW THAT'S IRONIC! YOU USUALLY HAVE A HARD TIME KEEPING IT SHUT!

SALLY! CALL CHUCK ON THE RADIO AND TELL HIM TO TAXI BACK TO THE SHOP! I FORGOT TO CHECK SOMETHING!

HE JUST LEFT WITH THE PLANE!

I KNOW!

www.chickenwingscomics.com

BUT... TAXI? COULDN'T HE JUST DRIVE BACK HERE WITH THE PLANE?

ARE YOU READY FOR A SCARY MOVIE?

SURE! WHICH ONE IS IT? THE SILENCE OF THE LAMBS? THE SHINING?

HALLOWEEN? THE RING?

I DON'T KNOW! JULIO OUR MECHANIC GAVE IT TO ME AND HE SAID IT WAS THE SCARIEST MOVIE HE HAS EVER SEEN!

COOL!

CHUCK'S TAKE-OFFS AND LANDINGS – FILMED AND EDITED BY JULIO   RATED R!

HEY!!

© Michael and Stefan Strasser - 268

© Michael and Stefan Strasser - 269

www.chickenwingscomics.com

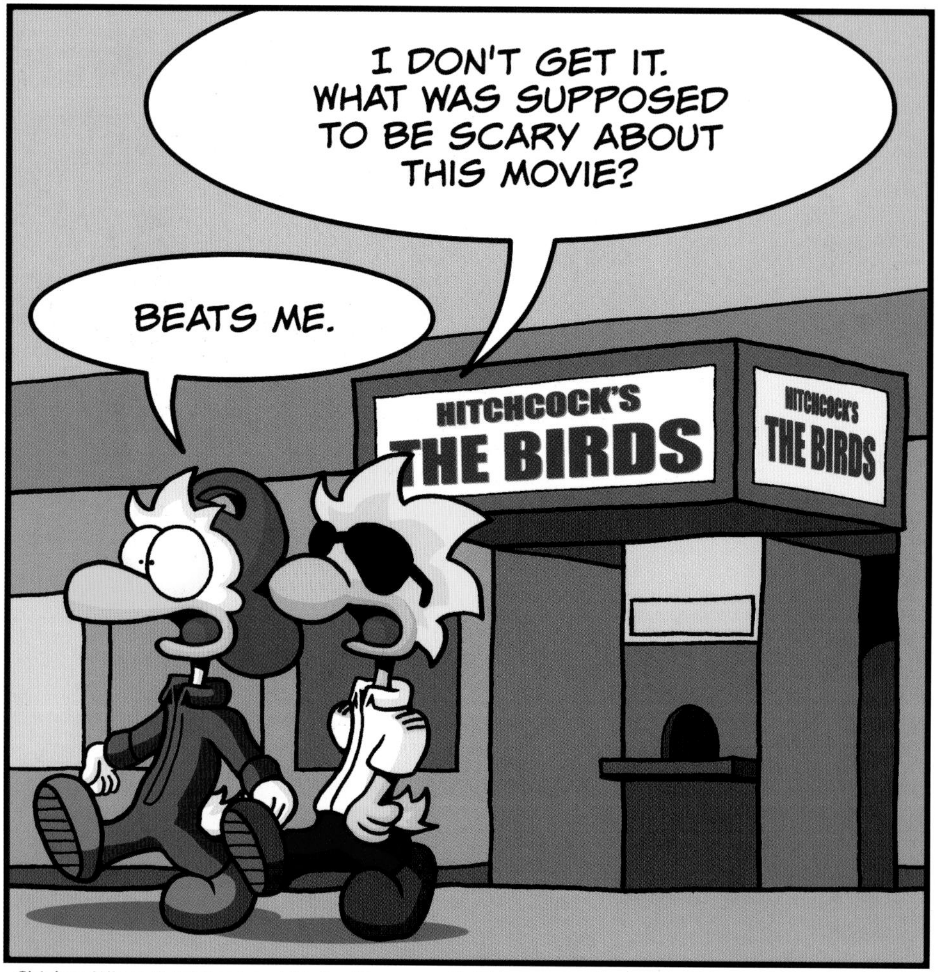
I DON'T GET IT. WHAT WAS SUPPOSED TO BE SCARY ABOUT THIS MOVIE?
BEATS ME.
HITCHCOCK'S THE BIRDS
HITCHCOCK'S THE BIRDS

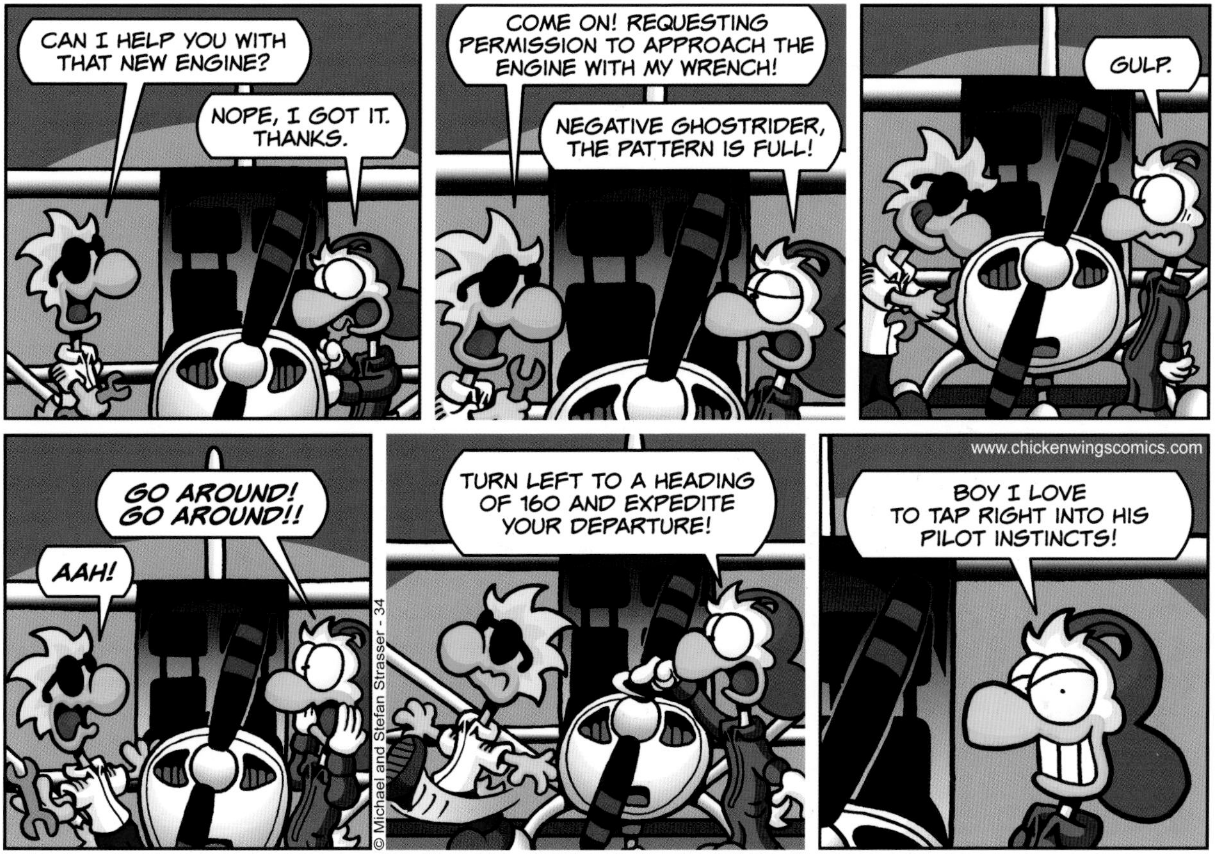
CAN I HELP YOU WITH THAT NEW ENGINE?
NOPE, I GOT IT. THANKS.
COME ON! REQUESTING PERMISSION TO APPROACH THE ENGINE WITH MY WRENCH!
NEGATIVE GHOSTRIDER, THE PATTERN IS FULL!
GULP.
www.chickenwingscomics.com
GO AROUND! GO AROUND!!
AAH!
© Michael and Stefan Strasser - 34
TURN LEFT TO A HEADING OF 160 AND EXPEDITE YOUR DEPARTURE!
BOY I LOVE TO TAP RIGHT INTO HIS PILOT INSTINCTS!

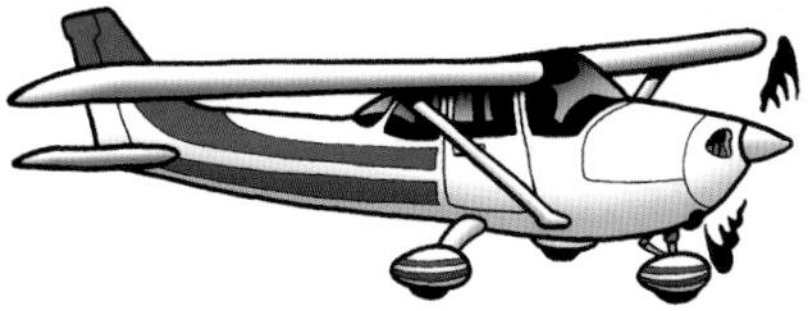

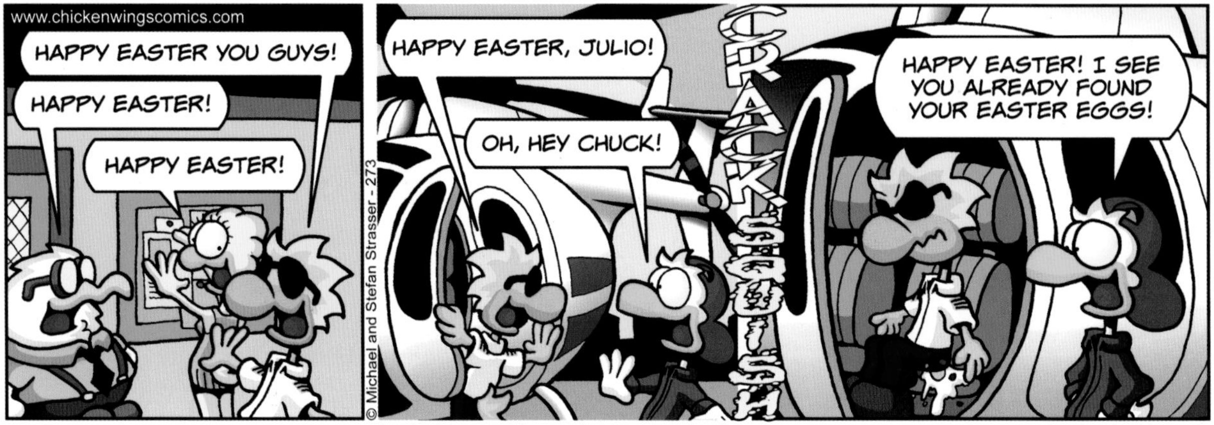
www.chickenwingscomics.com
HAPPY EASTER YOU GUYS!
HAPPY EASTER!
HAPPY EASTER!
© Michael and Stefan Strasser - 273
HAPPY EASTER, JULIO!
OH, HEY CHUCK!
CRACK!
HAPPY EASTER! I SEE YOU ALREADY FOUND YOUR EASTER EGGS!

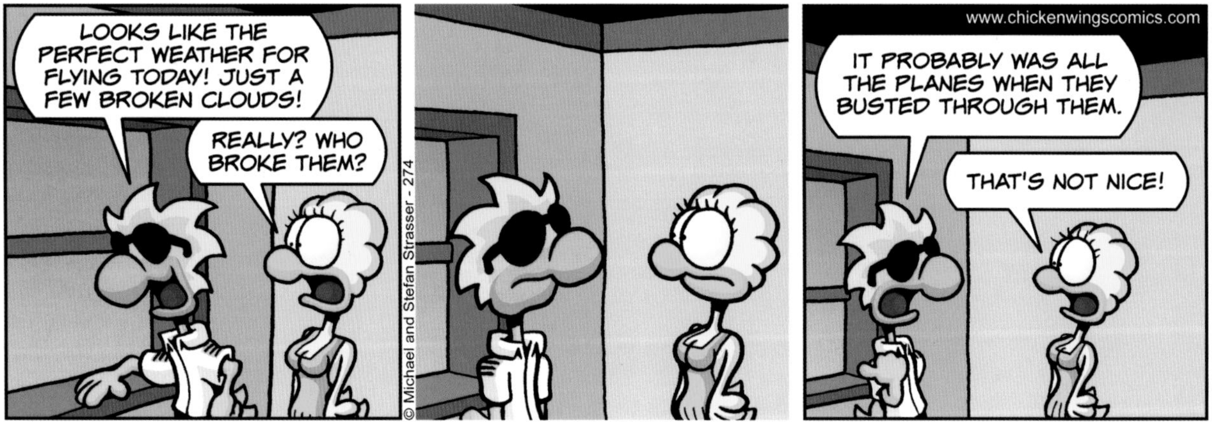
LOOKS LIKE THE PERFECT WEATHER FOR FLYING TODAY! JUST A FEW BROKEN CLOUDS!
REALLY? WHO BROKE THEM?
© Michael and Stefan Strasser - 274
www.chickenwingscomics.com
IT PROBABLY WAS ALL THE PLANES WHEN THEY BUSTED THROUGH THEM.
THAT'S NOT NICE!

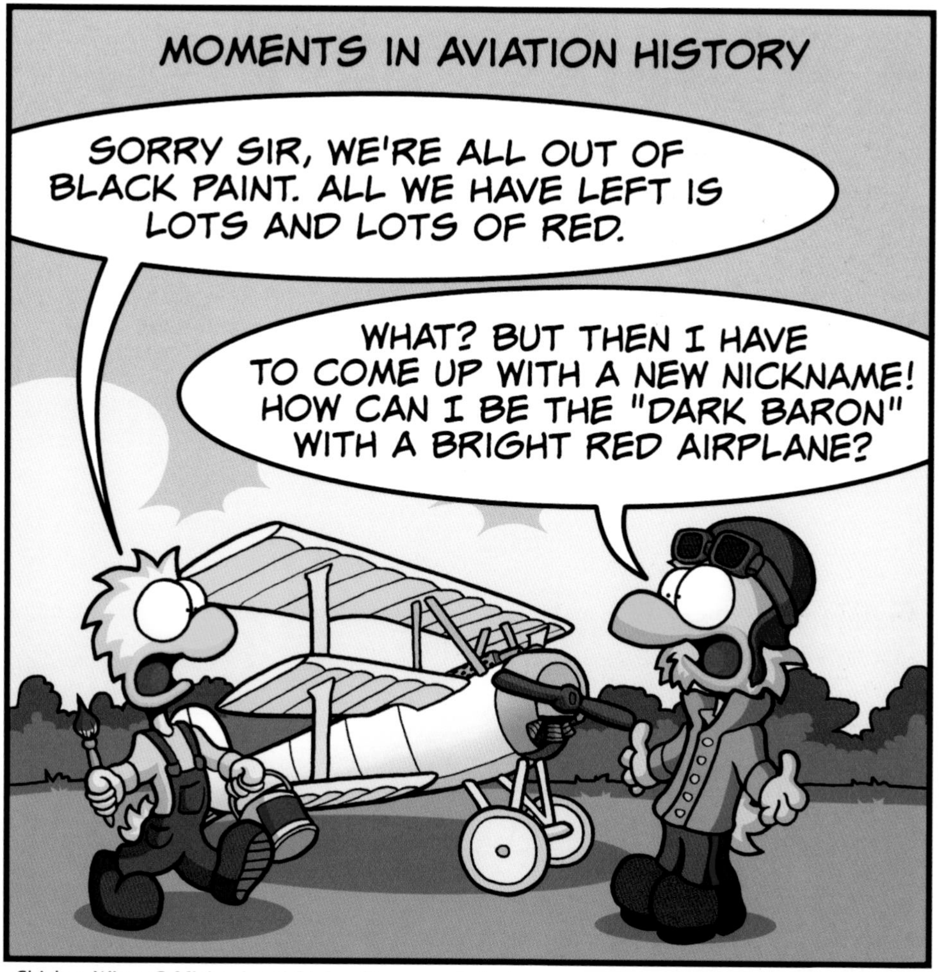
MOMENTS IN AVIATION HISTORY
SORRY SIR, WE'RE ALL OUT OF BLACK PAINT. ALL WE HAVE LEFT IS LOTS AND LOTS OF RED.
WHAT? BUT THEN I HAVE TO COME UP WITH A NEW NICKNAME! HOW CAN I BE THE "DARK BARON" WITH A BRIGHT RED AIRPLANE?

CHUCK, CAN YOU HAND ME THE MAP PLEASE?
SURE!
© Michael and Stefan Strasser - 276
SAY, THE "SHORTCUT" YOU WERE TALKING ABOUT... DOES IT GO THROUGH AREA 51?
AREA WHAT? IS THAT ONE OF THOSE WITH THE DASH MARKS ON THE EDGE? POSSIBLE, WHY?
www.chickenwingscomics.com
CHUCK, YOU THAT IS?
A WILD GUESS, REALLY.

HEY JULIO, I'M LEAKING OIL!
REALLY? HOW EMBARRASSING! LET ME TAKE A LOOK.
© Michael and Stefan Strasser - 279
www.chickenwingscomics.com
I MEAN THE *ENGINE* OF THE *AIRPLANE* IS LEAKING OIL.
RIGHT!

www.chickenwingscomics.com
© Michael and Stefan Strasser - 277
HI MOM! NO, I DID NOT BUY A REMOTE CONTROLLED HELICOPTER FOR 400 BUCKS DON'T BE RIDICULOUS!
NO! DON'T THROW IT AWAY OR SEND IT BACK! SINCE IT'S HERE, I'LL TAKE A LOOK AT IT FIRST.
MPFHTHIHIHI!
YOU *SO* ORDERED IT, DIDN'T YOU?
TOTALLY! IT'S GOING TO BE AWESOME!
YOU'RE *SO* GONNA BREAK IT, AREN'T YOU?
TOTALLY!

GOOD MORNING CHUCK! SO, HOW'S IT GOING WITH YOUR NEW REMOTE CONTROLLED HELICOPTER
OH, THAT LITTLE THING? IT WAS FUN FOR A WHILE, BUT I HAVE ALREADY GROWN WEARY OF IT.
© Michael and Stefan Strasser - 289
REALLY?
NOT AFTER ESTABLISHING A NEW WORLD RECORD THOUGH, I MIGHT ADD!
WHAT, LIKE "FROM COMPLETION TO COMPLETE DESTRUCTION IN LESS THAN FIVE SECONDS?"
DON'T BE RIDICULOUS!
IT TOOK ME SEVEN SECONDS.
www.chickenwingscomics.com

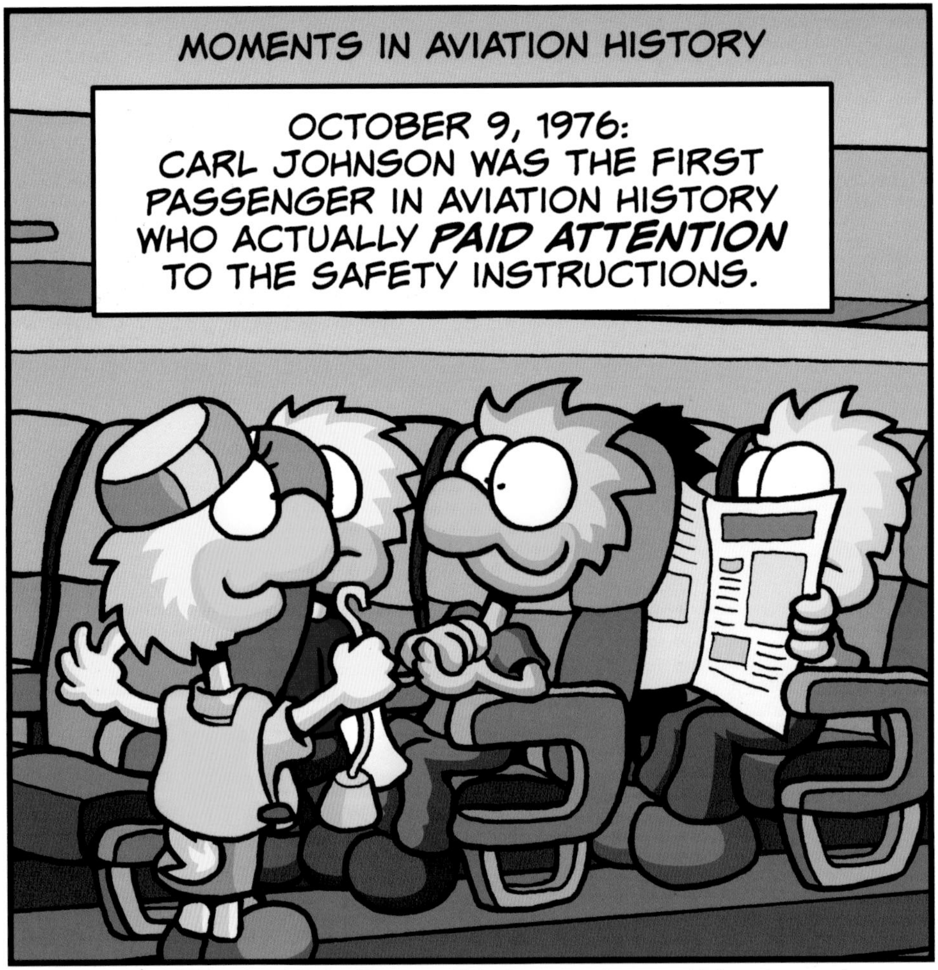
MOMENTS IN AVIATION HISTORY
OCTOBER 9, 1976:
CARL JOHNSON WAS THE FIRST
PASSENGER IN AVIATION HISTORY
WHO ACTUALLY PAID ATTENTION
TO THE SAFETY INSTRUCTIONS.

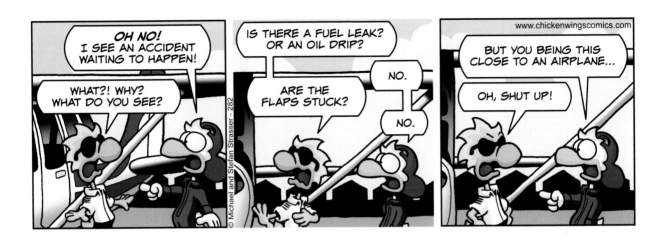

www.chickenwingscomics.com

Panel 1: OH NO! I SEE AN ACCIDENT WAITING TO HAPPEN!

WHAT?! WHY? WHAT DO YOU SEE?

Panel 2: IS THERE A FUEL LEAK? OR AN OIL DRIP?

ARE THE FLAPS STUCK?

NO.

NO.

Panel 3: BUT YOU BEING THIS CLOSE TO AN AIRPLANE...

OH, SHUT UP!

© Michael and Stefan Strasser - 282

www.chickenwingscomics.com

Panel 4: CHUCK, SALLY TOLD ME THAT AN NTSB ACCIDENT INVESTIGATOR CALLED HERE TODAY.

REALLY? WHAT DID HE WANT?

I DON'T KNOW!

Panel 5: HE PROBABLY WANTED TO SYNC UP HIS CALENDAR WITH YOUR FLIGHT SCHEDULE!

VERY FUNNY! HOW DO YOU KNOW HE DIDN'T CALL TO OFFER ME A JOB?

LIKE THEY'D HIRE YOU!

Panel 6: QUITE THE CONTRARY! CHUCK WOULD MAKE A GREAT INVESTIGATOR! AFTER ALL HE'S FAMILIAR WITH ALL ASPECTS OF "PILOT ERROR"!

© Michael and Stefan Strasser - 278

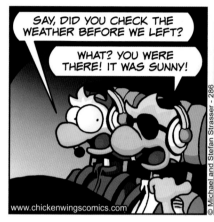

SAY, DID YOU CHECK THE WEATHER BEFORE WE LEFT?
WHAT? YOU WERE THERE! IT WAS SUNNY!
www.chickenwingscomics.com
© Michael and Stefan Strasser - 286
I MEAN, DID YOU CALL THE FLIGHT SERVICE STATION?
OH! UHM... WELL... TECHNICALLY, NO.
BUT DON'T YOU WORRY! I'LL JUST CALL THEM TWICE BEFORE OUR FLIGHT BACK!

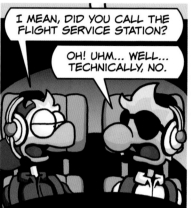

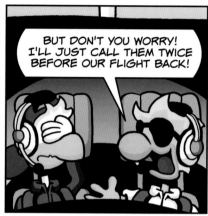

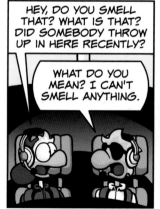

HEY, DO YOU SMELL THAT? WHAT IS THAT? DID SOMEBODY THROW UP IN HERE RECENTLY?
WHAT DO YOU MEAN? I CAN'T SMELL ANYTHING.
SERIOUSLY! MAYBE SOME SMALL ANIMAL DIED BEHIND THE PANEL OR SOMETHING. I HAVE TO CHECK IT OUT!
I'M SURE IT'S NOTHING!
DON'T!
OH!
© Michael and Stefan Strasser - 292
www.chickenwingscomics.com
SORRY, I DIDN'T MEAN TO INSULT YOU OR NOTHING.
WHAT? ***YOU*** NEVER TAKE OFF ***YOUR*** SHOES DURING FLIGHT?

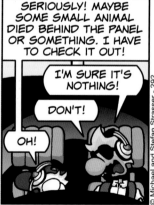

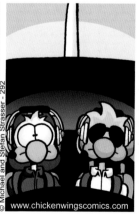

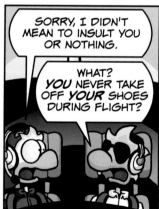

www.chickenwingscomics.com

HEY CHUCK, THERE'S A GUY FROM THE FAA IN THE OFFICE. I THINK HE'S LOOKING FOR YOU!

SEE YA!

POOF!

© Michael and Stefan Strasser - 280

WORKS EVERY TIME!

HEHEHE!

CHUCK, THERE'S A GUY IN A FUNNY LOOKING UNIFORM IN THE OFFICE WHO'S LOOKING FOR YOU!

OH NO! THAT MUST BE THAT GUY FROM THE FAA!

© Michael and Stefan Strasser - 281

www.chickenwingscomics.com

BUT WORRY NOT! I WILL TAKE CARE OF THIS MATTER FOR YOU!

THANKS! LATER!

SWOOSH!

I WONDER IF SOME DAY HE WILL ASK ME WHICH UNIFORM THAT GUY WAS WEARING!

GOOD THING HE ALWAYS PAYS HIS PIZZA WITH HIS CREDIT CARD!

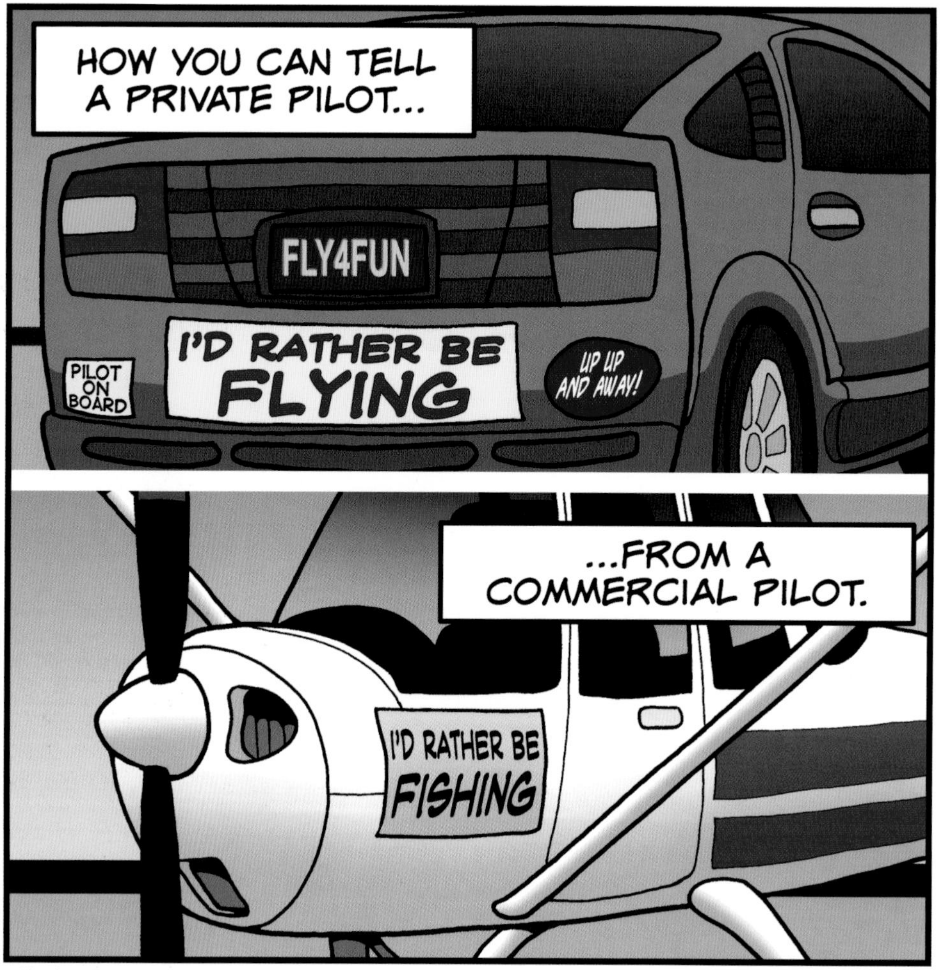
HOW YOU CAN TELL A PRIVATE PILOT...
FLY4FUN
PILOT ON BOARD
I'D RATHER BE FLYING
UP UP AND AWAY!
...FROM A COMMERCIAL PILOT.
I'D RATHER BE FISHING

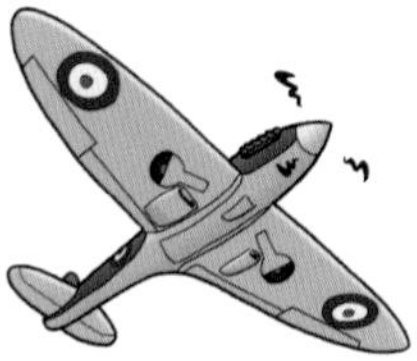

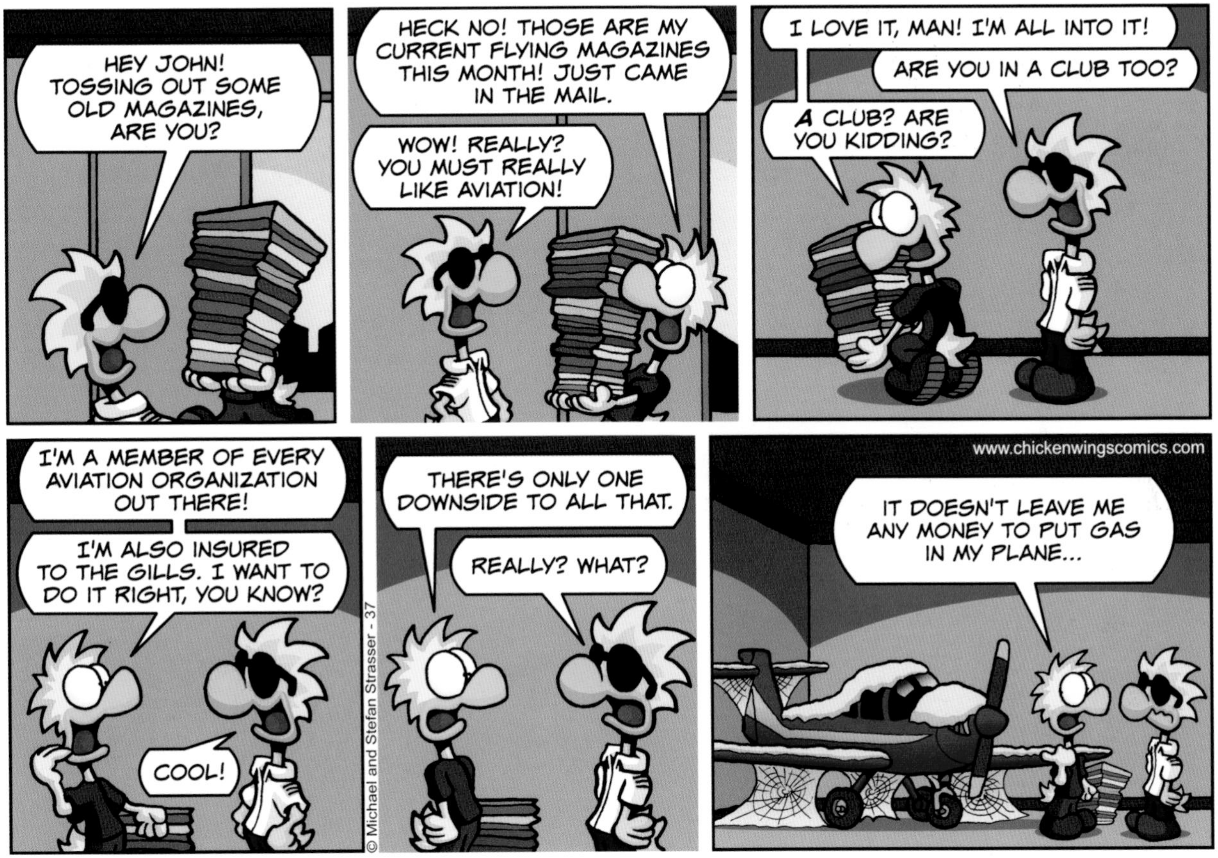
HEY JOHN! TOSSING OUT SOME OLD MAGAZINES, ARE YOU?
HECK NO! THOSE ARE MY CURRENT FLYING MAGAZINES THIS MONTH! JUST CAME IN THE MAIL.
WOW! REALLY? YOU MUST REALLY LIKE AVIATION!
I LOVE IT, MAN! I'M ALL INTO IT!
ARE YOU IN A CLUB TOO?
A CLUB? ARE YOU KIDDING?
I'M A MEMBER OF EVERY AVIATION ORGANIZATION OUT THERE!
I'M ALSO INSURED TO THE GILLS. I WANT TO DO IT RIGHT, YOU KNOW?
COOL!
© Michael and Stefan Strasser - 37
THERE'S ONLY ONE DOWNSIDE TO ALL THAT.
REALLY? WHAT?
www.chickenwingscomics.com
IT DOESN'T LEAVE ME ANY MONEY TO PUT GAS IN MY PLANE...

www.chickenwingscomics.com
CAN YOU HOLD THIS BATTERY FOR JUST ONE SECOND?
OKAY!
© Michael and Stefan Strasser - 283
HEY GUYS!
HEY NOBU! WHAT'S UP?
AAARGH!!
SMASH!
! OUCH! GRR!
OOPS, SORRY!
HAHA! THAT'S WHAT YOU CALL "BATTERY AND ASSAULT"!
YOU DID SAY "JUST ONE SECOND", THOUGH.

READY?
LET'S FLY!
© Michael and Stefan Strasser - 293
VROOOM
BRAZOOOM
www.chickenwingscomics.com
LET'S LAND!!

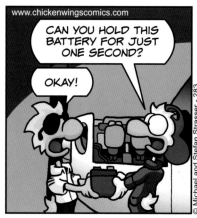

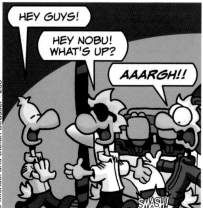

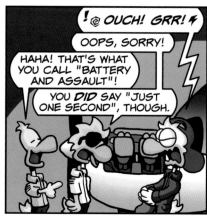

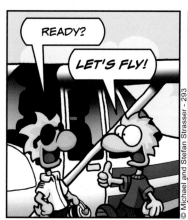

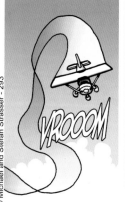

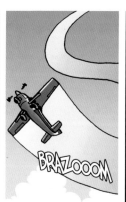

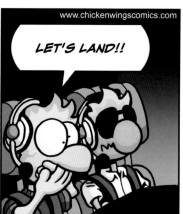

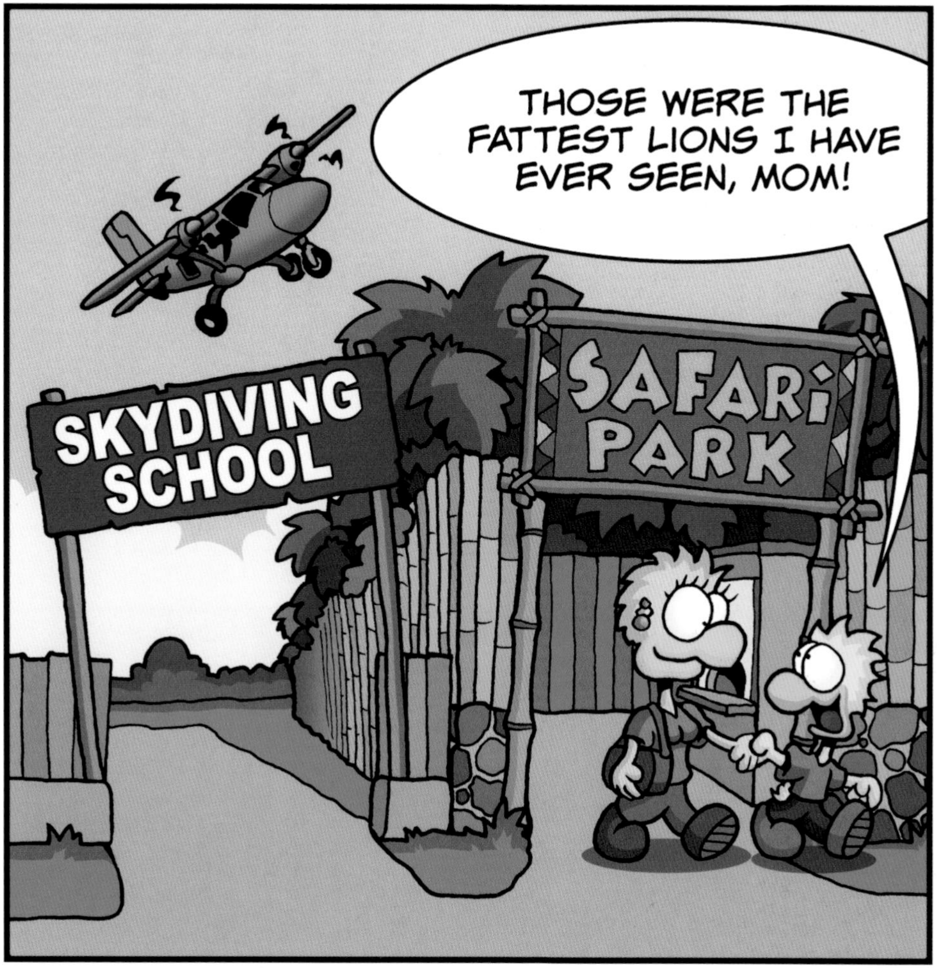
THOSE WERE THE FATTEST LIONS I HAVE EVER SEEN, MOM!
SKYDIVING SCHOOL
SAFARI PARK

WAIT BEFORE YOU PICK UP THE PHONE! IF IT'S THE FAA, TELL THEM I'M OUT IN A MEETING.
IF IT'S MY ACCOUNTANT, TELL HIM I'M ON THE OTHER LINE AND I'LL CALL HIM BACK.
RING! RING! RING!
© Michael and Stefan Strasser - 295
IF IT'S MY LAWYER, DENTIST, THE IRS OR THE BANK, JUST TELL THEM I'M NOT HERE.
RING! RING! RING!
www.chickenwingscomics.com
OOH, NOW LOOK AT THAT! IT STOPPED RINGING.
OH GOOD! PROBLEM SOLVED!

WAIT, WAIT! BEFORE YOU PICK UP THE PHONE... IF IT'S...
OKAY, OKAY!
RING! RING! RING!
© Michael and Stefan Strasser - 296
www.chickenwingscomics.com
WHY DON'T YOU JUST TELL ME WHO YOU ***WILL*** BE HERE FOR?
THE BAKERY, THE PIZZA PLACE ...AND MAYBE MY WIFE.
BOY, I'M SURE GLAD WE HAVE OUR PRIORITIES STRAIGHT OVER HERE.
RING! RING! RING!

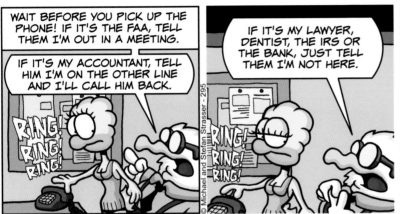

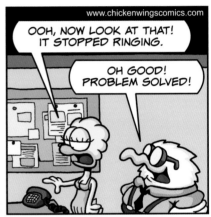

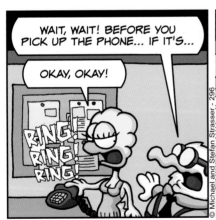

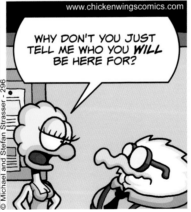

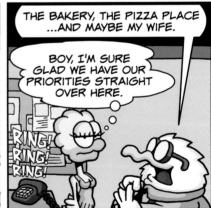

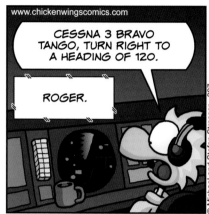

www.chickenwingscomics.com
CESSNA 3 BRAVO TANGO, TURN RIGHT TO A HEADING OF 120.
ROGER.
© Michael and Stefan Strasser - 297
CESSNA 3 BRAVO TANGO, I NEED YOU TO TURN RIGHT TO A HEADING OF 120 IMMEDIATELY!
BUT SIR, I **AM** AT A HEADING OF 120!
NO, YOU'RE NOT!
OH, WAIT! THAT'S MY AIRSPEED!
CHUCK, IS THAT YOU?

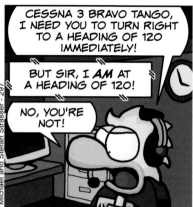

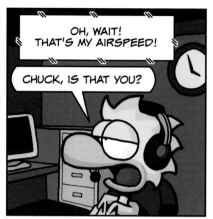

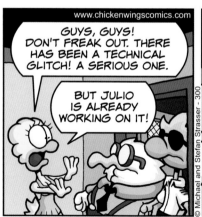

www.chickenwingscomics.com
GUYS, GUYS! DON'T FREAK OUT. THERE HAS BEEN A TECHNICAL GLITCH! A SERIOUS ONE.
BUT JULIO IS ALREADY WORKING ON IT!
© Michael and Stefan Strasser - 300
IS IT WHAT I THINK IT IS?
IT IS.
OH NO! BUT THAT IS OUR COMPANY'S MOST VALUABLE ASSET!
HE'S ALMOST GOT IT FIXED!
WE CAN RESUME NORMAL OPERATIONS. THE COFFEE MACHINE IS REPAIRED!
THANK GOODNESS!

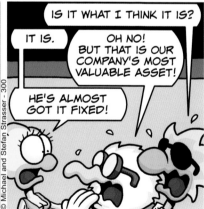

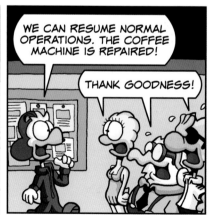

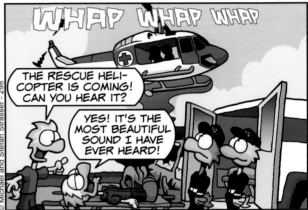

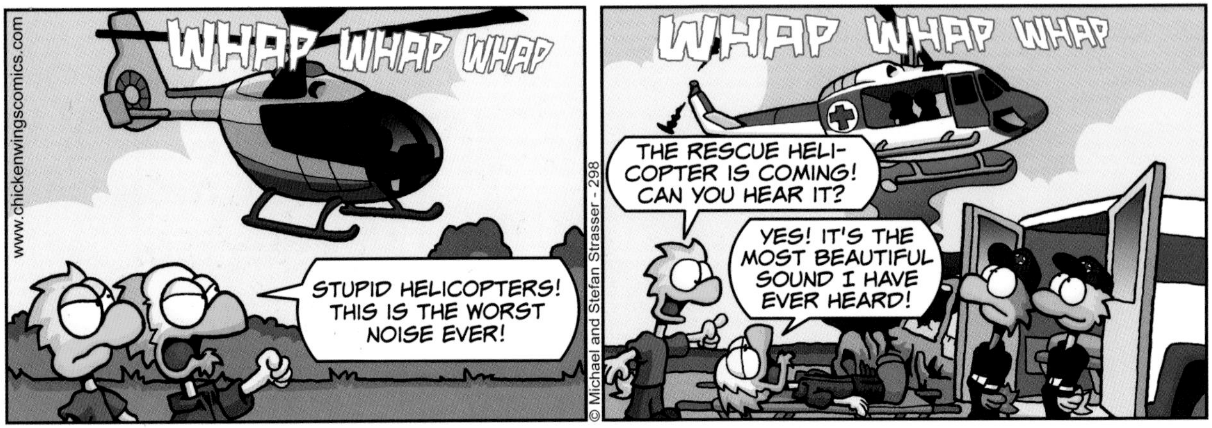

www.chickenwingscomics.com
WHAP WHAP WHAP
STUPID HELICOPTERS! THIS IS THE WORST NOISE EVER!
© Michael and Stefan Strasser - 298
WHAP WHAP WHAP
THE RESCUE HELI-COPTER IS COMING! CAN YOU HEAR IT?
YES! IT'S THE MOST BEAUTIFUL SOUND I HAVE EVER HEARD!

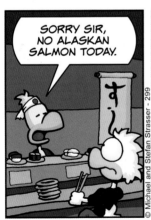

SORRY SIR, NO ALASKAN SALMON TODAY.
© Michael and Stefan Strasser - 299
HERE'S THE PACKAGE WITH YOUR MOM'S CHRISTMAS COOKIES THAT YOU'VE BEEN WAITING FOR!
BUT IT'S *JUNE!*
www.chickenwingscomics.com
GOOD NEWS, BILLY! YOUR NEW KIDNEY IS ALREADY ON THE SHIP AND WILL BE HERE BY OCTOBER!
ISN'T THIS GREAT? EVER SINCE WE WON THE LAWSUIT IT'S PEACE AND QUIET!
NOT A SINGLE PLANE IN THE SKY!

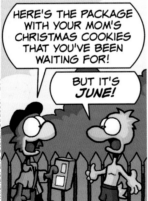

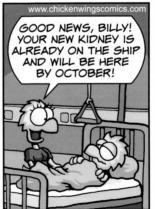

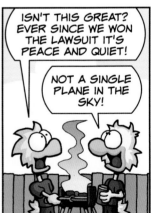

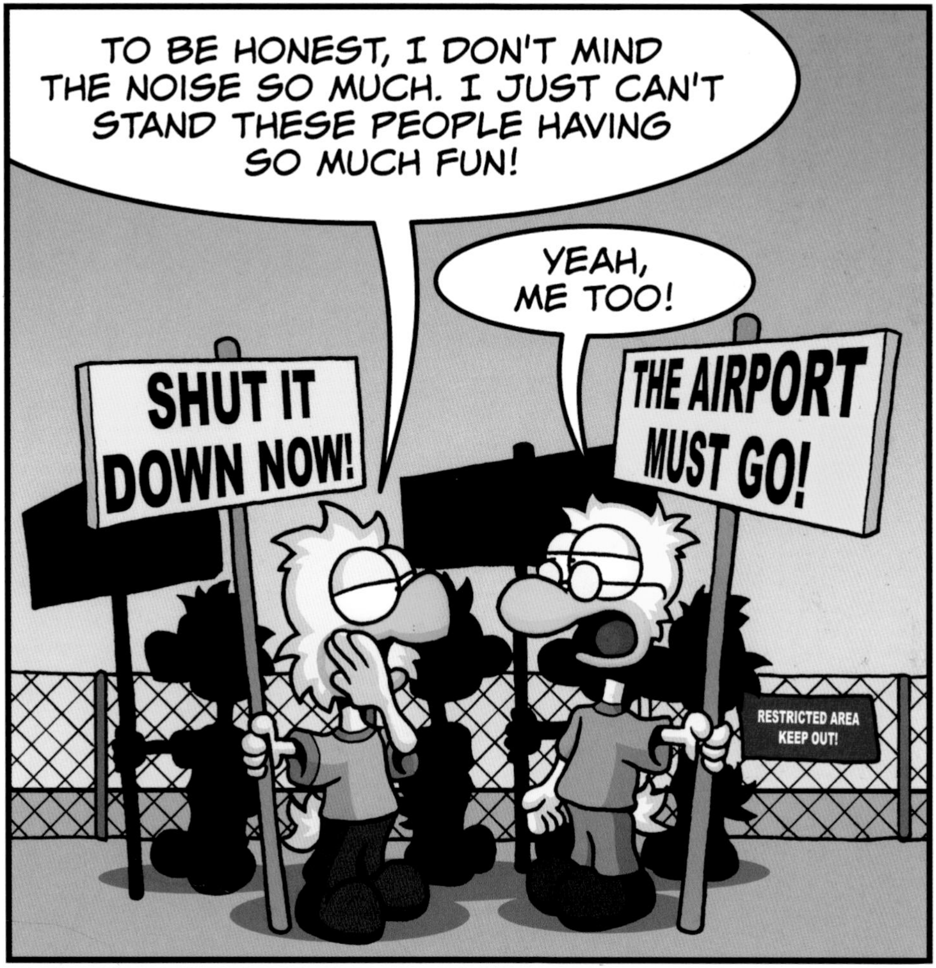
TO BE HONEST, I DON'T MIND THE NOISE SO MUCH. I JUST CAN'T STAND THESE PEOPLE HAVING SO MUCH FUN!
YEAH, ME TOO!
SHUT IT DOWN NOW!
THE AIRPORT MUST GO!
RESTRICTED AREA KEEP OUT!

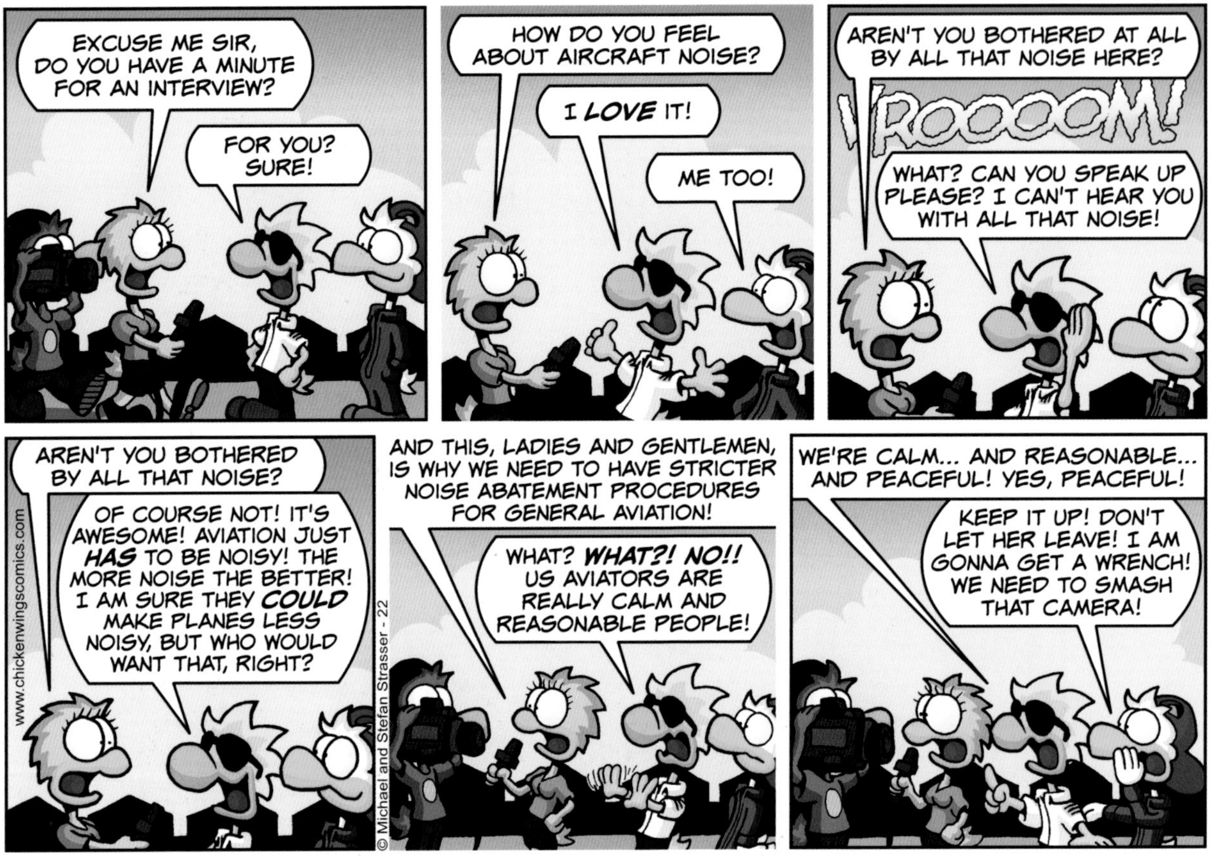
EXCUSE ME SIR, DO YOU HAVE A MINUTE FOR AN INTERVIEW?
FOR YOU? SURE!
HOW DO YOU FEEL ABOUT AIRCRAFT NOISE?
I LOVE IT!
ME TOO!
AREN'T YOU BOTHERED AT ALL BY ALL THAT NOISE HERE?
VROOOOM!
WHAT? CAN YOU SPEAK UP PLEASE? I CAN'T HEAR YOU WITH ALL THAT NOISE!
AREN'T YOU BOTHERED BY ALL THAT NOISE?
OF COURSE NOT! IT'S AWESOME! AVIATION JUST HAS TO BE NOISY! THE MORE NOISE THE BETTER! I AM SURE THEY COULD MAKE PLANES LESS NOISY, BUT WHO WOULD WANT THAT, RIGHT?
www.chickenwingscomics.com
© Michael and Stefan Strasser - 22
AND THIS, LADIES AND GENTLEMEN, IS WHY WE NEED TO HAVE STRICTER NOISE ABATEMENT PROCEDURES FOR GENERAL AVIATION!
WHAT? WHAT?! NO!! US AVIATORS ARE REALLY CALM AND REASONABLE PEOPLE!
WE'RE CALM... AND REASONABLE... AND PEACEFUL! YES, PEACEFUL!
KEEP IT UP! DON'T LET HER LEAVE! I AM GONNA GET A WRENCH! WE NEED TO SMASH THAT CAMERA!

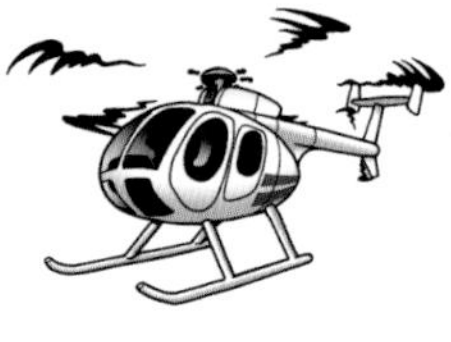

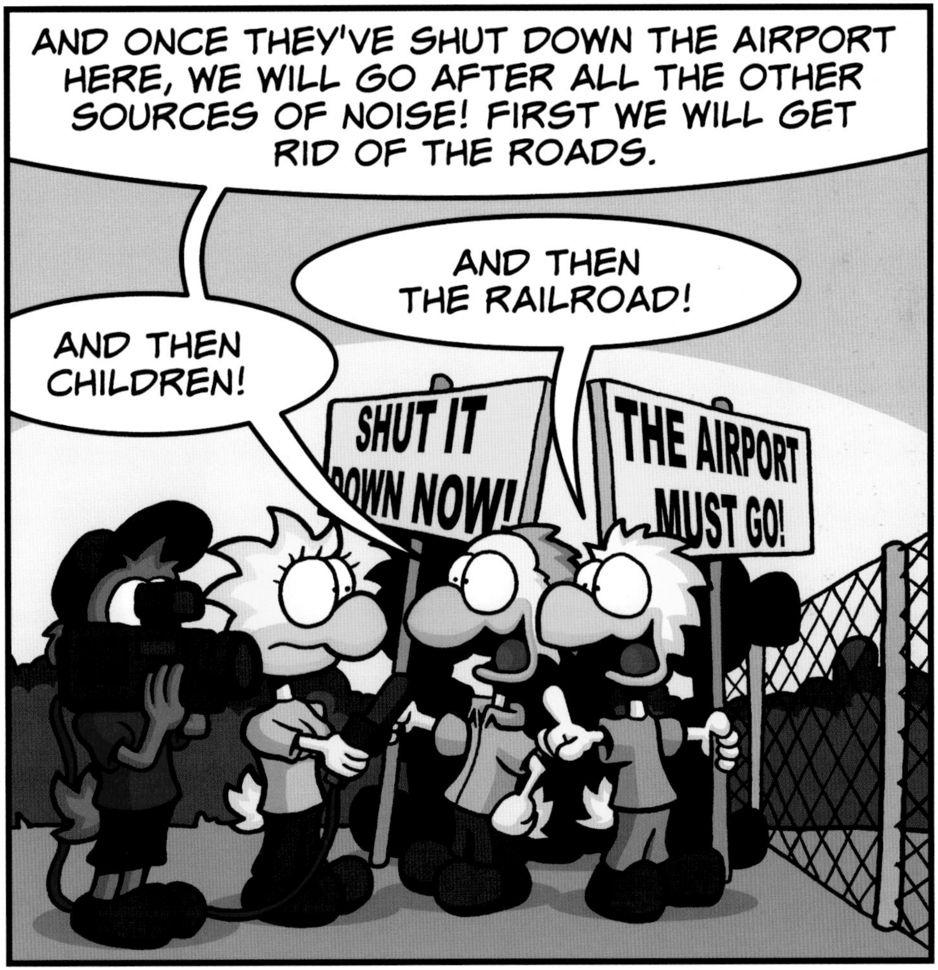
AND ONCE THEY'VE SHUT DOWN THE AIRPORT HERE, WE WILL GO AFTER ALL THE OTHER SOURCES OF NOISE! FIRST WE WILL GET RID OF THE ROADS.
AND THEN THE RAILROAD!
AND THEN CHILDREN!
SHUT IT DOWN NOW!
THE AIRPORT MUST GO!

www.chickenwingscomics.com
LOOK WHAT I GOT!
WHOA!! WHO-A! YOU DIDN'T TAKE THIS OUT OF ANY OF MY PLANES, DID YOU?
© Michael and Stefan Strasser - 347
NO, SILLY! LET ME GIVE YOU A HINT: ONLY 17 MORE TO GO!
WHY DIDN'T YOU GET "THE WHOLE SET", LIKE WITH CYLINDERS, DRIVE-SHAFT, HOUSING AND STUFF, YOU KNOW THE "USUAL"?
REALLY? WHY DIDN'T I GO OUT AND JUST BUY THE WHOLE PLANE?
WELL...
LIKE THAT MAKES ANY SENSE!

www.chickenwingscomics.com
HEY JULIO! CHECK OUT WHAT I ACQUIRED TO AID ME IN MY NOBLE QUEST!
YAY, YOU FOUND A RUSTY OLD WRENCH.
© Michael and Stefan Strasser - 348
HARDLY, INFIDEL! I'M DISAPPOINTED THAT YOU OF ALL PEOPLE DON'T KNOW WHAT THIS IS!
OKAY, ENLIGHTEN ME!
THIS IS AN ORIGINAL WRENCH THEY ORIGINALLY USED ON THE ORIGINAL CORSAIR IN THE ORIGINAL PACIFIC WAR!
WOW, HOW ORIGINAL!

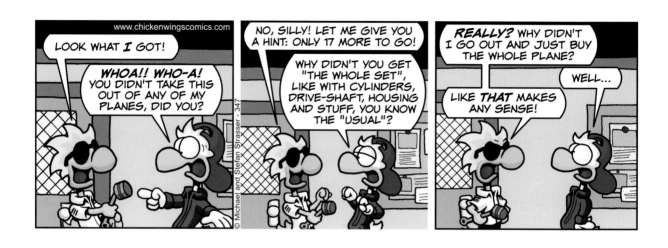

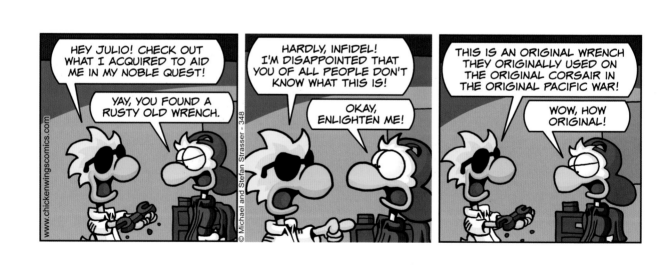

WELL, JUST MAKE SURE YOU DON'T DROP IT, HAHA!
WHERE DID YOU FIND IT ANYWAY?
ON EBAY.
© Michael and Stefan Strasser - 349
WHAT?!
I CAN'T BELIEVE YOU SPENT MONEY ON AN OLD SALTWATER-DAMAGED ONE INCH WRENCH!
WRONG!
www.chickenwingscomics.com
OH?
I BOUGHT THE WHOLE SET!
OH.

SNAP
UH-OH.
CRACK!
DAMN!
© Michael and Stefan Strasser - 350
CRUMBLE
SIGH...
www.chickenwingscomics.com
UHM, JULIO, CAN I BORROW YOUR WRENCH SET?

www.chickenwingscomics.com
THIS IS A DECISION WE SHOULD MAKE AS A TEAM. SO WHAT DO YOU SAY? SHALL WE DO IT?
YES!!
OKAY, WE WILL GO FOR THE SUPERSIZE FAMILY PIZZA! EXTRA ANCHOVIES!
© Michael and Stefan Strasser - 333

www.chickenwingscomics.com
JULIO, I GOT A BUNCH OF QUESTIONS FOR YOU! I NEED SOME ADVICE! FIRST OF ALL...
YOU KNOW WHAT, JASON, I ACTUALLY DO HAVE SOME ADVICE FOR YOU!
COOL!
INSTEAD OF BUGGING ME ALL DAY WHILE I'M WORKING, YOU SHOULD TRY TO BE A LITTLE BIT MORE LIKE CHUCK, AND DO WHAT HE ALWAYS DOES WHEN HE IS WORKING!
REALLY? WHAT?
GET LOST!
HEY!
HEY!
© Michael and Stefan Strasser - 315

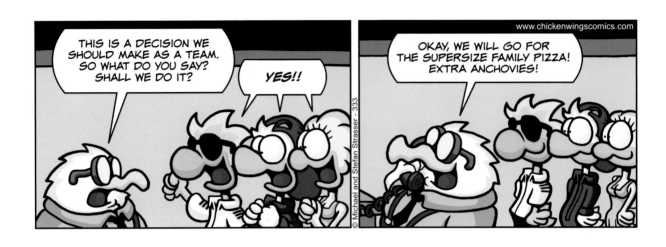

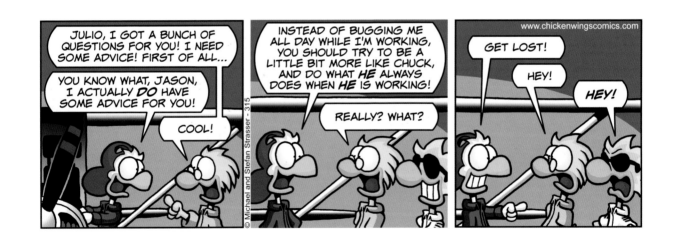

HOW DO THEY DETERMINE HOW LONG TO MAKE THE ROTOR BLADES?
SEE, WHAT THEY DO IS...
AND, HOW DO THEY KNOW **HOW MANY** BLADES THEY NEED?
© Michael and Stefan Strasser - 308
WELL, THE ENGINEERS...
HOW DO THEY KNOW HOW FAST THE BLADES NEED TO SPIN?
KEEP YOUR HANDS ON THE CONTROL, JASON.
www.chickenwingscomics.com
IF SPAIN IS A DEMOCRACY, WHY DO THEY STILL HAVE A KING?

© Michael and Stefan Strasser
SIGH!
www.chickenwingscomics.com
WHAT'S UP, JASON? NO QUESTIONS? ARE YOU OKAY?
I NEED TO PEE!

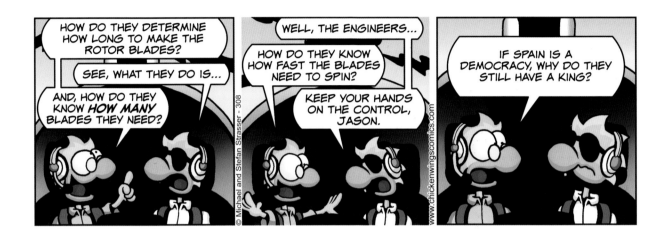

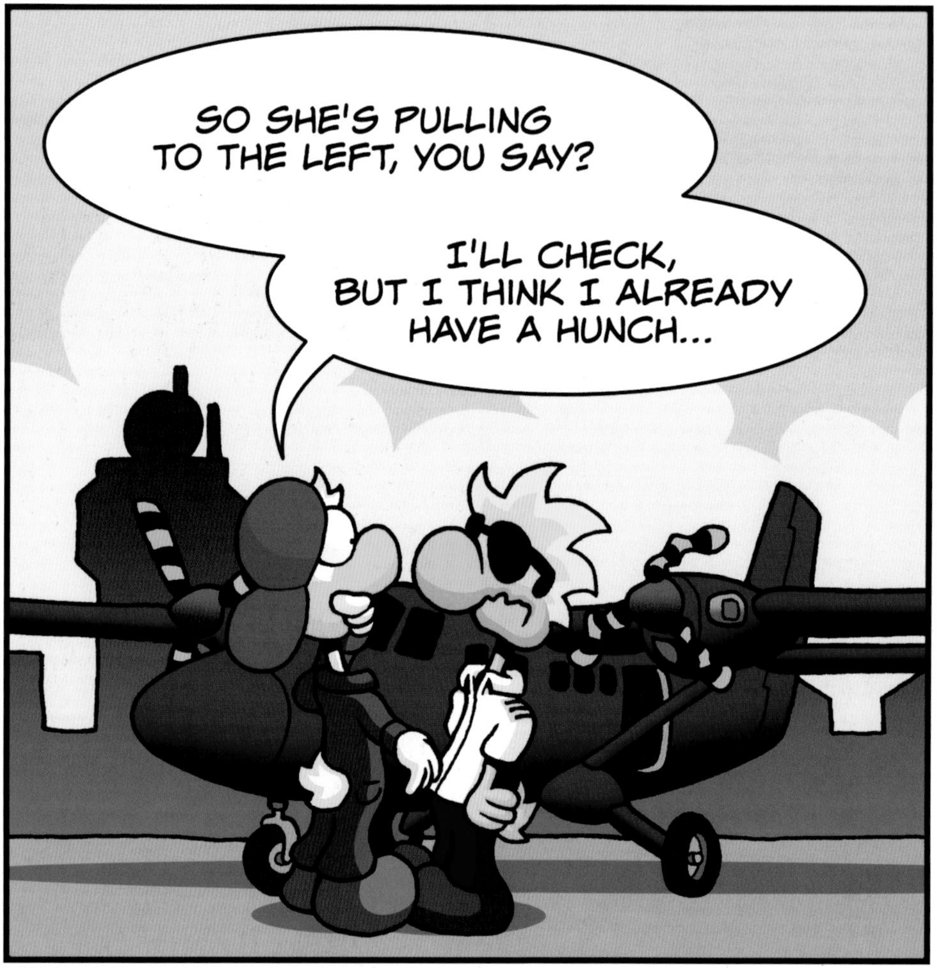
SO SHE'S PULLING TO THE LEFT, YOU SAY?
I'LL CHECK, BUT I THINK I ALREADY HAVE A HUNCH...

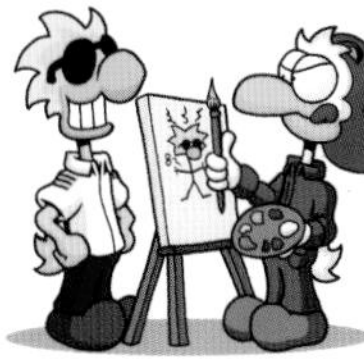

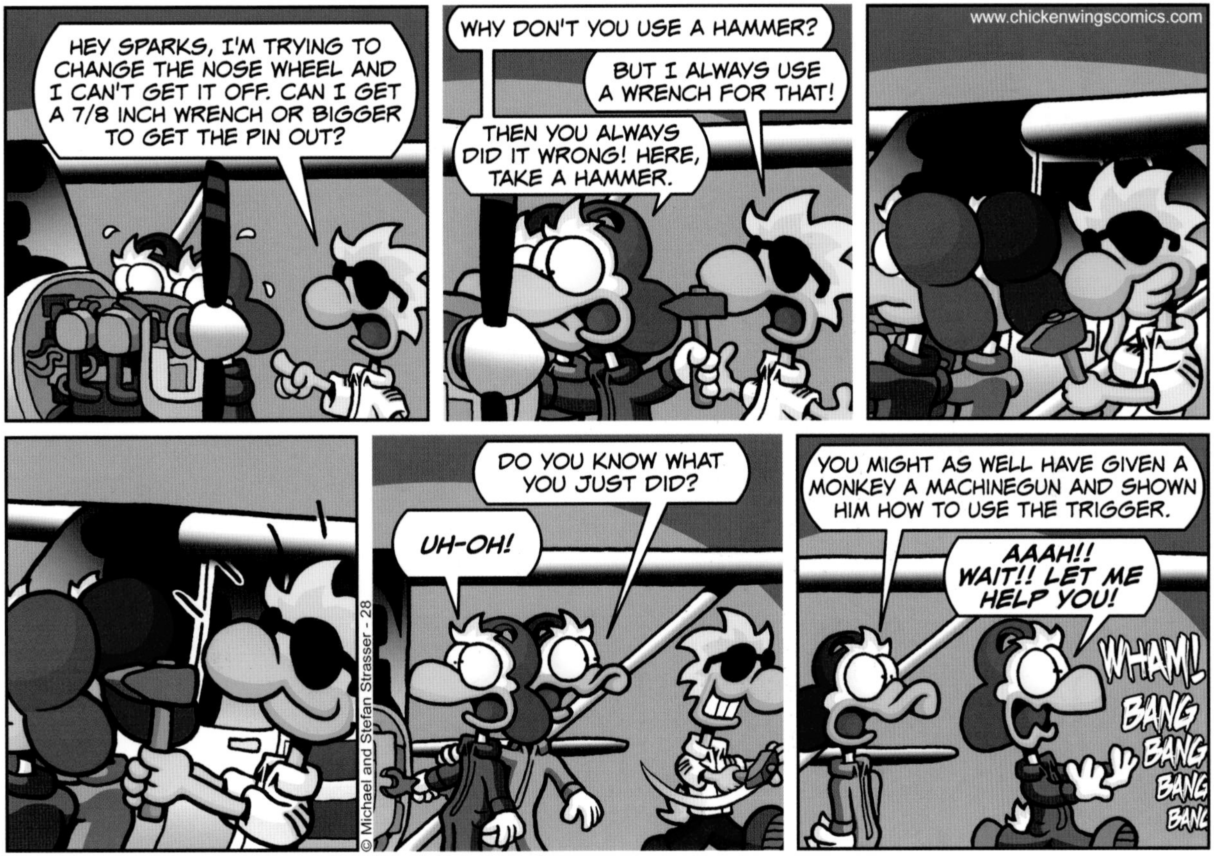
www.chickenwingscomics.com
HEY SPARKS, I'M TRYING TO CHANGE THE NOSE WHEEL AND I CAN'T GET IT OFF. CAN I GET A 7/8 INCH WRENCH OR BIGGER TO GET THE PIN OUT?
WHY DON'T YOU USE A HAMMER?
BUT I ALWAYS USE A WRENCH FOR THAT!
THEN YOU ALWAYS DID IT WRONG! HERE, TAKE A HAMMER.
© Michael and Stefan Strasser - 28
DO YOU KNOW WHAT YOU JUST DID?
UH-OH!
YOU MIGHT AS WELL HAVE GIVEN A MONKEY A MACHINEGUN AND SHOWN HIM HOW TO USE THE TRIGGER.
AAAH!! WAIT!! LET ME HELP YOU!
WHAM!
BANG
BANG
BANG
BANG

HEY JULIO! SURPRISE! WE'VE CLEANED UP THE HANGAR FOR YOU!
AND WE NEATLY SORTED AND ORGANIZED ALL YOUR TOOLS!
NO NEED TO THANK US, WE ENJOYED DOING IT!
YOU DID WHAT?!
© Michael and Stefan Strasser - 304
ARE YOU CRAZY?! HOW AM I SUPPOSED TO FIND MY STUFF NOW?!
JUST KIDDING!
YEAH, SERIOUSLY... AS IF WE WOULD EVER CLEAN THE HANGAR! HAHA!
JEEZ! I HATE YOU GUYS! ON SO MANY LEVELS!
PANT PANT
www.chickenwingscomics.com

www.chickenwingscomics.com
HEY HANS, WE WOULD LIKE TO BUY A NEW MAGNETO FOR THE CESSNA.
© Michael and Stefan Strasser - 316
WHAT? HA! DO YOU THINK MONEY IS GROWING ON TREES? NO WAY!
AND I'M SURE WE DON'T EVEN NEED A NEW ONE!
MA... MA... MAGNETO...
AVIATION FOR DUMMIES

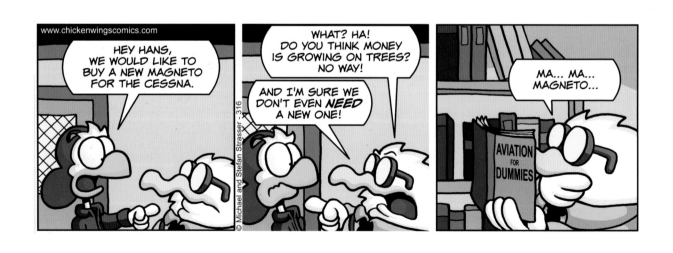

www.chickenwingscomics.com
WELCOME TO A BRAND NEW REALITY TV SHOW!
TO ALL GATES
SECURITY
I DON'T THINK WE'RE GONNA MAKE IT...
2 H 15 MIN FROM THIS POINT
© Michael and Stefan Strasser - 317
GATE C25
HERE IS YOUR NEXT CHALLENGE: WE SWITCHED GATES ON YOU AND YOU HAVE ONLY TEN MINUTES TO FIND THE NEW GATE!
LADIES AND GENTLEMEN, OUR AIR CONDITION IS BROKEN AND THE DOOR WON'T OPEN. WILL YOU BE ABLE TO ADAPT TO LIVING IN A METAL TUBE PARKED ON A HOT TARMAC?
TUNE IN AGAIN NEXT WEEK FOR ANOTHER EPISODE OF
SURVIVOR LAX

WHAT ARE YOU DOING IN MY HANGAR?
I AM BUILDING A SODA-CAN SUPERCHARGER TO GET MORE POWER ON TAKE-OFF WITH OLD 3BT.
NO WAY!
© Michael and Stefan Strasser - 330
RELAX! I'VE SEEN THIS DONE ON MYTHBUSTERS!
DON'T THE MYTH-BUSTERS ALWAYS SAY NOT TO TRY ANYTHING THEY DO AT HOME?
www.chickenwingscomics.com
I KNOW! THAT'S WHY I AM USING YOUR HANGAR!

WOW, CHUCK! YOU CAN PULL OFF A DECENT LANDING AFTER ALL! THAT MUST HAVE BEEN THE BEST ONE I'VE EVER SEEN!
UHM... THANK YOU, TOWER.
© Michael and Stefan Strasser - 321
www.chickenwingscomics.com
ALRIGHT!! DON'T BE SMUG ABOUT IT!

HEY JULIO, I HAVE A QUESTION! WHEN THE RUDDER JAMS WHILE YOU...
OH! I CAN SEE YOU'RE WORKING. I WON'T BOTHER YOU THEN!
© Michael and Stefan Strasser - 382
www.chickenwingscomics.com
CHILDREN! THEY GROW UP SO FAST.
I AM SO PROUD!

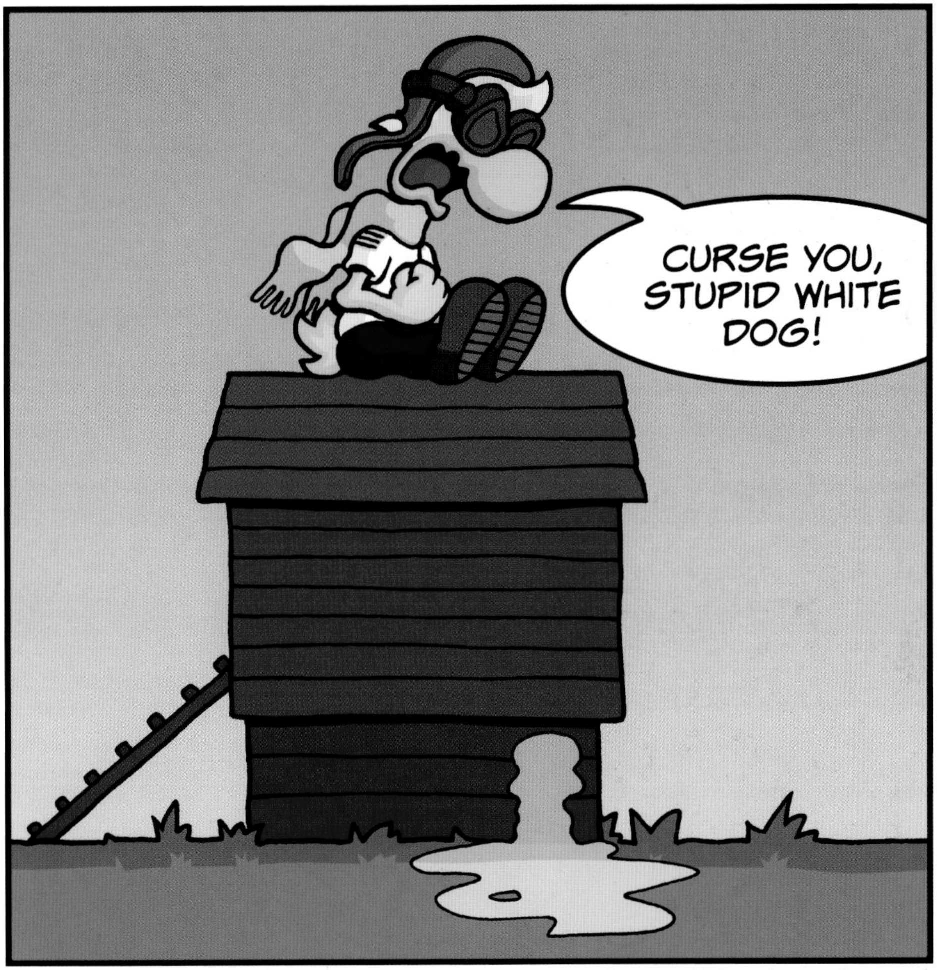
CURSE YOU, STUPID WHITE DOG!

DUDE, I HAVE AN IDEA! LET'S BUZZ THE TOWER!

AWESOME! LET'S DO IT!

TOP GUN STYLE!

AWESOME!

YEEHAW!!

BRRRR

EAT THIS!

© Michael and Stefan Strasser - 324

www.chickenwingscomics.com

OH NO! DID YOU HEAR THAT? DO WE HAVE A BEE IN HERE AGAIN?

DUDE, I LOVE FOREIGN AIRLINES! FREE BEER IS AWESOME!

FRAULEIN WAITRESS! BRING US SOME MORE BOOZE!

WOOHOO! PARTY!!

© Michael and Stefan Strasser - 339

GUYS, I AM HOLDING A SLEEPING BABY, AND IF YOU WAKE IT UP, I WILL PASS IT BACK TO YOU.

GULP!

www.chickenwingscomics.com

OH SUGAR! I DROPPED A STITCH!

SSSHH!!

www.chickenwingscomics.com
CHUCK! THIS IS THE THIRD TIME YOU'RE LATE THIS WEEK! YOU KNOW WHAT THAT MEANS?
UHM... IT'S WEDNESDAY?
© Michael and Stefan Strasser - 320
NO! IT MEANS I'VE JUST ABOUT HAD IT! HOW COME RAY AND NOBU OVER THERE ALWAYS SHOW UP EARLY?
WELL, ***THEIR*** OFFICE HAS EIGHT EMPLOYEES BUT ONLY SIX PARKING SPOTS.
OH! HM... FOOD FOR THOUGHT!

CHECK OUT MY NEW R/C MODEL AIRPLANE!
NICE! LOOKS LIKE ONE FROM THE TWENTY-SECOND AIRBORNE DIVISION!
© Michael and Stefan Strasser - 322
www.chickenwingscomics.com
HUH? WHY? YOU MEAN THE ***EIGHTY***-SECOND AIRBORNE DIVISION?
NO, WHAT I MEAN IS, I WOULD BE SURPRISED IF IT STAYED AIRBORNE FOR ***MORE THAN TWENTY SECONDS!***

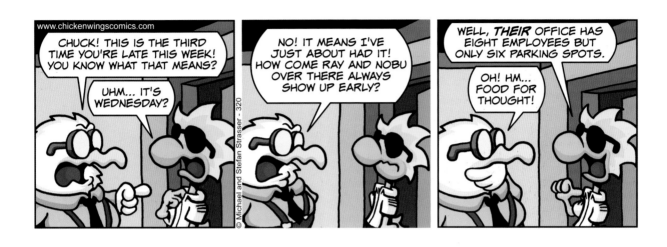

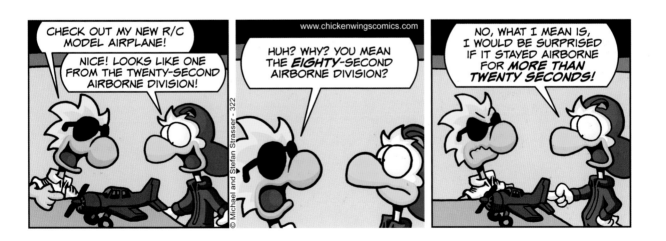

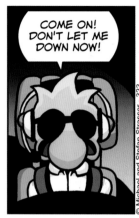

COME ON! DON'T LET ME DOWN NOW!
© Michael and Stefan Strasser - 323
COME ON!
COME AWWN!!!
LIFT OFF! WE HAVE A LIFT OFF!!
www.chickenwingscomics.com

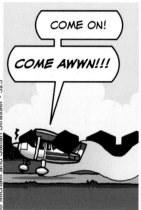

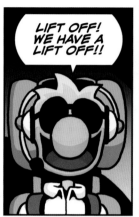

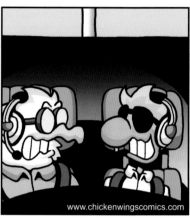

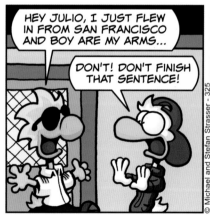

HEY JULIO, I JUST FLEW IN FROM SAN FRANCISCO AND BOY ARE MY ARMS...
DON'T! DON'T FINISH THAT SENTENCE!
© Michael and Stefan Strasser - 325
THIS JOKE WAS ALREADY OLD BEFORE DA VINCI INVENTED THE FIRST FLYING MACHINE!
I CAN'T HEAR IT ANYMORE!
www.chickenwingscomics.com
...TIRED.
AAARGH!!
REALLY? DID SAN FRANCISCO ALREADY EXIST BACK THEN?

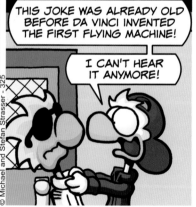

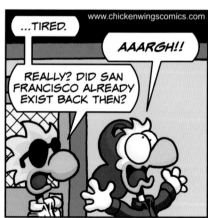

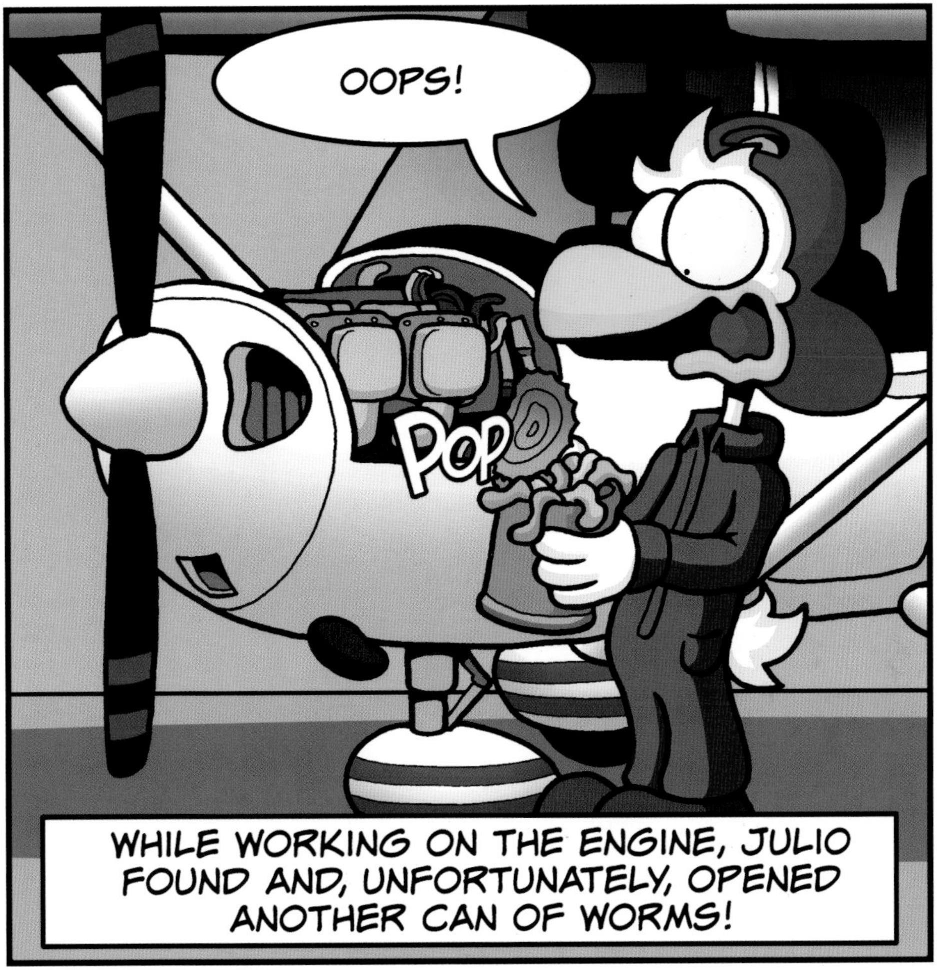
OOPS!
POP
WHILE WORKING ON THE ENGINE, JULIO FOUND AND, UNFORTUNATELY, OPENED ANOTHER CAN OF WORMS!

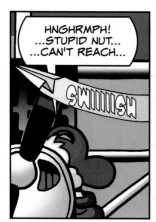

HNGHRMPH! ...STUPID NUT... ...CAN'T REACH...
SWIIIIISH
ZOOM
www.chickenwingscomics.com
PING!
© Michael and Stefan Strasser - 352
WHAT?! I HAVE TO STAY CURRENT SOMEHOW, SINCE YOUR INSPECTIONS TAKE FOREVER!

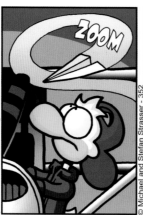

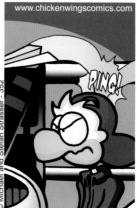

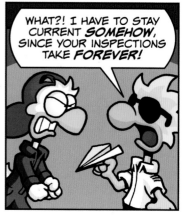

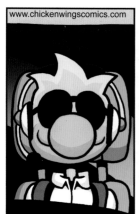

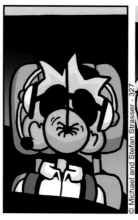

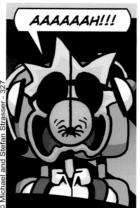

www.chickenwingscomics.com
© Michael and Stefan Strasser - 327
AAAAAAH!!!
CHECK IT OUT! I HAVE NEVER SEEN ANYBODY PULL THAT OFF BEFORE!
WOW! I WISH I WAS ONLY HALF AS GOOD AS THIS GUY!

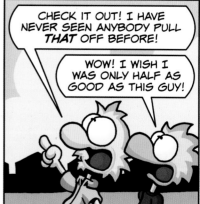

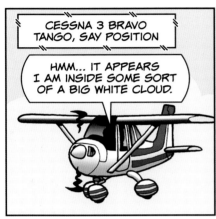

CESSNA 3 BRAVO TANGO, SAY POSITION
HMM... IT APPEARS I AM INSIDE SOME SORT OF A BIG WHITE CLOUD.
© Michael and Stefan Strasser - 346
YOU DON'T SAY?! HOW ABOUT FILING A FLIGHT PLAN?
NO WORRIES! I CAN'T SEE ANY OTHER PLANES IN HERE!
www.chickenwingscomics.com
CHUCK, IS THAT YOU?

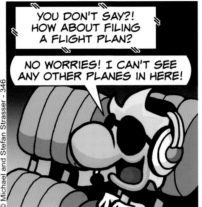

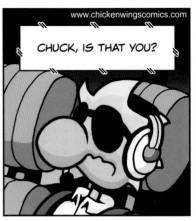

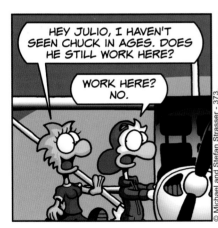

HEY JULIO, I HAVEN'T SEEN CHUCK IN AGES. DOES HE STILL WORK HERE?
WORK HERE? NO.
© Michael and Stefan Strasser - 373
WHAT?! WHAT HAPPENED? DID HE GET FIRED?
www.chickenwingscomics.com
OH! NO, NO! HE'S STILL "EMPLOYED" HERE. I JUST NEVER SEE HIM DO ACTUAL "WORK"!
I SEE!

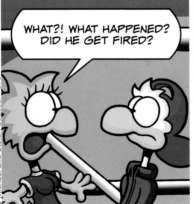

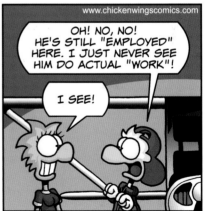

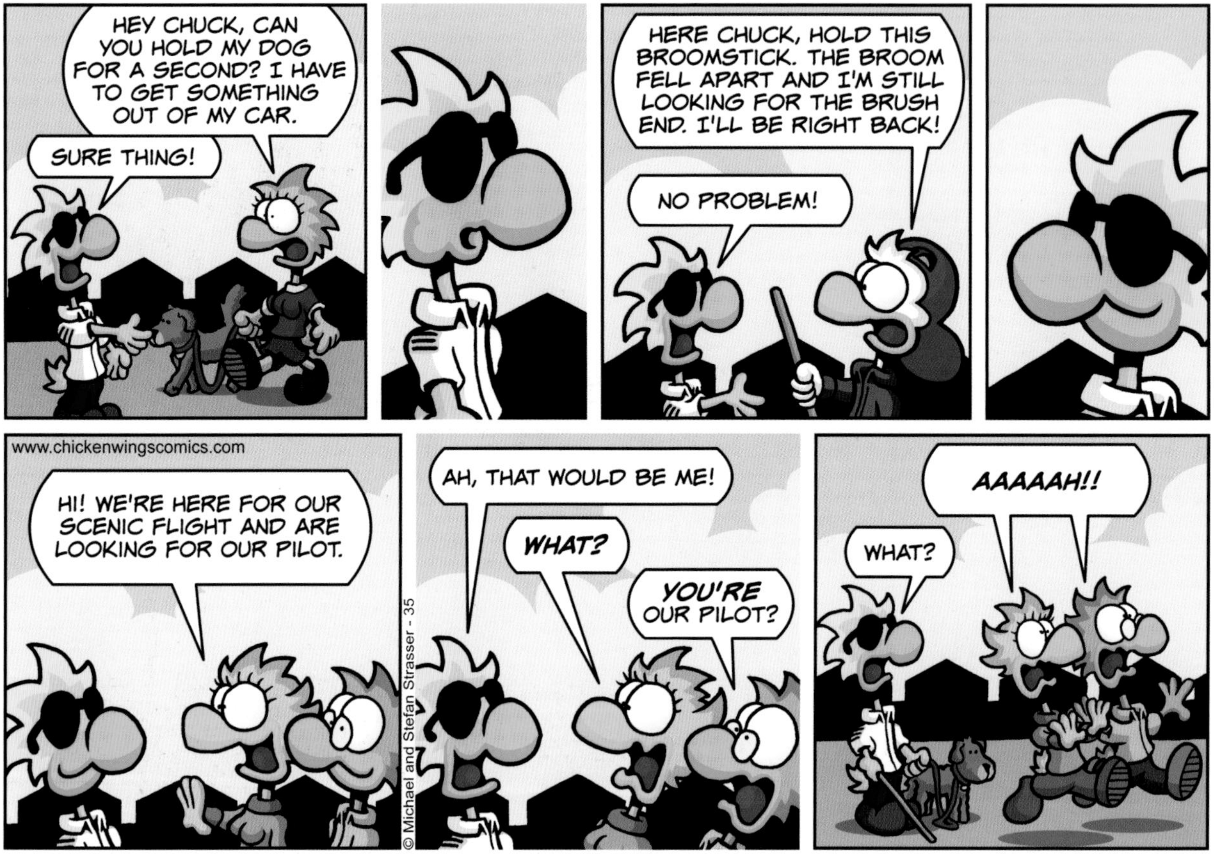
HEY CHUCK, CAN YOU HOLD MY DOG FOR A SECOND? I HAVE TO GET SOMETHING OUT OF MY CAR.
SURE THING!
HERE CHUCK, HOLD THIS BROOMSTICK. THE BROOM FELL APART AND I'M STILL LOOKING FOR THE BRUSH END. I'LL BE RIGHT BACK!
NO PROBLEM!
www.chickenwingscomics.com
HI! WE'RE HERE FOR OUR SCENIC FLIGHT AND ARE LOOKING FOR OUR PILOT.
© Michael and Stefan Strasser - 35
AH, THAT WOULD BE ME!
WHAT?
YOU'RE OUR PILOT?
WHAT?
AAAAAH!!

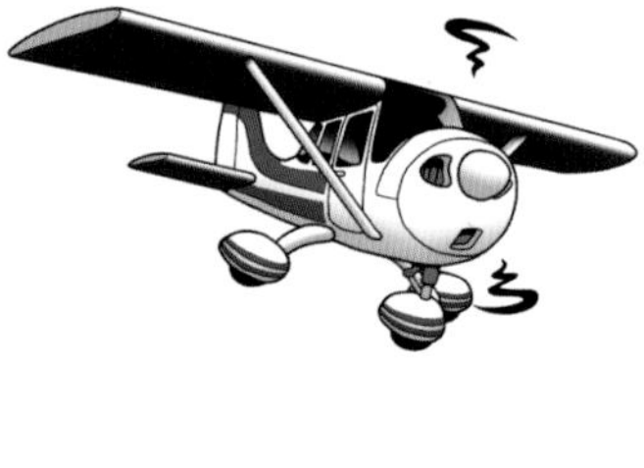

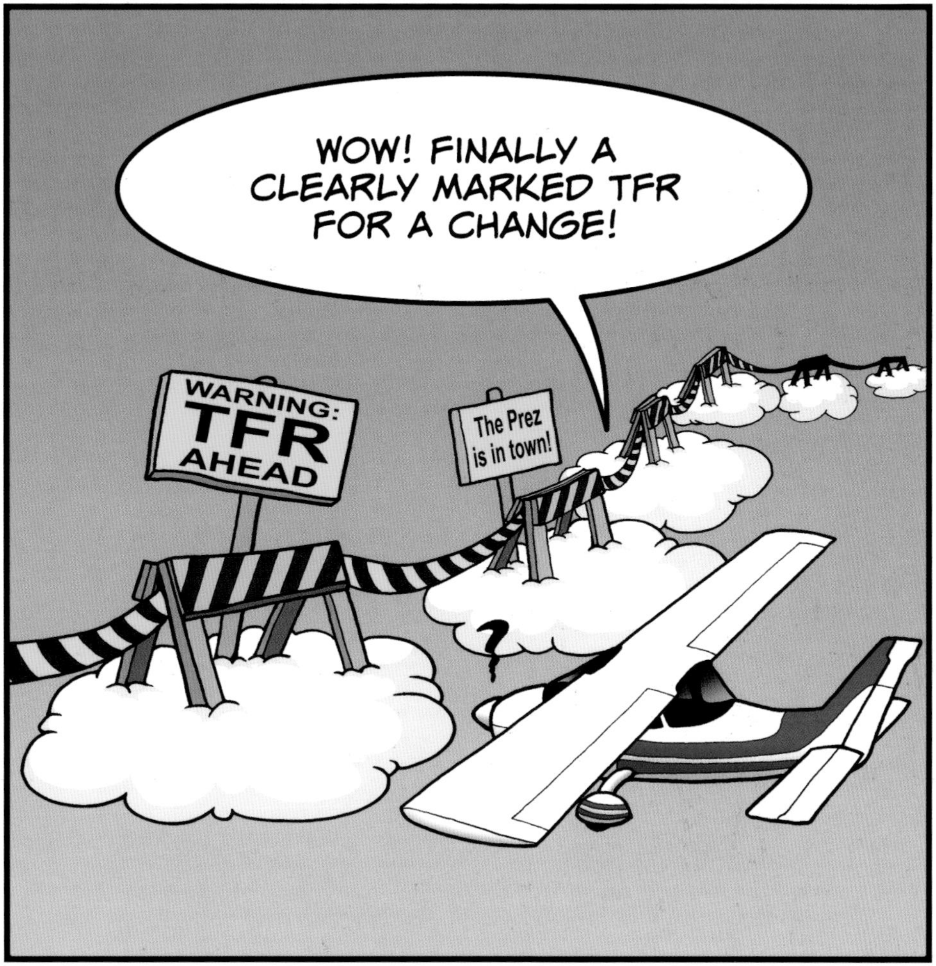
WOW! FINALLY A CLEARLY MARKED TFR FOR A CHANGE!
WARNING: TFR AHEAD
The Prez is in town!
?

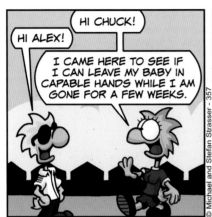

HI ALEX!
HI CHUCK!
I CAME HERE TO SEE IF I CAN LEAVE MY BABY IN CAPABLE HANDS WHILE I AM GONE FOR A FEW WEEKS.
© Michael and Stefan Strasser - 357
REALLY?
YEAH. YOU KNOW, RUN UP THE ENGINE EVERY WEEK, MAKE SURE EVERYTHING IS OKAY.
COOL!
www.chickenwingscomics.com
SO... UHM... IS JULIO HERE?

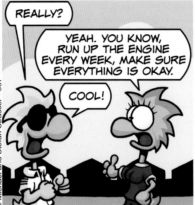

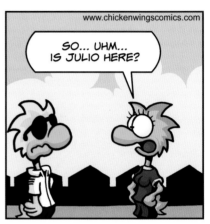

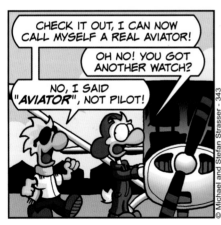

CHECK IT OUT, I CAN NOW CALL MYSELF A REAL AVIATOR!
OH NO! YOU GOT ANOTHER WATCH?
NO, I SAID "*AVIATOR*", NOT PILOT!
© Michael and Stefan Strasser - 343
AND?
UHM... NEW SUNGLASSES?
www.chickenwingscomics.com
A SCARF! ARE YOU BLIND?
OH BROTHER, YES! I SEE THE SCARF. I WAS JUST HOPING IT WAS ONLY MY IMAGINATION.

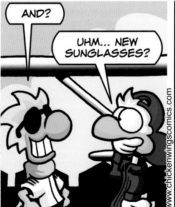

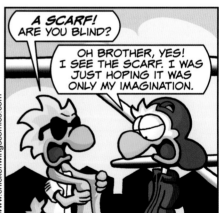

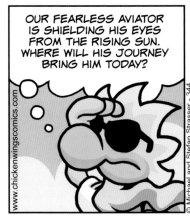

OUR FEARLESS AVIATOR IS SHIELDING HIS EYES FROM THE RISING SUN. WHERE WILL HIS JOURNEY BRING HIM TODAY?
www.chickenwingscomics.com
THE ENGINE IS HUMMING AND THE WIND IS RUSHING THROUGH HIS HAIR, AS OUR HERO SCANS HIS SIX FOR ENEMY FIGHTER PLANES, WHEN...
© Michael and Stefan Strasser - 344
WHAT IN THE WORLD ARE YOU DOING?
UHM... JUST CATCHING SOME FRESH AIR.

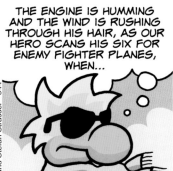

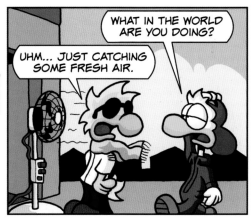

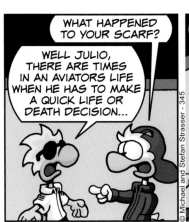

WHAT HAPPENED TO YOUR SCARF?
WELL JULIO, THERE ARE TIMES IN AN AVIATORS LIFE WHEN HE HAS TO MAKE A QUICK LIFE OR DEATH DECISION...
© Michael and Stefan Strasser - 345
UH OH! HANS, IS THAT YOU IN THERE?
YES, AND I AM GONNA BE A WHILE!
MEN
CLICK
OH BOY, LOOKS LIKE THERE'S A LIMIT TO HOW MUCH SAUSAGE ONE CAN EAT AND I HAVE FOUND IT...
HANG ON, HERE WE GO!
www.chickenwingscomics.com
... AND I CHOSE LIFE!

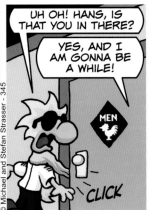

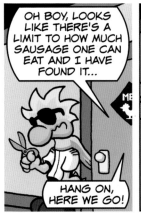

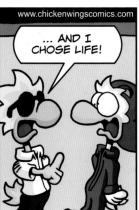

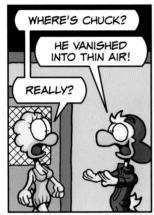

WHERE'S CHUCK?
HE VANISHED INTO THIN AIR!
REALLY?
YEAH, SEE, THE DENSITY ALTITUDE IS EXTREMELY HIGH TODAY! HAHAHA!
HUH?
© Michael and Stefan Strasser - 356
THAT MEANS THE ATMOSPHERIC PRESSURE IS EXTREMELY LOW.
www.chickenwingscomics.com
HE'S OUT FLYING.
AH!

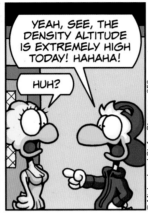

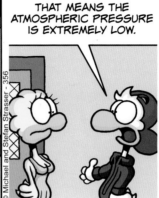

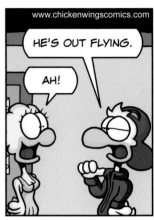

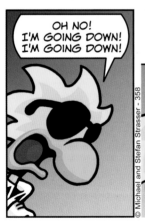

OH NO! I'M GOING DOWN! I'M GOING DOWN!
© Michael and Stefan Strasser - 358
AAH! I'M SUDDENLY YANKED UPWARDS!! WHAT'S GOING ON?!
AND DOWN AGAIN!! THE CONTROLS HAVE NO EFFECT AT ALL!
www.chickenwingscomics.com
ARE YOU DONE?
UHM, YEAH.

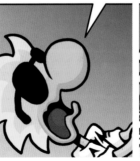

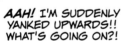

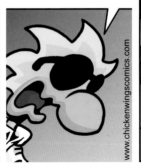

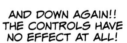

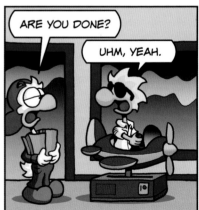

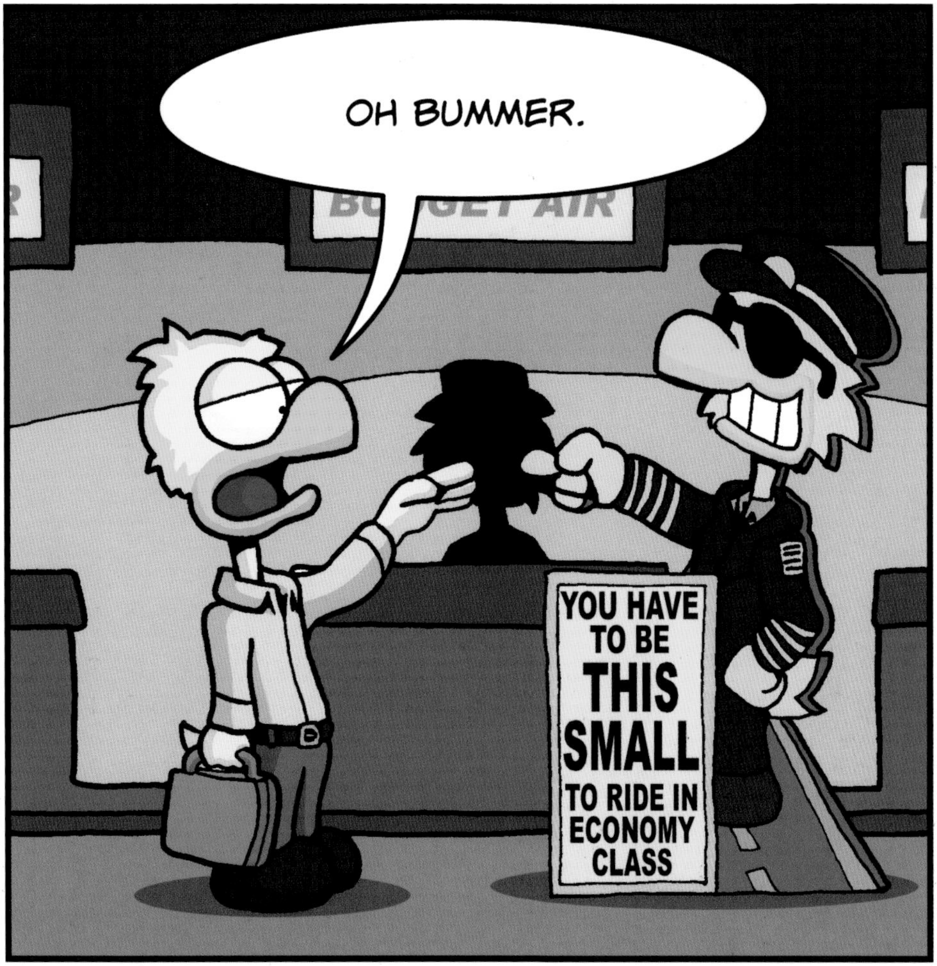
OH BUMMER.
YOU HAVE TO BE THIS SMALL TO RIDE IN ECONOMY CLASS

HEY JULIO, LET'S GO MAKE SOME PROFIT!
GREAT IDEA! LET'S!
PROFIT, HERE WE COME!
www.chickenwingscomics.com
© Michael and Stefan Strasser - 359
FINALLY MY EMPLOYEES ARE CATCHING ON TO OUR COMPANY PHILOSOPHY! I AM ALMOST PROUD OF THEM!
I GOT TEN BUCKS ON MAVERICK!
ARE YOU SURE? HE FINISHED LAST THE LAST TEN RACES!
I KNOW, BUT I LIKE THE NAME!

HI! I AM NEW IN THIS TOWN! COULD YOU GIVE ME DIRECTIONS TO YOUR APARTMENT?
GREAT! THAT'S THE SAME LINE YOU USED ON ME LAST TIME!
© Michael and Stefan Strasser - 360
I DID?
YES!
BYE NOW!
www.chickenwingscomics.com
WAIT!!
DID IT WORK?

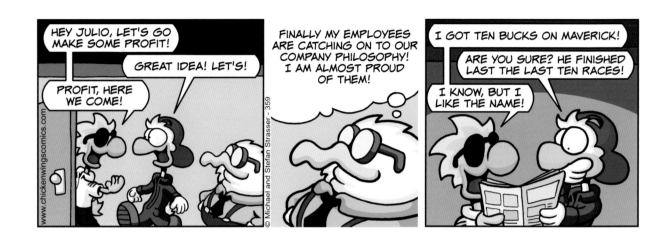

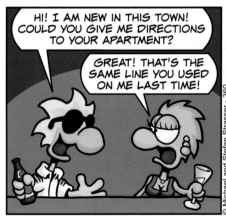

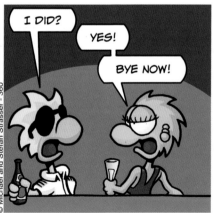

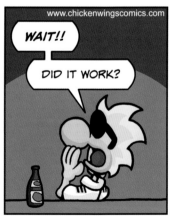

AND THEN THEY MADE ME STAY IN THE HOLDING PATTERN UNTIL I ALMOST RAN OUT OF FUEL!
I'M SORRY!
© Michael and Stefan Strasser - 361
DON'T BE SORRY. I MADE IT BACK OKAY! NO NEED TO APOLOGIZE!
www.chickenwingscomics.com
NO, BUT I WANT TO APOLOGIZE FOR THE FANCY DINNER YOU'RE HAVING TO PAY, EVEN THOUGH I AM NOT ENJOYING IT AT ALL.

CHUCK, I AM TRACKING YOUR FLIGHT AND IT LOOKS LIKE YOU'RE 90 DEGREES OFF COURSE.
WHAT? NO, I AM NOT!
© Michael and Stefan Strasser - 362
YOU'RE SUPPOSED TO GO NORTH, BUT YOU'RE FLYING EAST.
BUT MY COMPASS SAYS NORTH!
www.chickenwingscomics.com
WHAT'S GOING ON?
CHUCK IS SUPPOSED TO TAKE THIS REFRIGERATOR-MAGNET SALESMAN NORTH, BUT FOR SOME REASON HE'S WAY OFF COURSE!
HUH! I WONDER WHY THAT IS!

www.chickenwingscomics.com
BOING
BOING
© Michael and Stefan Strasser - 363
TOWER, CAN YOU TELL ME WHAT TIME I LANDED?
CERTAINLY, CHUCK! YOU LANDED PRECISELY AT 1500 HOURS, 12 MINUTES AND 12 SECONDS AND 17 SECONDS AND 19 SECONDS!

SAY CHUCK, BY THE WAY, DO YOU HAVE A MANUAL FOR YOUR WATCH?
SURE! I NEVER USE IT, BUT LET ME SHOW YOU.
© Michael and Stefan Strasser - 364
ARE YOU SERIOUS?
WHAT? IT'S AN AVIATOR PRO 3000 LINKED TO ZULU TIME. WHAT DID YOU EXPECT?
A SMALLER MANUAL?
HERE, START WITH THIS FIRST.
www.chickenwingscomics.com
MANUAL? THIS IS JUST THE INDEX!

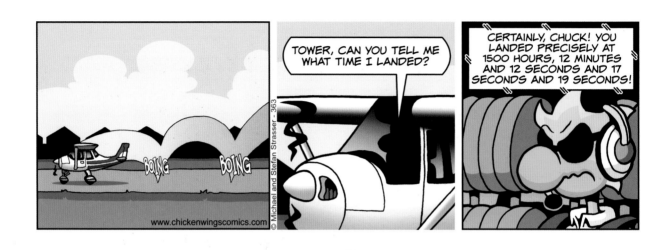

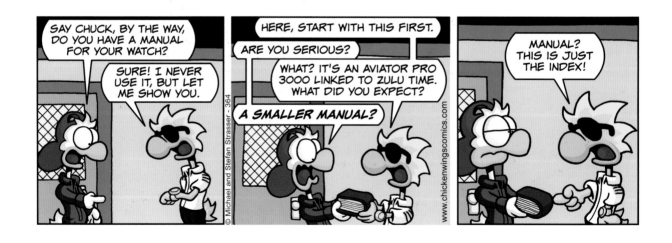

SENIOR CONTROLLER DAVIS WAS VERY SURPRISED, WHEN FLIGHT 488 SUDDENLY FELL OFF THE RADAR.
ATC coffee supply status:
mocca: OK
cappucino: OK
latte: stock warning
NW488
140° 10300ft
640kts -None-

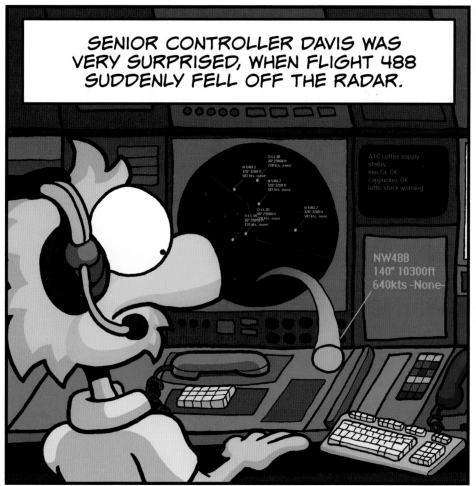

DID YOU HEAR ABOUT THIS NEW PILOT SHOP? DOES ANYONE OF YOU KNOW WHERE IT IS?
OOH, I KNOW! I KNOW!
YOU GO UP THE BIG STREET FROM HERE UNTIL... DO YOU KNOW WHERE THE "FLOWA POWA" FLOWER SHOP IS? IT'S RIGHT NEXT TO WHERE I GET MY NAILS DONE. THEY ALWAYS HAVE SUCH NICE FLOWERS IN FRONT OF THEIR SHOP.
THERE'S ALSO AN UP AND DOWN BURGER JOINT NEXT TO IT.
I THINK I KNOW THAT ONE!
WELL, ***ANYWAY***, YOU STILL HAVE TO GO FURTHER THAN THAT!
DO YOU KNOW THE "RAGTIME" BOUTIQUE?
UHM... NO.
YOU HAVE TO TURN LEFT THERE.
OR RIGHT!
© Michael and Stefan Strasser - 24
THIS SIDE!
AND THEN THERE'S THIS CHESTNUT TREE BETWEEN THE CHINESE PLACE AND THE SHOE SHOP. IF YOU SEE THAT, YOU'RE ALREADY TOO FAR.
www.chickenwingscomics.com
JULIO?
GO NORTH FROM THE AIRPORT, TURN EAST ON 5TH STREET, AND IT'S HALF A MILE DOWN ON THE SOUTH SIDE.
THANK YOU!

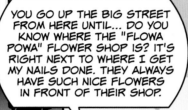

WELL, THAT GUY IS NO HELP!

WHAT HAPPENED?

SLAM!

MY EYES ARE GETTING WORSE, BUT I CAN'T GET MY DOCTOR TO WRITE A PRESCRIPTION.

NO WAY! FOR THICKER GLASSES?

© Michael and Stefan Strasser - 365

www.chickenwingscomics.com

WHAT? NO, SILLY! FOR A BIGGER TV!

SO CAPTAIN, WHEN DO I GET MY PEANUTS?

WHAT, YOU DIDN'T GET YOUR PAYCHECK YET?

www.chickenwingscomics.com

HAHAHA!

HAHAHA!

© Michael and Stefan Strasser - 370

KIND OF SAD, ACTUALLY...

SIGH!

CRASH!
WHAM!
OOF!
© Michael and Stefan Strasser - 366
SALLY!! WHY AM I LAYING ON THE FLOOR?!
BOSS
OH, I MEANT TO TELL YOU! I MOVED YOUR CHAIR, TO MAKE YOUR OFFICE MORE FENG SHUI!
I THOUGHT I TOLD YOU TO ORDER PIZZA, NOT GO ALL CHINESE ON ME!
BOSS
www.chickenwingscomics.com

EXPLAIN TO ME ONE MORE TIME. WHY DID YOU MOVE ALL MY FURNITURE AROUND AGAIN?
© Michael and Stefan Strasser - 367
TO MAKE IT MORE FENG SHUI.
CHOP SUEY?
FENG SHUI!
www.chickenwingscomics.com
WHAT DOES RAW FISH HAVE TO DO WITH MY FURNITURE?!

OW! DOES THIS FLOWER-POT HAVE TO STAND RIGHT IN FRONT OF THE DOOR?
YES! ACCORDING TO FENG SHUI, THAT'S THE PERFECT SPOT.
PANG!
FENG SHUI? ARE YOU SERIOUS? YOU BELIEVE IN THAT SUPERSTICIOUS NONSENSE?
YOU DON'T?
OF COURSE NOT! I ONLY BELIEVE IN THINGS I CAN SEE AND PROOF!
© Michael and Stefan Strasser - 368
www.chickenwingscomics.com
REALLY?
WELL, THAT'S JUST THE WAY I AM. I'M A SCORPIO, YOU KNOW?
AH!

SIGH.
WHAT'S WRONG? ARE YOU SICK?
NO. THIS PLANE JUST DOESN'T FEEL VERY FENG SHUI, YOU KNOW?
© Michael and Stefan Strasser - 369
YOU DON'T SAY. WHAT WOULD YOU RECOMMEND?
I WOULD TAKE OUT THESE FLOORBOARDS AND REPLACE THEM WITH MARBLE STONES. AND MOVE THE SEATS BACK FURTHER.
www.chickenwingscomics.com
OLD MR. SHUI DIDN'T KNOW MUCH ABOUT WEIGHT AND BALANCE, DID HE?

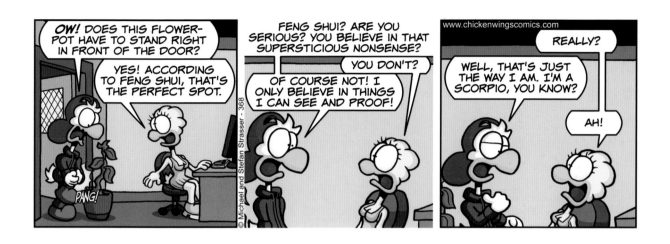

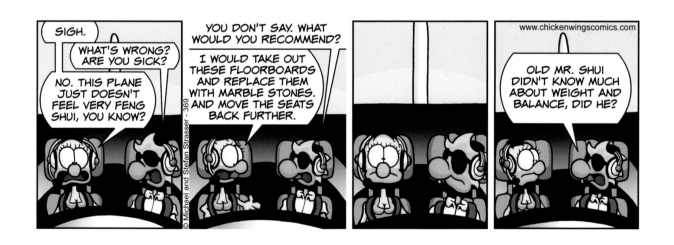

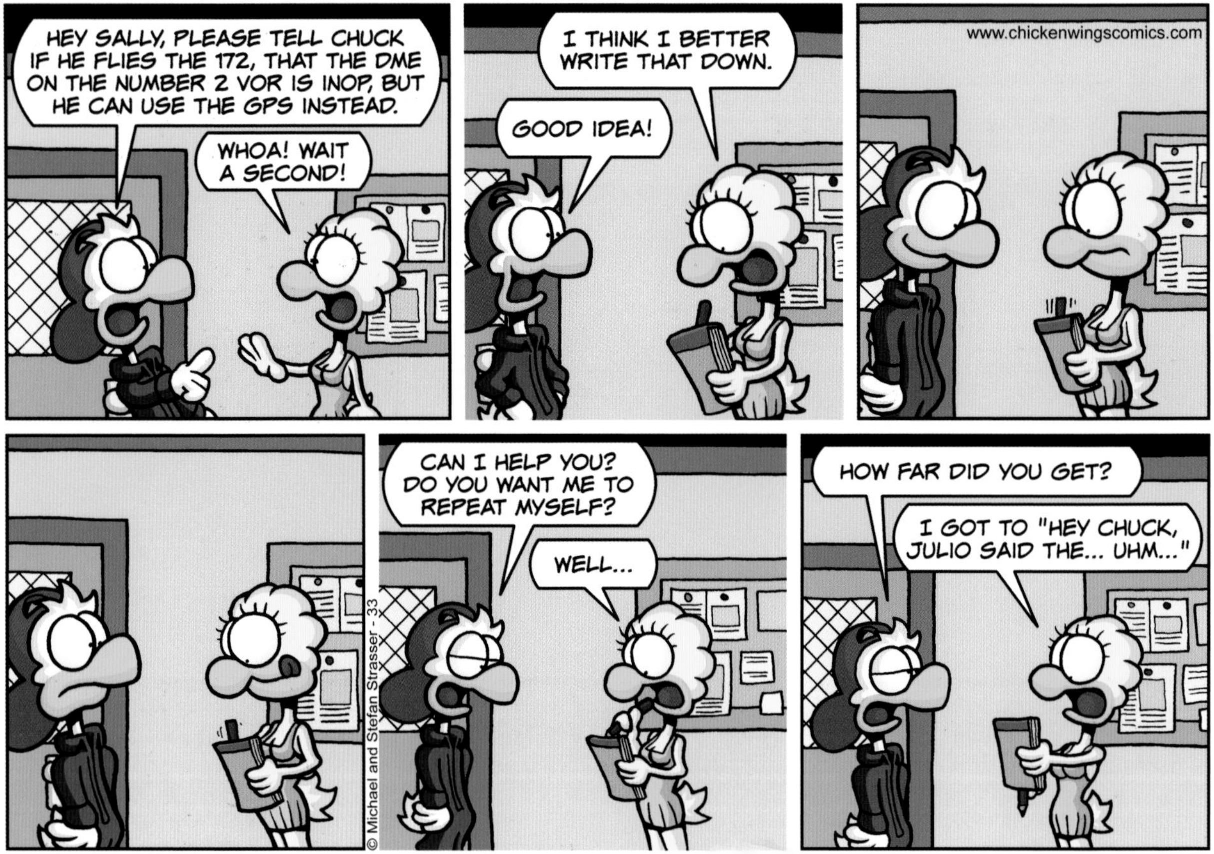
HEY SALLY, PLEASE TELL CHUCK IF HE FLIES THE 172, THAT THE DME ON THE NUMBER 2 VOR IS INOP, BUT HE CAN USE THE GPS INSTEAD.
WHOA! WAIT A SECOND!
I THINK I BETTER WRITE THAT DOWN.
GOOD IDEA!
www.chickenwingscomics.com
© Michael and Stefan Strasser - 33
CAN I HELP YOU? DO YOU WANT ME TO REPEAT MYSELF?
WELL...
HOW FAR DID YOU GET?
I GOT TO "HEY CHUCK, JULIO SAID THE... UHM..."

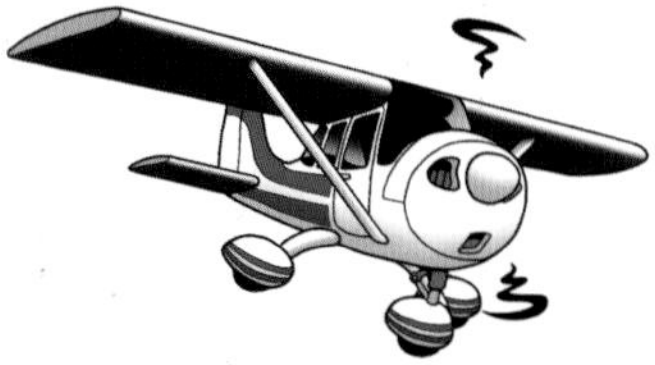

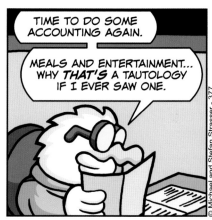

TIME TO DO SOME ACCOUNTING AGAIN.
MEALS AND ENTERTAINMENT... WHY THAT'S A TAUTOLOGY IF I EVER SAW ONE.
© Michael and Stefan Strasser - 377
I THINK I BETTER MAKE SOME SUBDIVISIONS FOR SUCH AN IMPORTANT ITEM.
www.chickenwingscomics.com
LET'S SEE, THERE'S MARBLE CAKE, CREAM CAKE, CHOCOLATE CAKE...

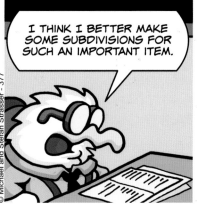

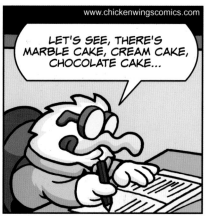

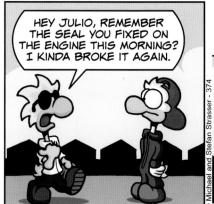

HEY JULIO, REMEMBER THE SEAL YOU FIXED ON THE ENGINE THIS MORNING? I KINDA BROKE IT AGAIN.
© Michael and Stefan Strasser - 374
THERE'S OIL ALL OVER THE PLACE. WOULD YOU MIND CLEANING IT UP? HERE, TAKE THIS RAG, IT'S ALREADY OILY.
SPLOT
www.chickenwingscomics.com
GEEZ, MR. GRUMPY! SOMEBODY'S IN A BAD MOOD TODAY.

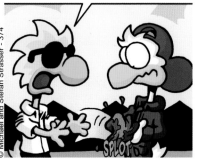

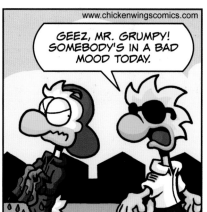

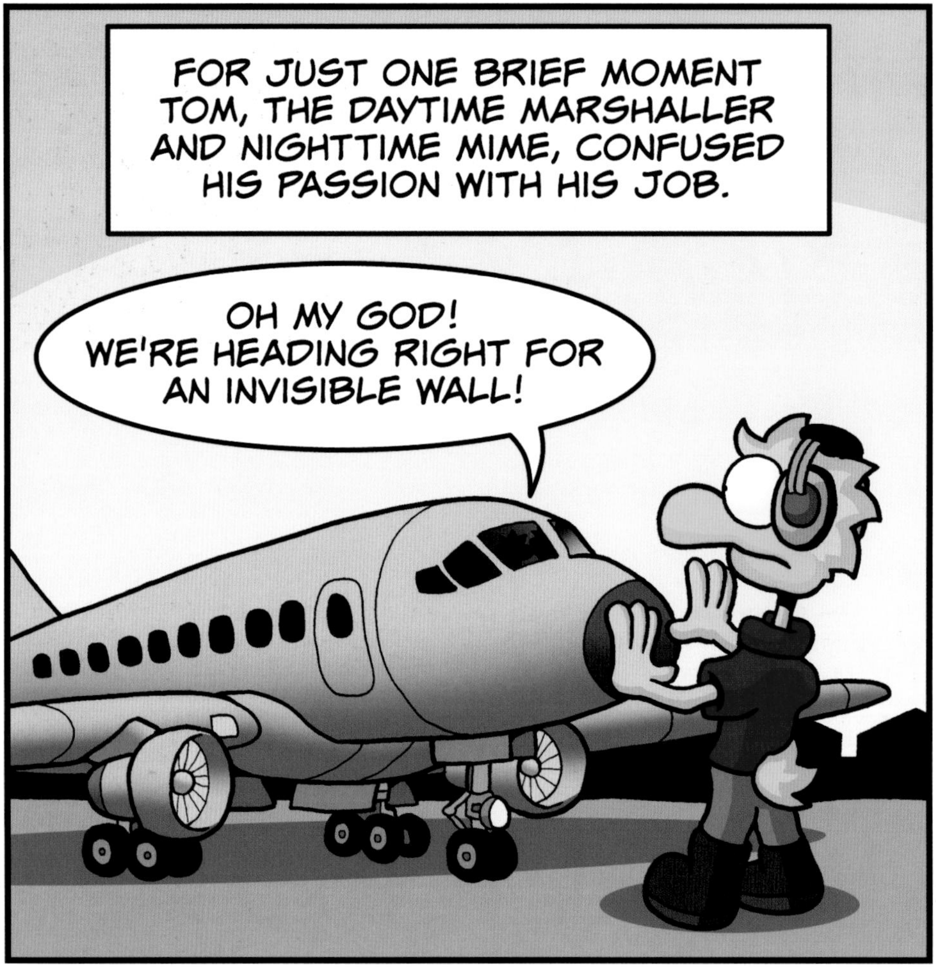
FOR JUST ONE BRIEF MOMENT TOM, THE DAYTIME MARSHALLER AND NIGHTTIME MIME, CONFUSED HIS PASSION WITH HIS JOB.
OH MY GOD! WE'RE HEADING RIGHT FOR AN INVISIBLE WALL!

WHAT? YOU BROKE THE FLAP LEVER AGAIN?!
YES, WELL, IT'S A DELICATE BALANCE OF NATURE, ISN'T IT?
HUH? WHAT?
© Michael and Stefan Strasser - 375
I BREAK 'EM YOU FIX 'EM!
SHOULDN'T THE BALANCE RATHER BE "YOU FLY THEM, I MANTAIN THEM"?
www.chickenwingscomics.com
WELL, OBVIOUSLY YOU DON'T UNDERSTAND ANYTHING ABOUT NATURE!

AW MAN. IT'S GOING TO TAKE ME ALL DAY TO FIX THAT!
REALLY? IT ONLY TOOK ME FIVE SECONDS TO BREAK IT!
© Michael and Stefan Strasser - 376
WHAT?! IT'S NOT MY FAULT I'M MORE EFFICIENT THAN YOU!
www.chickenwingscomics.com
AND MORE LEVEL-HEADED!

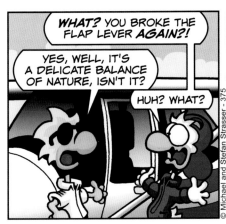

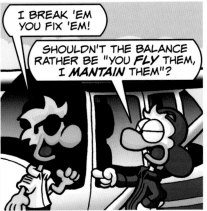

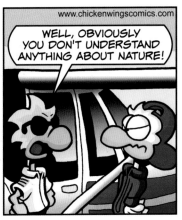

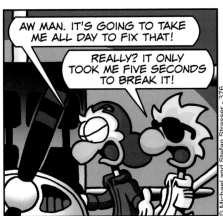

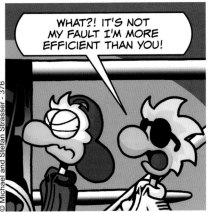

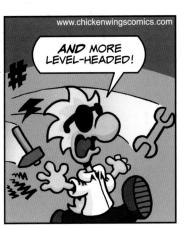

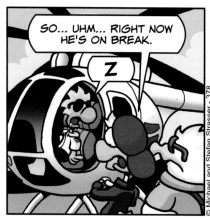

SO... UHM... RIGHT NOW HE'S ON BREAK.
Z
© Michael and Stefan Strasser - 378
www.chickenwingscomics.com
Z
AND NOW HE'S BACK ON DUTY.
Z
YOU'RE RIGHT. YOU CAN'T TELL THE DIFFERENCE!

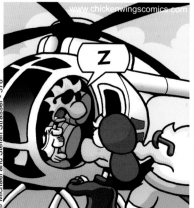

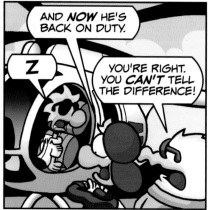

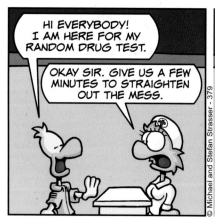

HI EVERYBODY! I AM HERE FOR MY RANDOM DRUG TEST.
OKAY SIR. GIVE US A FEW MINUTES TO STRAIGHTEN OUT THE MESS.
© Michael and Stefan Strasser - 379
MESS?
WELL, ONE OF YOU PILOTS JUST KNOCKED OVER THE TABLE WITH ALL THE SAMPLES AND WE HAVE PEE EVERYWHERE.
www.chickenwingscomics.com
CHUCK, IS THAT YOU?

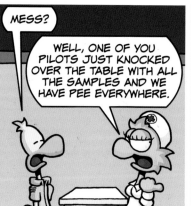

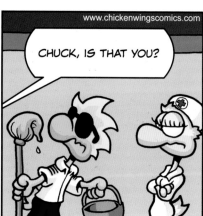

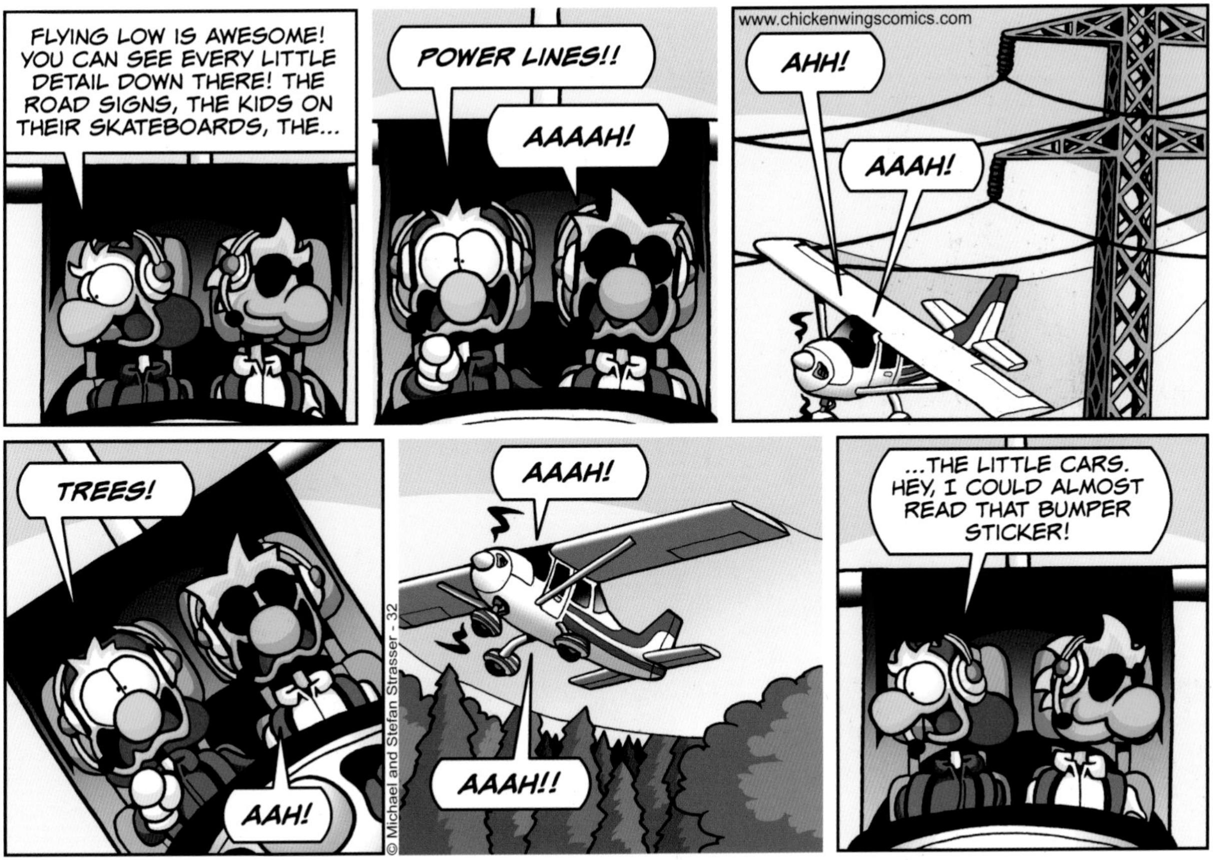
www.chickenwingscomics.com
FLYING LOW IS AWESOME! YOU CAN SEE EVERY LITTLE DETAIL DOWN THERE! THE ROAD SIGNS, THE KIDS ON THEIR SKATEBOARDS, THE...
POWER LINES!!
AAAAH!
AHH!
AAAH!
TREES!
AAH!
© Michael and Stefan Strasser - 32
AAAH!
AAAH!!
...THE LITTLE CARS. HEY, I COULD ALMOST READ THAT BUMPER STICKER!

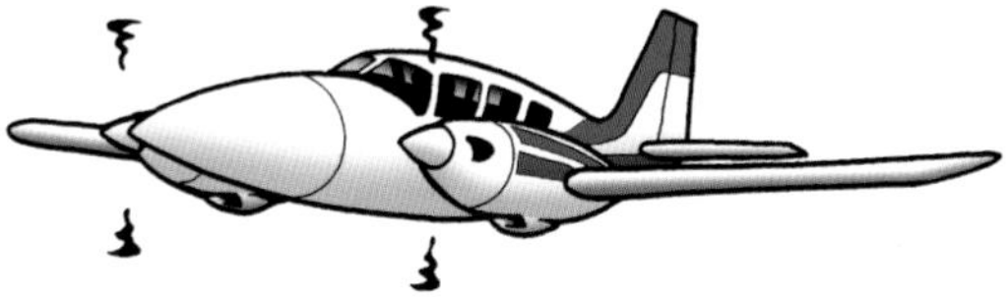

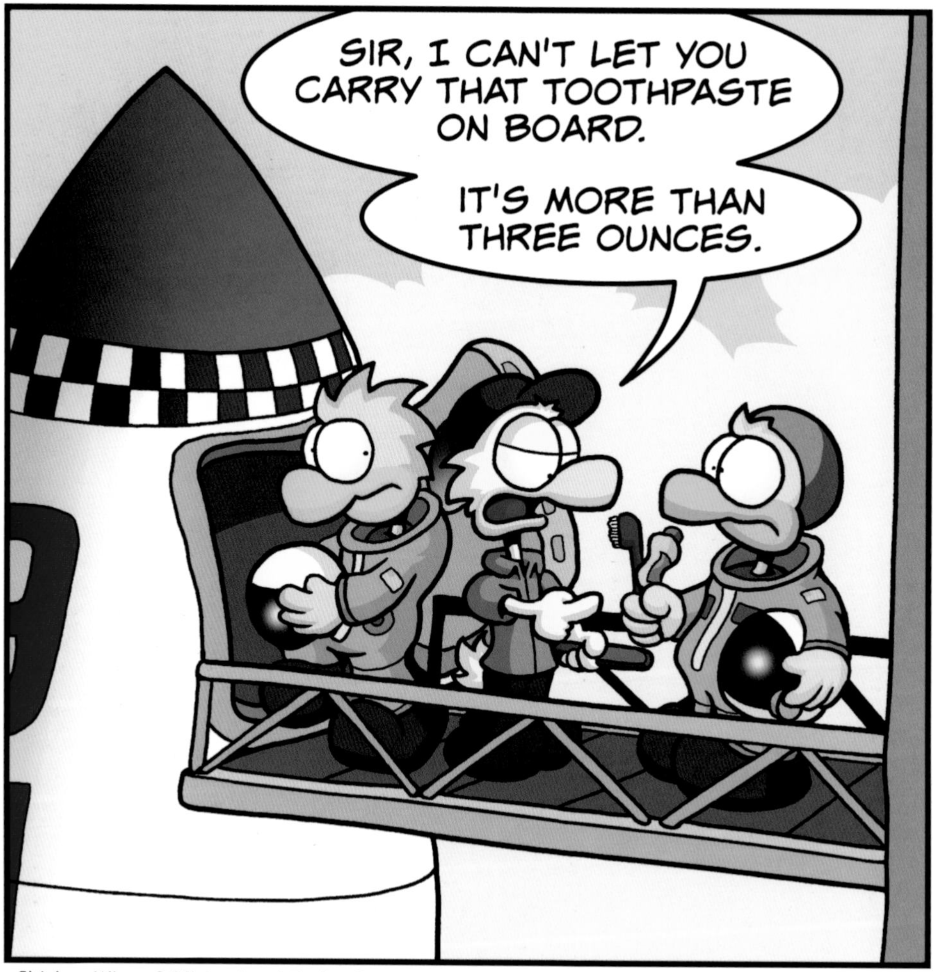
SIR, I CAN'T LET YOU CARRY THAT TOOTHPASTE ON BOARD.
IT'S MORE THAN THREE OUNCES.

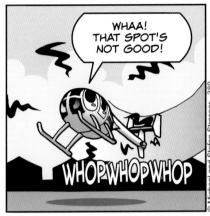

WHAA! THAT SPOT'S NOT GOOD!
WHOPWHOPWHOP
© Michael and Stefan Strasser - 380
COME ON! SET IT DOWN ALREADY!
NO, HERE'S NOT GOOD EITHER.
www.chickenwingscomics.com
AH, I GET IT! **THAT** IS WHAT THE 20 MINUTE FUEL RESERVE IS FOR? TO FIND THE PERFECT PARKING SPOT?
SHUT UP, JULIO!

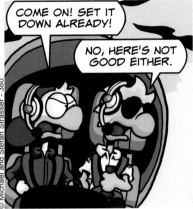

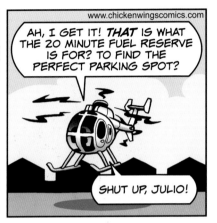

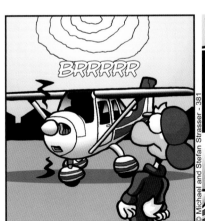

BRRRRR
© Michael and Stefan Strasser - 381
www.chickenwingscomics.com
SWOOSH
WE NEED AN AIR CONDITION IN THIS THING.
EEEWW!

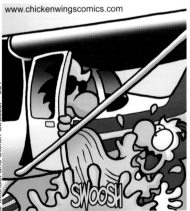

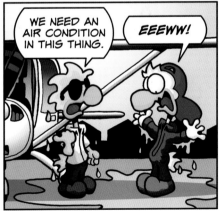

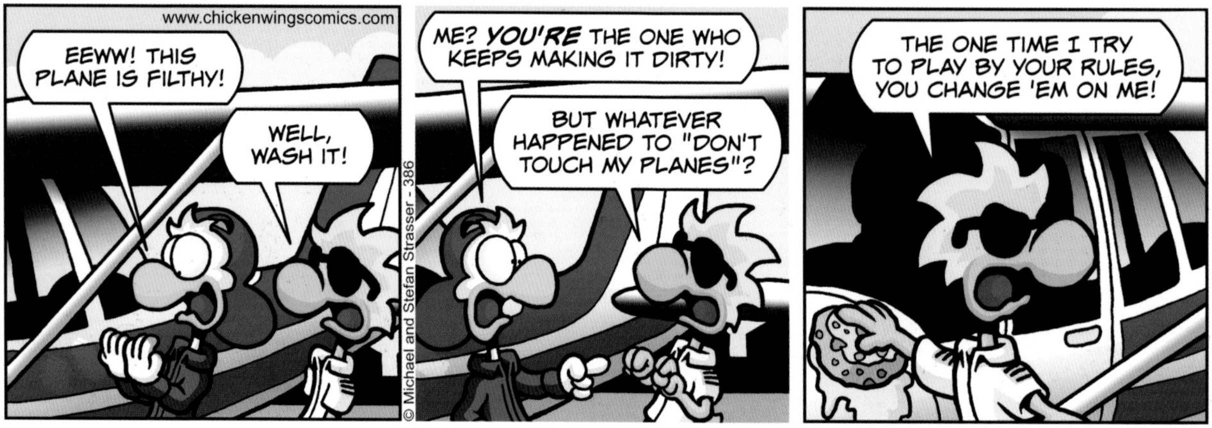
www.chickenwingscomics.com
EEWW! THIS PLANE IS FILTHY!
WELL, WASH IT!
© Michael and Stefan Strasser - 386
ME? YOU'RE THE ONE WHO KEEPS MAKING IT DIRTY!
BUT WHATEVER HAPPENED TO "DON'T TOUCH MY PLANES"?
THE ONE TIME I TRY TO PLAY BY YOUR RULES, YOU CHANGE 'EM ON ME!

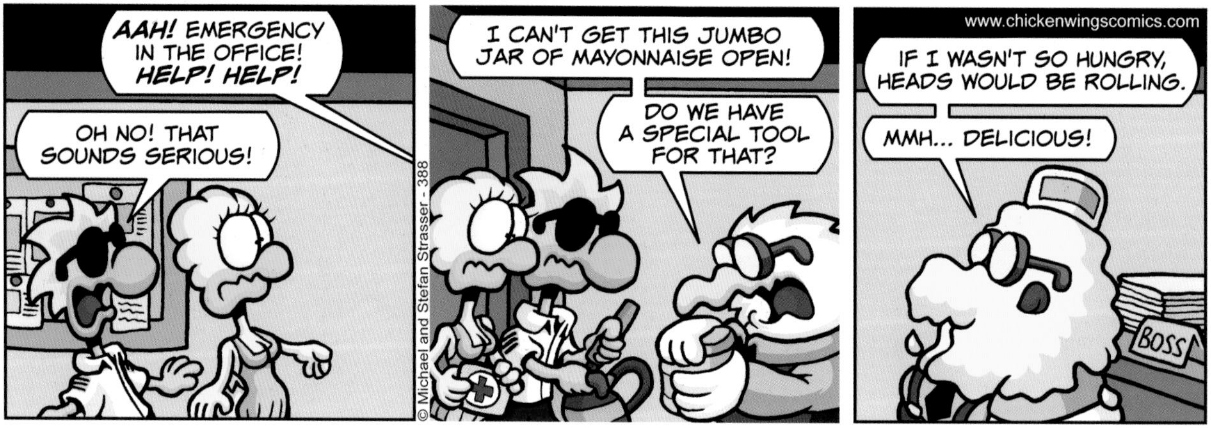
AAH! EMERGENCY IN THE OFFICE! HELP! HELP!
OH NO! THAT SOUNDS SERIOUS!
© Michael and Stefan Strasser - 388
I CAN'T GET THIS JUMBO JAR OF MAYONNAISE OPEN!
DO WE HAVE A SPECIAL TOOL FOR THAT?
www.chickenwingscomics.com
IF I WASN'T SO HUNGRY, HEADS WOULD BE ROLLING.
MMH... DELICIOUS!
BOSS

www.chickenwingscomics.com
HA! I LAUGH AT YOU STONE-AGE AVIATORS WITH YOUR VINTAGE GAS GUZZLERS!
OH YEAH, HAN SOLO? WHAT MAKES YOU SO SPECIAL?
© Michael and Stefan Strasser - 337
I BUILT MY OWN ELECTRIC POWERED AIRPLANE! IT'S THE WAY OF THE FUTURE, YOU KNOW?
THAT IS ACTUALLY QUITE IMPRESSIVE!
IT IS, ISN'T IT?
HOW FAR DOES IT GO?
WELL, SO FAR I HAVEN'T LEFT THE TRAFFIC PATTERN.
BUT I HAVE A LONGER EXTENSION CORD ON ORDER!

BOY, I JUST HAD THE WORST DAY! FIRST I DECIDED TO CLEAN THE BELLY OF THE PIPER. IT WAS DISGUSTING! THEN I LOOKED INSIDE THE TAIL AND FOUND NOT ONLY GRIME AND STUCK PULLEYS, BUT RATS!
© Michael and Stefan Strasser - 340
I HAD TO REMOVE THE RATS NEST AND CLEAN UP ALL THE POOP! IT WAS GROSS!
TRY TO BEAT THAT, LITTLE FLYBOY!
www.chickenwingscomics.com
I TRIED TO INSTALL VISTA ALL DAY.
EEW! YOU WIN!

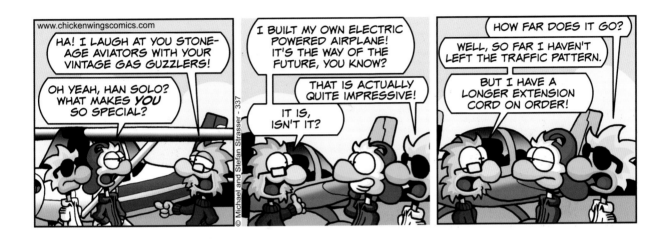

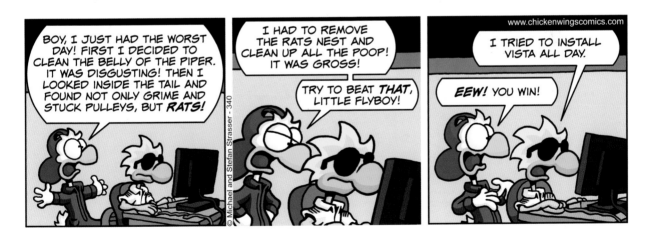

ARE YOU SERIOUS? YOU COULDN'T HAVE THOUGHT ABOUT THIS BEFORE WE PUT THE SUIT ON?
BUT I DIDN'T HAVE TO GO BACK THEN...

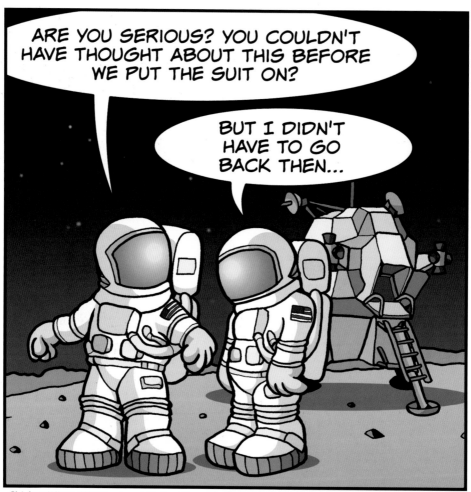

SO BECOMING AN ASTRONAUT IS MY MAIN GOAL. FLYING PLANES IS JUST A STEPPING STONE TO HONE MY SKILLS.
UNBELIEVABLE!
© Michael and Stefan Strasser - 389
OH YEAH, YOU CAN BELIEVE HIM! HE'S IN THE SPACE PROGRAM, ALRIGHT!
COOL!
www.chickenwingscomics.com
HIS CURRENT RANK IS SPACE CADET!
HAHAHA!

DO YOU WANT ME TO TOP HER OFF?
GOSH NO! ARE YOU MAD?
UEL
© Michael and Stefan Strasser - 390
JUST BRING HER UP TO 10%.
'CUZ OF THE FUEL PRICES, HUH?
www.chickenwingscomics.com
NO, BECAUSE I LIKE TO FLY HER AT A FUEL TO AIR RATIO OF 1:10!

BOY, PRICES REALLY HAVE GONE UP LATELY...
AVGAS PRICES
200 gal. .....your soul
160 gal. .....your firstborn son
120 gal. .....an arm and a leg
l. .....an arm
gal. .....your house
40 gal. .....a leg
20 gal. .....your car

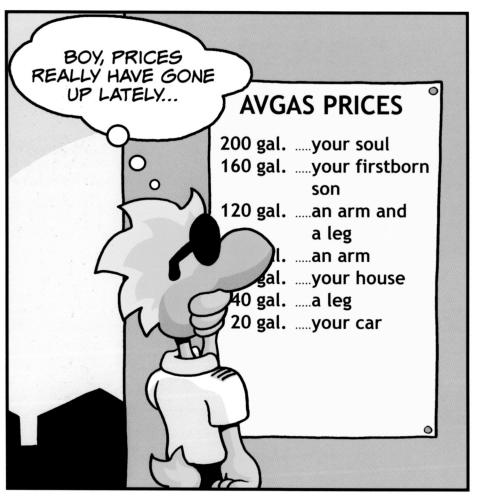

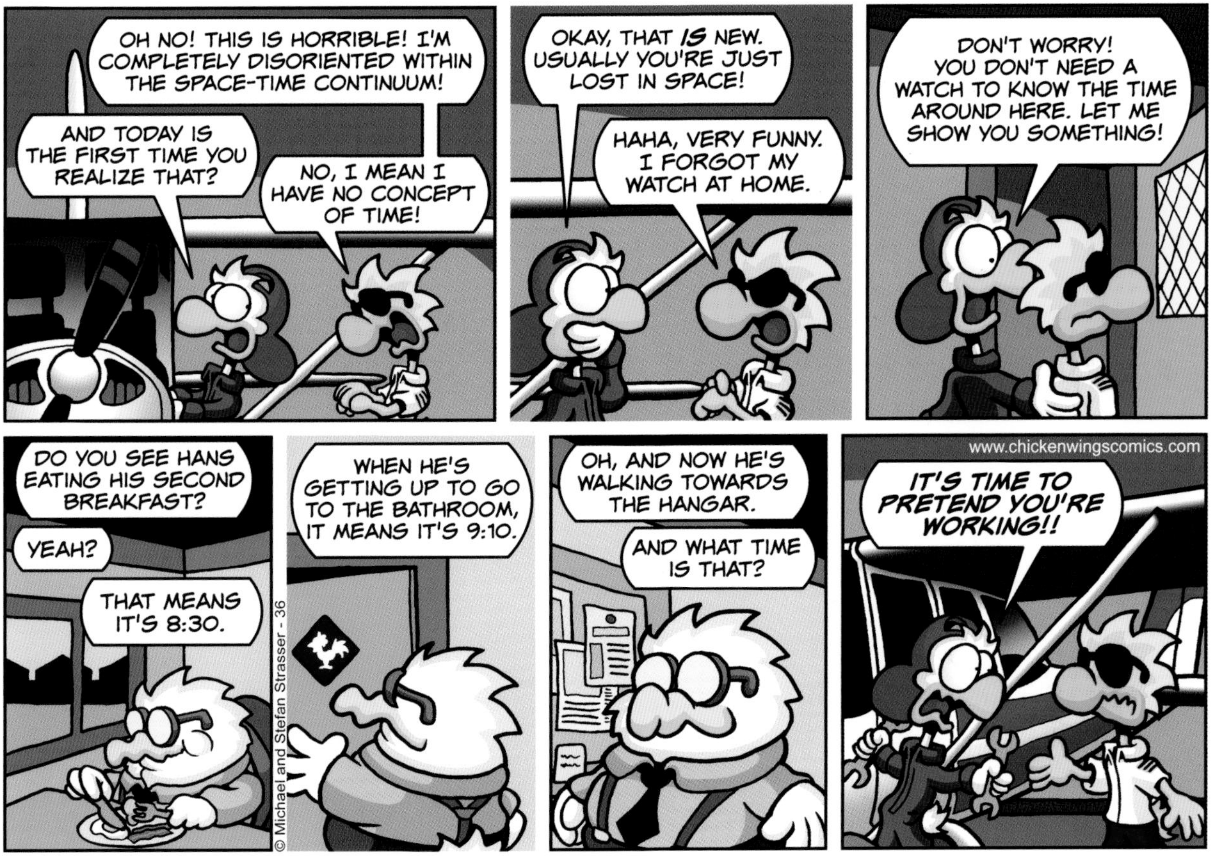
AND TODAY IS THE FIRST TIME YOU REALIZE THAT?
OH NO! THIS IS HORRIBLE! I'M COMPLETELY DISORIENTED WITHIN THE SPACE-TIME CONTINUUM!
NO, I MEAN I HAVE NO CONCEPT OF TIME!
OKAY, THAT *IS* NEW. USUALLY YOU'RE JUST LOST IN SPACE!
HAHA, VERY FUNNY. I FORGOT MY WATCH AT HOME.
DON'T WORRY! YOU DON'T NEED A WATCH TO KNOW THE TIME AROUND HERE. LET ME SHOW YOU SOMETHING!
DO YOU SEE HANS EATING HIS SECOND BREAKFAST?
YEAH?
THAT MEANS IT'S 8:30.
© Michael and Stefan Strasser - 36
WHEN HE'S GETTING UP TO GO TO THE BATHROOM, IT MEANS IT'S 9:10.
OH, AND NOW HE'S WALKING TOWARDS THE HANGAR.
AND WHAT TIME IS THAT?
www.chickenwingscomics.com
IT'S TIME TO PRETEND YOU'RE WORKING!!

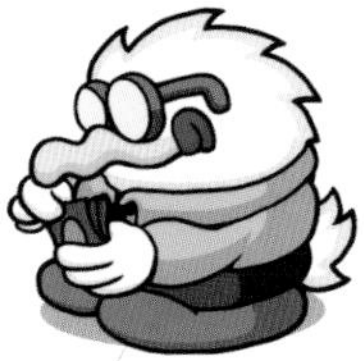

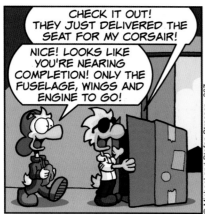

CHECK IT OUT! THEY JUST DELIVERED THE SEAT FOR MY CORSAIR!
NICE! LOOKS LIKE YOU'RE NEARING COMPLETION! ONLY THE FUSELAGE, WINGS AND ENGINE TO GO!
© Michael and Stefan Strasser - 267
HA! I AM UNTOUCHED BY YOUR MOCKERY, INFIDEL! I AM GONNA SIT IN THIS SEAT AS MUCH AS I CAN, SO I CAN GET USED TO IT!
AND? ALREADY USED TO IT?
GETTING THERE... CAN YOU HAND ME DOWN MY BURGER PLEASE?
www.chickenwingscomics.com

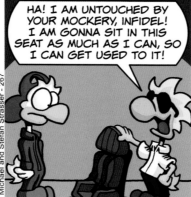

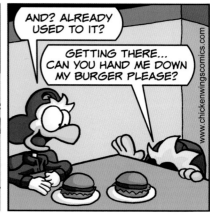

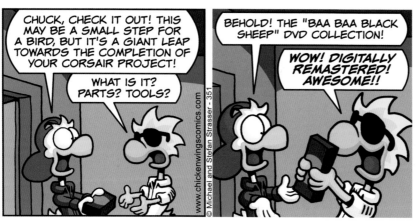

CHUCK, CHECK IT OUT! THIS MAY BE A SMALL STEP FOR A BIRD, BUT IT'S A GIANT LEAP TOWARDS THE COMPLETION OF YOUR CORSAIR PROJECT!
WHAT IS IT? PARTS? TOOLS?
www.chickenwingscomics.com
© Michael and Stefan Strasser - 351
BEHOLD! THE "BAA BAA BLACK SHEEP" DVD COLLECTION!
WOW! DIGITALLY REMASTERED! AWESOME!!
THANKS!
THIS SHOULD KEEP HIM OUT OF MY HANGAR FOR A COUPLE OF WEEKS AT LEAST... HEHEHE...
SWOOSH

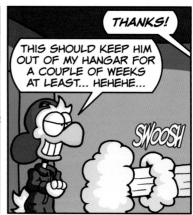

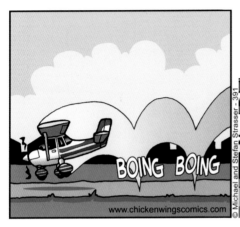

BOING BOING
www.chickenwingscomics.com
© Michael and Stefan Strasser - 391
OH BOY, I'M GOING TO HAVE TO CHECK THE LANDING GEAR AFTER THIS ONE. WHY CAN'T HE EVER PULL OFF A SMOOTH LANDING?
DID YOU JUST SAY SOMETHING?
YES, I SAID "SMOOTH LANDING!"
THANKS!

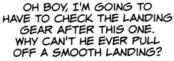

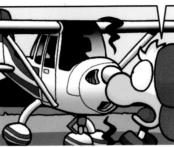

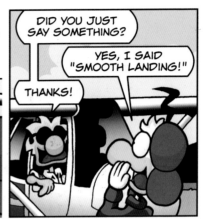

AH... DUCT TAPE! WHERE WOULD I BE WITHOUT YOU?
© Michael and Stefan Strasser - 392
JULIO! THE HANGAR DOOR DOESN'T LOCK AGAIN. YOU NEED TO FIX IT, PRONTO! BUT THIS TIME GET IT RIGHT!
www.chickenwingscomics.com
AH... DUCT TAPE!

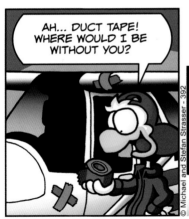

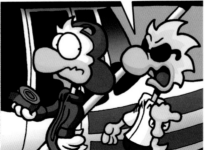

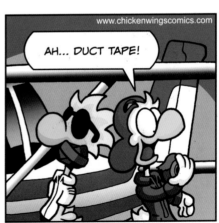

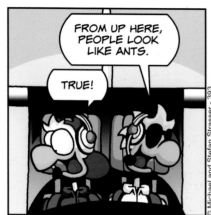

FROM UP HERE, PEOPLE LOOK LIKE ANTS.
TRUE!
© Michael and Stefan Strasser - 393
www.chickenwingscomics.com
ACTUALLY, MORE LIKE ARMY ANTS.
HUH?
UNKNOWN AIRCRAFT, YOU ARE IN RESTRICTED MILITARY AIRSPACE. TURN BACK IMMEDIATELY!
SIGH!

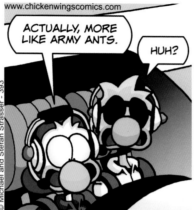

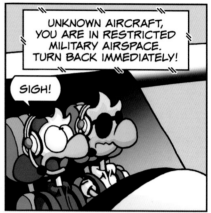

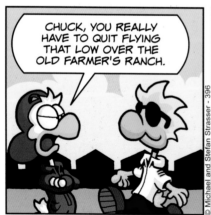

CHUCK, YOU REALLY HAVE TO QUIT FLYING THAT LOW OVER THE OLD FARMER'S RANCH.
© Michael and Stefan Strasser - 396
COME ON! IT'S SO MUCH FUN CHASING THE COWS!
THAT MAY BE THE CASE, BUT HE HAS A PRETTY BIG GUN AND IS A GOOD SHOT.
www.chickenwingscomics.com
HOW DO YOU KNOW?

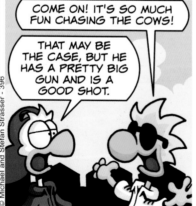

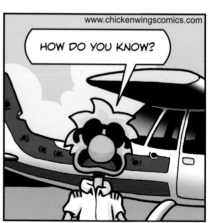

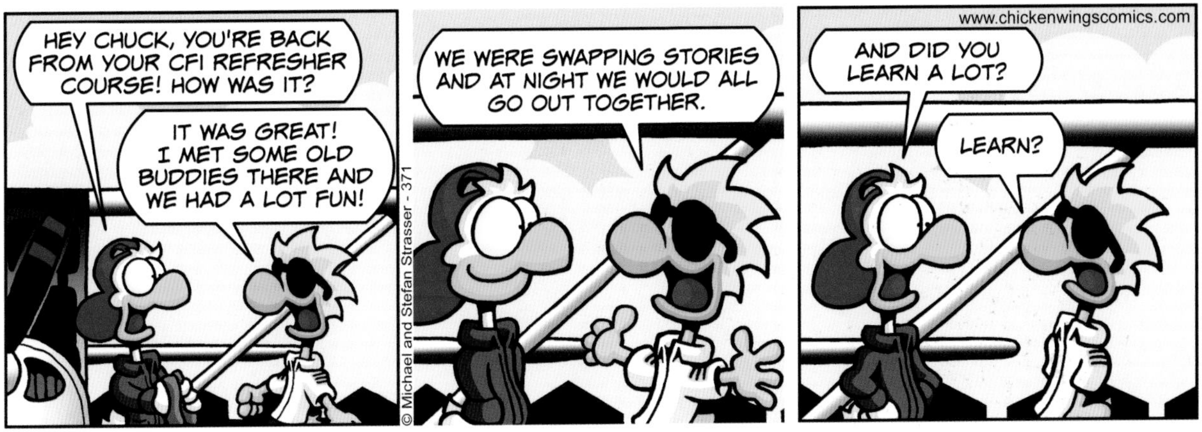
HEY CHUCK, YOU'RE BACK FROM YOUR CFI REFRESHER COURSE! HOW WAS IT?
IT WAS GREAT! I MET SOME OLD BUDDIES THERE AND WE HAD A LOT FUN!
© Michael and Stefan Strasser - 371
WE WERE SWAPPING STORIES AND AT NIGHT WE WOULD ALL GO OUT TOGETHER.
www.chickenwingscomics.com
AND DID YOU LEARN A LOT?
LEARN?

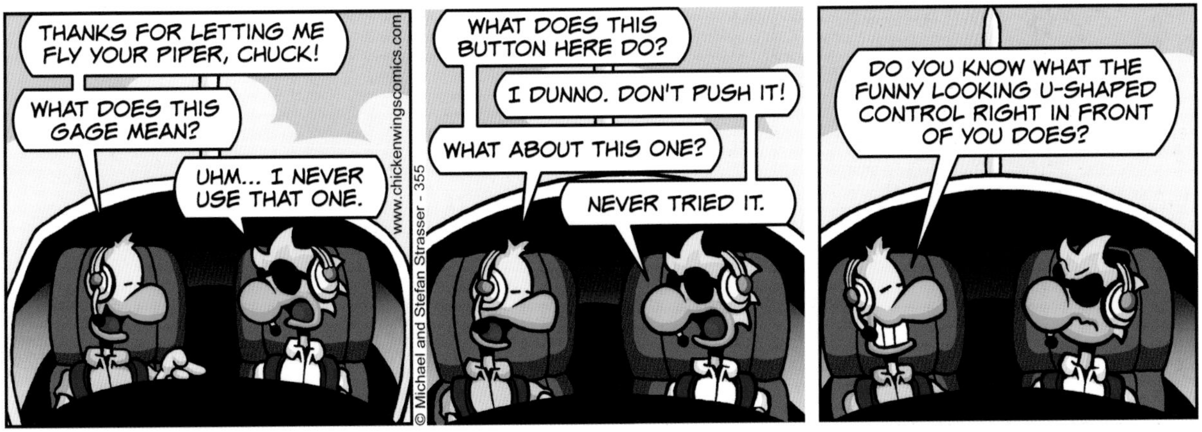
THANKS FOR LETTING ME FLY YOUR PIPER, CHUCK!
WHAT DOES THIS GAGE MEAN?
UHM... I NEVER USE THAT ONE.
www.chickenwingscomics.com
© Michael and Stefan Strasser - 355
WHAT DOES THIS BUTTON HERE DO?
I DUNNO. DON'T PUSH IT!
WHAT ABOUT THIS ONE?
NEVER TRIED IT.
DO YOU KNOW WHAT THE FUNNY LOOKING U-SHAPED CONTROL RIGHT IN FRONT OF YOU DOES?

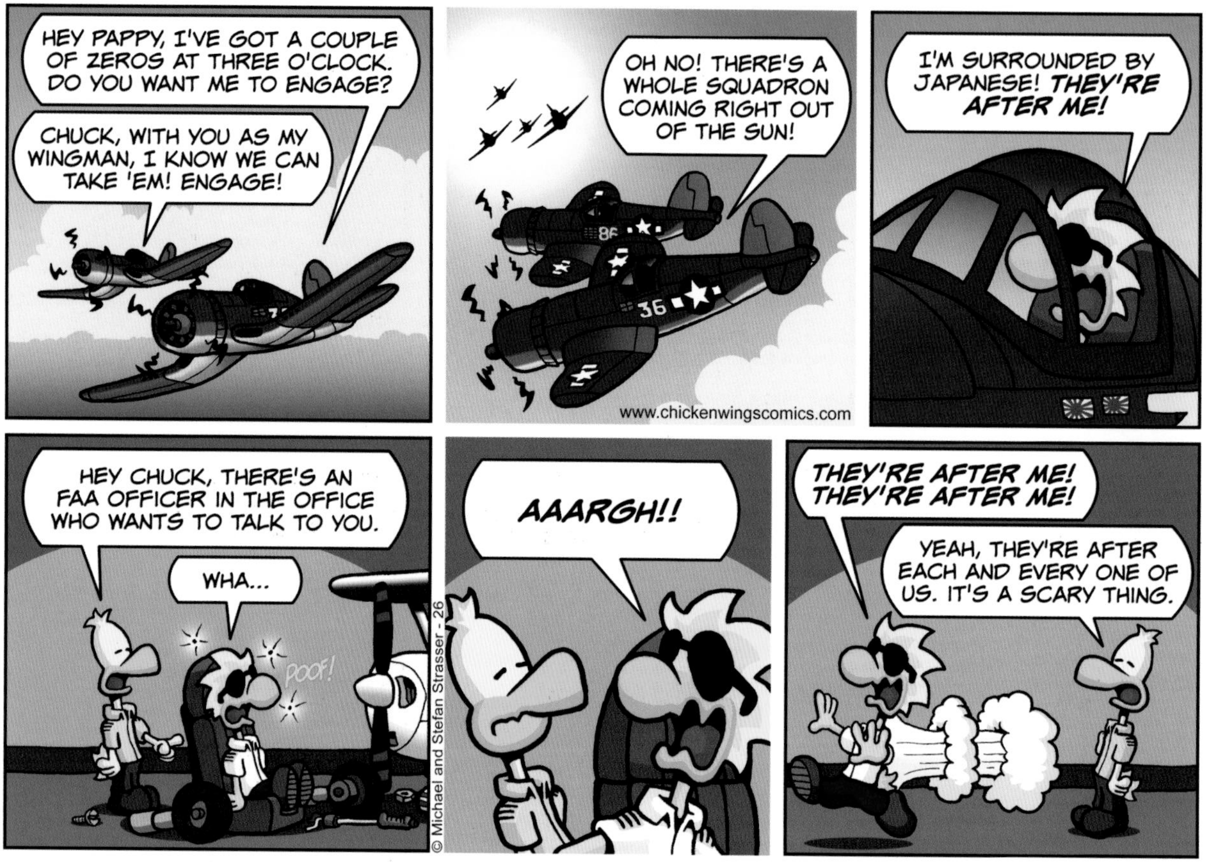
HEY PAPPY, I'VE GOT A COUPLE OF ZEROS AT THREE O'CLOCK. DO YOU WANT ME TO ENGAGE?
CHUCK, WITH YOU AS MY WINGMAN, I KNOW WE CAN TAKE 'EM! ENGAGE!
OH NO! THERE'S A WHOLE SQUADRON COMING RIGHT OUT OF THE SUN!
www.chickenwingscomics.com
I'M SURROUNDED BY JAPANESE! THEY'RE AFTER ME!
HEY CHUCK, THERE'S AN FAA OFFICER IN THE OFFICE WHO WANTS TO TALK TO YOU.
WHA...
POOF!
© Michael and Stefan Strasser - 26
AAARGH!!
THEY'RE AFTER ME! THEY'RE AFTER ME!
YEAH, THEY'RE AFTER EACH AND EVERY ONE OF US. IT'S A SCARY THING.

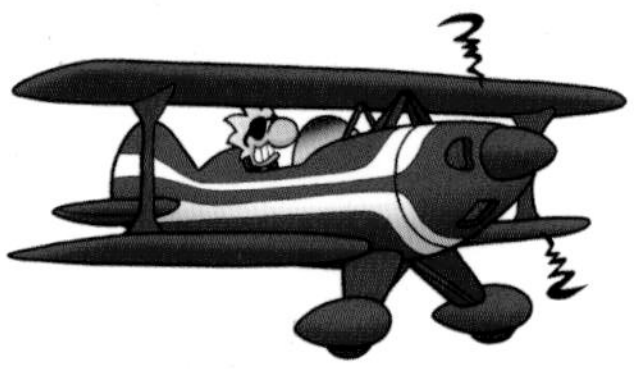

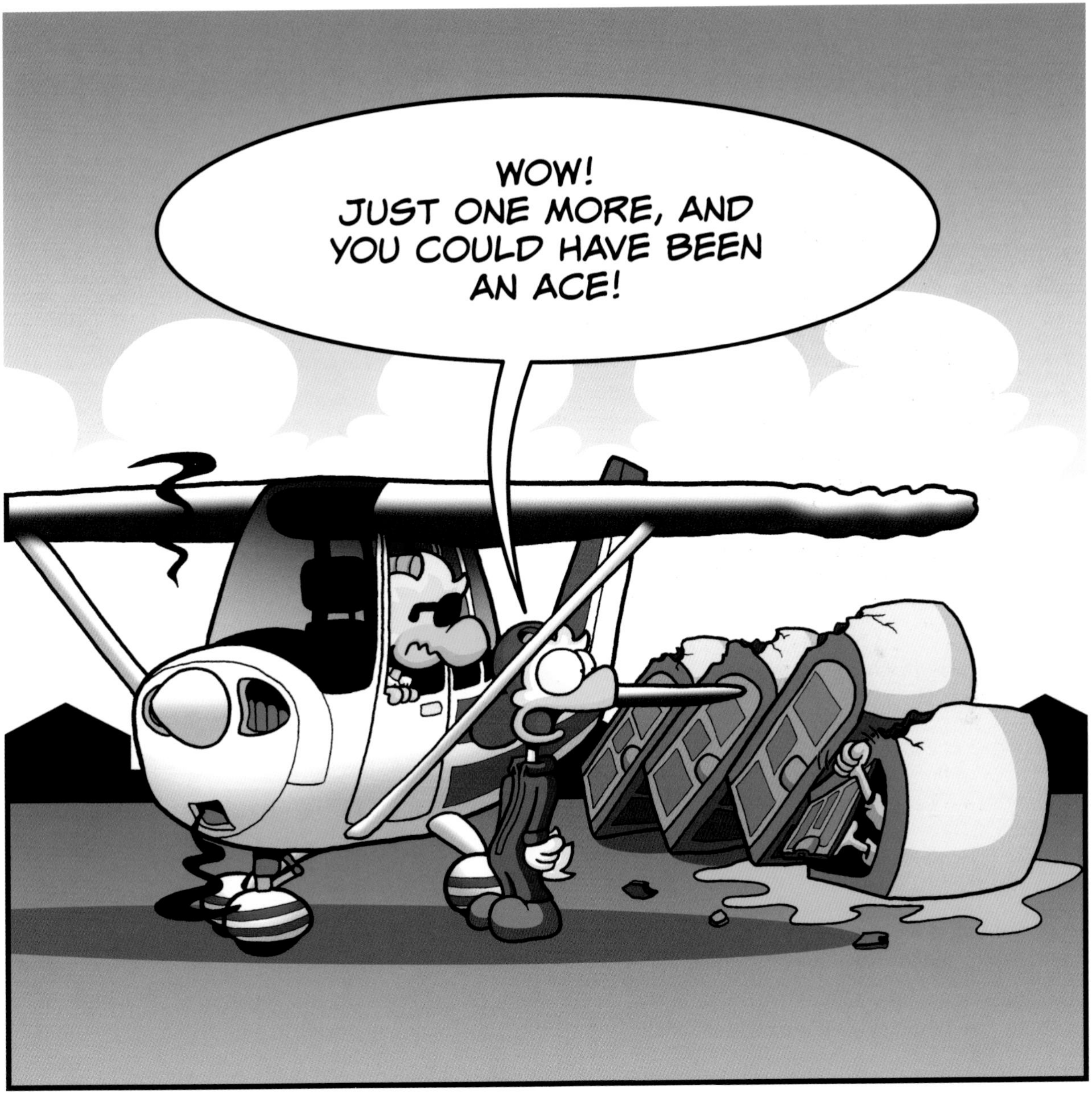
WOW!
JUST ONE MORE, AND
YOU COULD HAVE BEEN
AN ACE!

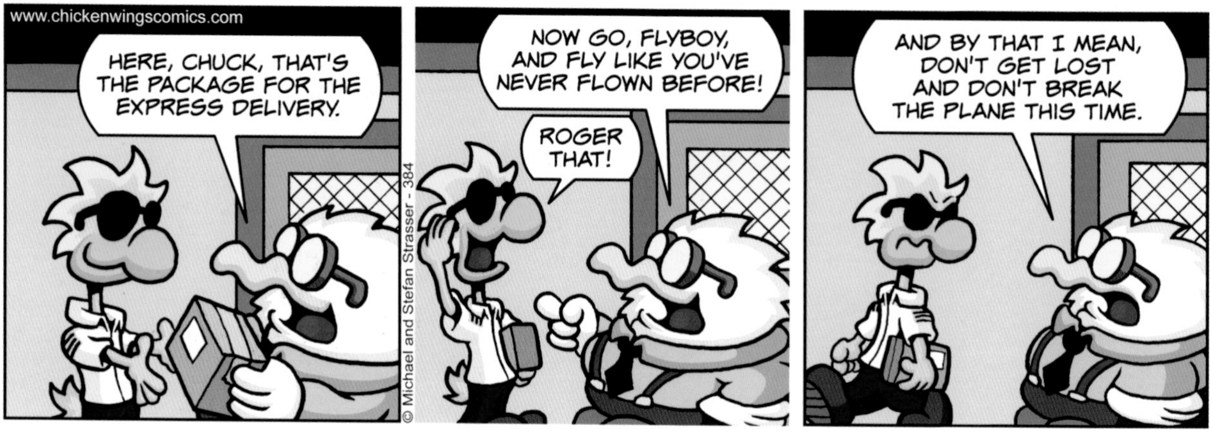
www.chickenwingscomics.com
HERE, CHUCK, THAT'S THE PACKAGE FOR THE EXPRESS DELIVERY.
© Michael and Stefan Strasser - 384
NOW GO, FLYBOY, AND FLY LIKE YOU'VE NEVER FLOWN BEFORE!
ROGER THAT!
AND BY THAT I MEAN, DON'T GET LOST AND DON'T BREAK THE PLANE THIS TIME.

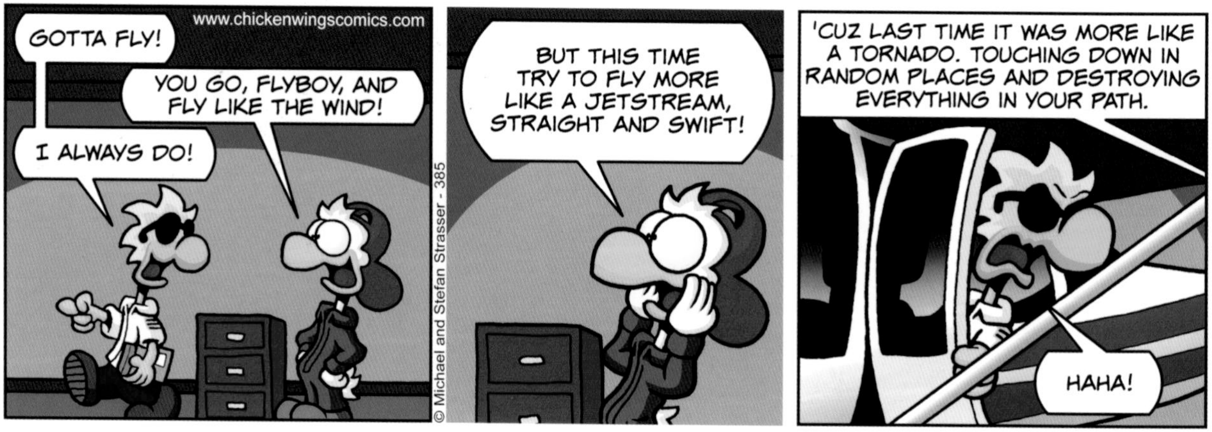
www.chickenwingscomics.com
GOTTA FLY!
YOU GO, FLYBOY, AND FLY LIKE THE WIND!
I ALWAYS DO!
© Michael and Stefan Strasser - 385
BUT THIS TIME TRY TO FLY MORE LIKE A JETSTREAM, STRAIGHT AND SWIFT!
'CUZ LAST TIME IT WAS MORE LIKE A TORNADO. TOUCHING DOWN IN RANDOM PLACES AND DESTROYING EVERYTHING IN YOUR PATH.
HAHA!

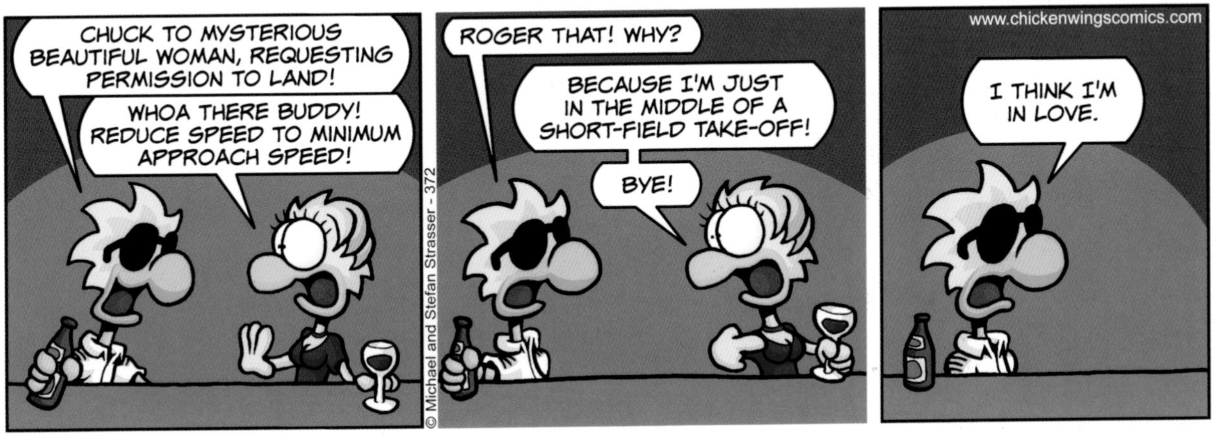
CHUCK TO MYSTERIOUS BEAUTIFUL WOMAN, REQUESTING PERMISSION TO LAND!
WHOA THERE BUDDY! REDUCE SPEED TO MINIMUM APPROACH SPEED!
© Michael and Stefan Strasser - 372
ROGER THAT! WHY?
BECAUSE I'M JUST IN THE MIDDLE OF A SHORT-FIELD TAKE-OFF!
BYE!
www.chickenwingscomics.com
I THINK I'M IN LOVE.

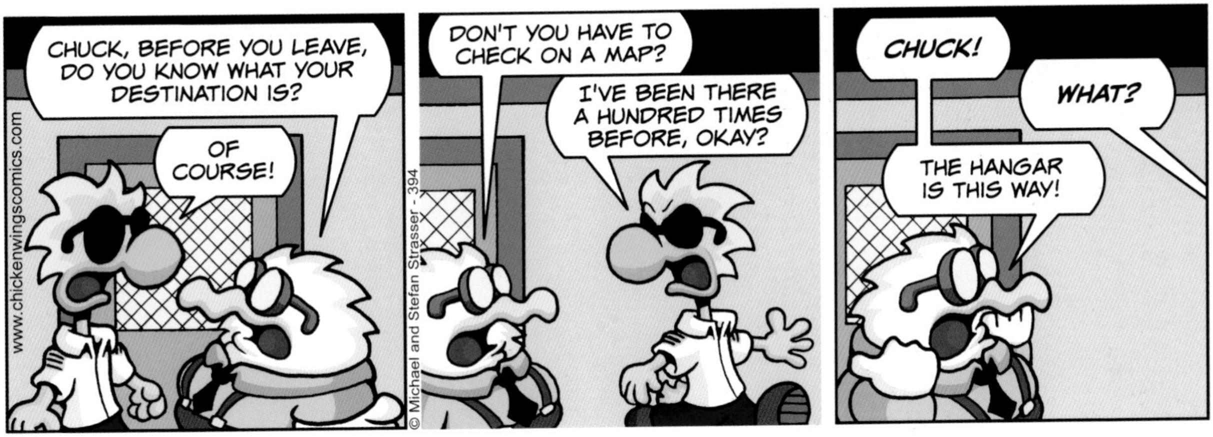
CHUCK, BEFORE YOU LEAVE, DO YOU KNOW WHAT YOUR DESTINATION IS?
OF COURSE!
www.chickenwingscomics.com
© Michael and Stefan Strasser - 394
DON'T YOU HAVE TO CHECK ON A MAP?
I'VE BEEN THERE A HUNDRED TIMES BEFORE, OKAY?
CHUCK!
WHAT?
THE HANGAR IS THIS WAY!

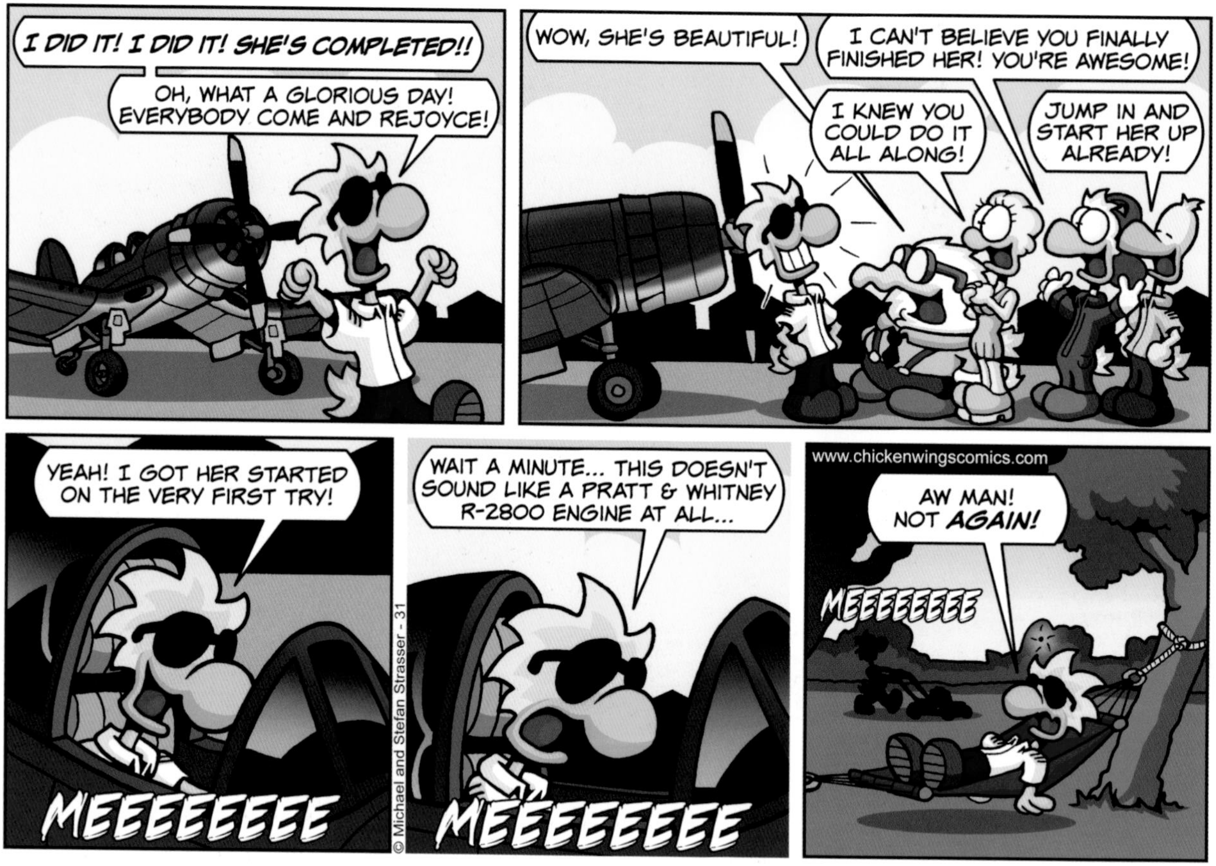
I DID IT! I DID IT! SHE'S COMPLETED!!
OH, WHAT A GLORIOUS DAY! EVERYBODY COME AND REJOYCE!
WOW, SHE'S BEAUTIFUL!
I CAN'T BELIEVE YOU FINALLY FINISHED HER! YOU'RE AWESOME!
I KNEW YOU COULD DO IT ALL ALONG!
JUMP IN AND START HER UP ALREADY!
YEAH! I GOT HER STARTED ON THE VERY FIRST TRY!
MEEEEEEEEE
© Michael and Stefan Strasser - 31
WAIT A MINUTE... THIS DOESN'T SOUND LIKE A PRATT & WHITNEY R-2800 ENGINE AT ALL...
MEEEEEEEEE
www.chickenwingscomics.com
AW MAN! NOT AGAIN!
MEEEEEEEE

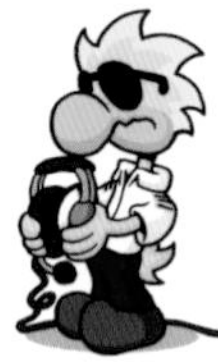

Meet the Roost Air Crew!

Chuck is bright, colorful and full of ambition. He flies everything and anything, likes to tell stories, wears his sunglasses all the time, has a big watch and a big mouth. Like the the typical pilot, he is a womanizer, or rather a "chickenizer", but he always ends up alone thanks to his inability to think before he speaks. He is an optimistic and positive character with a can-do-attitude that even extends to all the things he can't do. In his mind he's a virtuous and dauntless king of the skies. In reality, he only made it to chief pilot by being the company's only pilot on staff!

Julio is a really great guy. He is the typical aircraft mechanic who can fix everything from a helicopter turbine engine to the coffee machine in the office. He doesn't talk too much and doesn't really like pilots a lot. They tend to break "his" planes and never treat them the way he would like. His nickname is "Sparks", which seems to have originated from an unlucky hand with electricity, so he's not very proud of it.

Sally is always motivated and in high spirits, but unfortunately aviation seems to be sort of a foreign language to her. Being the only woman in this company and working in a male-dominated industry is not always easy, even more so when you're all thumbs with technical stuff. But she makes up for that with her character. And because she can make some killer coffee that can keep pilots awake for two nights in a row, and she's the only one who has at least a rudimental overview of the paperwork, she is indispensable to Roost Air.

Hans inherited the company from his uncle and used to run a yogurt factory before. But seriously, there can't be that much difference between yogurt and airplanes, right? He has a slight German accent which he can't always hide and he has little clue of what is really going on. It almost seems like his resourceful management strategies are the main cause of things going wrong and turning complicated. Sounds familiar, you say?

Nobu is the pilot from the company next door. He is Japanese but has been living in the US long enough to really master the language and to get used to a Roost-Air style of corporate culture. Being a professional pilot too, he is one of the few who can relate to Chuck. But he also rarely misses an opportunity to poke fun at him. His full name is Nobutada Yakitori, but since nobody can pronounce it right, they call him Nobu.

Jason is Chuck's flight student. He is very interested in everything related to aviation and has serious difficulties to hold his curiosity in check. While Sally and Hans love him, because he owns a chocolate factory, and Chuck can usually endure Jasons inquisitive manner, he often drives Julio crazy with his drumfire of questions.

Alex is a private pilot and owns her own Pitts Special aerobatic plane. She likes to keep it in Roost-Air's hangar and has Julio help her with the maintenance. Alex is a really cool "chick" that has no problems hanging with the boys, except maybe one of them. That one is Chuck, which you probably guessed. He has a major crush on her as well as her airplane, but keeps getting shot down hard at every approach he makes. His chances of ever flying that beautiful yellow biplane are probably zero.

Ray is the mechanic from the FBO next door and works together with Nobu. He is a pretty mellow duck from the south and there doesn't seem to be much he gets excited over. He is Julios partner in crime and shoulder to lean and cry on when it comes to mechanical questions or issues with his pilot.

Captain Ed is Chuck's uncle and also a pilot. But that's where the similarities end. He works as a captain for a major airline but is often burdened with straightening out the mess at Roost Air, trying to keep his nephew on the right track. Unlike Chuck he is known for his experience and his calm and positive manner.

ENCYCLOPEDIA

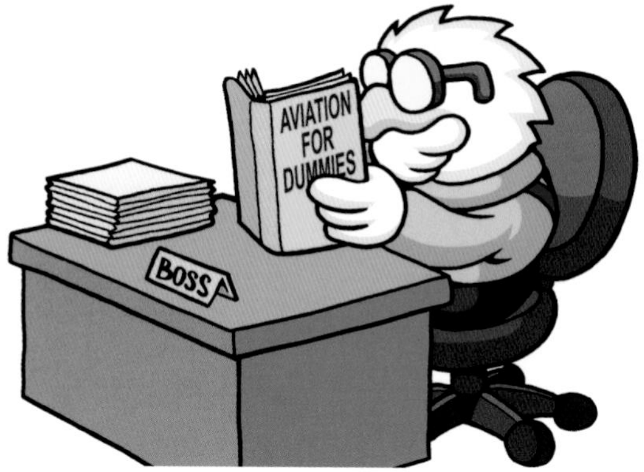
AVIATION
FOR
DUMMIES
BOSS

PILOT LINGO EXPLAINED

...a quick study guide for the non-aviator

$100 Hamburger When one buys a plane for personal use he or she might one day run out of "missions". If this occurs it has been common practice to find nice airport restaurants around the country side to justify the occasional Sunday trip. This will exercise the aircraft to keep it from becoming a hangar queen and by the time you fly to a restaurant have your burger and fly back in your own plane the meal will probably cost, well you guessed it, right around $100. (Actual cost and participation may vary depending on country and aircraft size).

100 Hour Inspection Every registered aircraft must be on some sort of maintenance schedule. The small planes Chuck flies usually have to be inspected after every 100 flight hours. (Imagine your car being inspected that often....pfew....)

Cessna 172 Little private piston engine plane, the one you see buzzing around at pretty much every airport. It's a good trainer too and therefore very common.

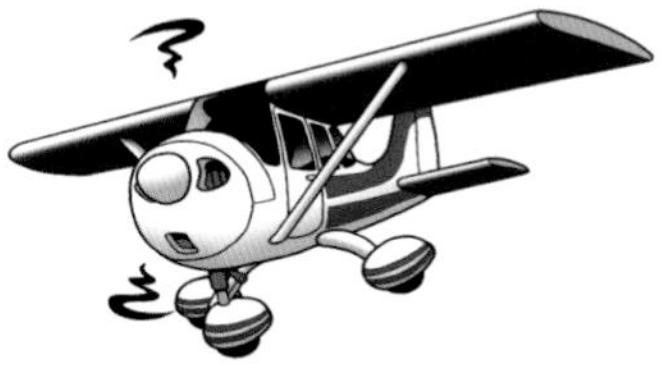

CFI CFI stands for "Certified Flight Instructor". To this day we have no idea how Chuck got certified and who in the world signed him off. But we are looking for that guy, seriously.

CG CG stands for "Center of Gravity". It's important to know because a plane can have some very funny flight characteristics or may not fly at all if the CG limits are exceeded (e.g. if Hans sits too far in the back of the plane).

Checkride A checkride is kind of like your final exam in school. After you are done with your flight training you have to take a knowledge test with an FAA examiner. Part of it is theoretical knowledge and if you can pass that part you go out and fly with him or her. Once he or she signs you off you can call yourself a certified pilot that same day. Commercial pilots also have recurring checkrides to make sure they still know what's going on.

Density Altitude Density Altitude is a theoretical value which is computed from existing temperature, and is an important factor in determining aircraft performance. When you go up in altitude, the air gets thinner and the aircraft has to work harder to keep flying since engine power output and aerodynamic lift all decrease. The air also gets thinner when the temperature increases. Now imagine a hot day at high altitude. The aircraft might be flying at 4,000ft for example but because it's warmer than normal (or standard) at that altitude, the aircraft "thinks" it's flying at 6,000ft.

DME DME stands for "Distance Measuring Equipment". It is an instrument that is able to tell you the distance to a certain point of reference (a VOR beacon). It is almost outdated nowadays because it is getting replaced with the much more accurate GPS technology.

F4-U Corsair The Vaught Corsair's most unique feature was the "bent" wing, the result of a marriage between the most powerful engine ever installed in a piston-engined fighter and one of the biggest propellers in the world. It vaught, oops-I-mean, fought, in the Pacific during WWII and we are both really big fans of this plane. Watching "Baa Baa Black Sheep" growing up has greatly influenced our young minds and might have contributed to the conception of Chicken Wings.

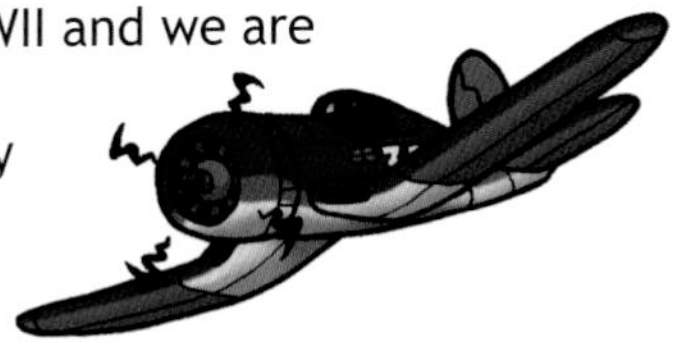

FAA Federal Aviation Administration or as pilots call them "the feds".

FBO FBO stands for Fixed-Base Operation. It's an aviation business that serves the general aviation industry with items such as fuel, fuel services, catering and customs.

FOD	Foreign Object Damage is damage caused by (usually and hopefully small) objects that get sucked in by the props or rotors and then hit and damage fan blades, engines, intakes, the airframe, or the props or rotors themselves.
IFR (actual IFR)	Instrument Flight Rules. It means that you're not allowed to play any instrument, even as small as a harmonica, while piloting an aircraft. Just kidding! Instrument Flight Rules are a huge set of regulations you have to abide by while flying under instruments only. It allows you to go through clouds and fog without having to look outside using and trusting your flight instruments. Obviously when there are a bunch of planes in the air without being able to see each other, the FAA needs to make sure everybody is on the same page. It takes a lot of training to learn how to fly IFR and you have to get a rating before you are allowed to go out and do it by yourself. When they say "actual IFR" it means that you're not only flying under IFR but that you are actually in the clouds with no ground reference and nothing but gray around you.
Magneto	The ignition system of an aircraft is usually powered by two magnetos that create the voltage spike for the spark plugs. That way the engine keeps running even if the battery or the alternator fails.
Maintenance Flight	A maintenance flight is a non-revenue flight after the aircraft was fixed or maintained to make sure all systems work correctly. In many instances the mechanic will go with the pilot to perform his tests since he knows what he is looking at. Julio always goes with Chuck because he just doesn't trust him.
NOTAM	NOTAM is short for "Notice to Airmen". It is a nifty information system that tells pilots about recent changes to any component in the National Airspace system. Let's say a runway get's repaved. The airport would put out a NOTAM that tells everybody when, why, where, and that kind of stuff. The pilot will (should) check for all NOTAMS concerning his route of flight and destination during his preflight planning.
NTSB	NTSB stands for "National Transportation Safety Board". One of their many jobs is to investigate aircraft accidents. Your goal as a pilot should be never to run into these guys unless it is at a bar. Of course our friend Chuck is well known amongst the NTSB crowd.

Piper Aztec The Piper Aztec, or what Chuck and Julio always refer to simply as "the Piper", is a small twin engine airplane build by Piper Aircraft. It has the wing on the bottom and one engine on each side.

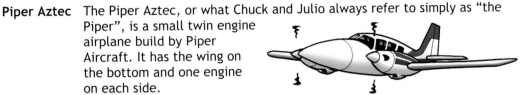

Pitot Tube A Pitot Tube is the sensor for measuring the airspeed. It is a little tube that sticks out of the airplane oriented into the direction of flight and looks like a forward facing spike. When the aircraft flies, air pressure builds up inside the pitot tube and this pressure is directly related to how fast the plane is going.

POI POI stands for "Principal Operations Inspector". Mortals and private pilots usually will never have to deal with these guys. They work for the FAA and inspect air carrier and charter operations and represent the link between the aviation companies chief pilots and Directors of Operations and the "feds".

Skyhawk See "Cessna 172".

Stall Warning Horn A stall warning horn is a system that warns the pilot before the plane "stalls" so he can react. "Stalling" means the airstream above the wing rips from the surface, so the wing suddenly has no lift and the airplane literally falls out of the sky. This can happen when the plane is going too slow or it's climbing with too steep of an angle. You can recover from a stall by building up speed again, but that takes altitude which you don't have on final approach for example, hence the warning system. If you want to know more about this you should get youself a flying handbook instead of a comic book with chickens flying airplanes.

Tachgage A tachgage or tachometer in aviation is an instrument that measures and indicates the revolutions per unit of time of a rotating mechanism. On Chucks little airplane it measures how fast his engine is turning, just like the rpm gage in a car. But a tachgage could also measure rotor rpm in a helicopter for example, and so on.

TFR TFR stands for "Temporary Flight Restriction". Whenever there is a specific hazard or condition the FAA may impose restrictions to protect persons or properties on the surface or in the air. What this fancy sentence means is that whenever there is a wildfire, or toxic spill, volcanic eruption, aircraft hijacking, a president in town, or a similar calamity (pun intended!), the FAA can create an area in which flight restrictions apply. And this again means they like to keep sightseeing airplanes and pilots like Chuck out of the area where "real professionals" do their job. Firefighting pilots operating within the TFR do not appreciate a confused "Chuck" crossing their path right when they are turning in and diving down for their dangerous water drop for example...

Top Gun Come on! Seriously? If you don't know what Top Gun is, you totally bought the wrong book!

Traffic Pattern A traffic pattern is the flight path planes have to follow when landing at or taking off from an airport. It helps keeping everybody on the same page so the planes don't run into each other when they curve in for their landing. At small airports you can often see little planes flying the same rectangular pattern while practicing their takeoffs and landings.

VOR VOR is another acronym (surprised?) and stands for "VHF Omni directional Range". Now, without going into what all that means, let's just say it's a navigational aid (thingy on the ground) that sends out a signal and, combined with an instrument in the cockpit, can help the pilot figure out where he is and where he is going. That is only if the pilot knows how to use it, which Chuck obviously doesn't.

Zulu Time Zulu Time is the international standardized time in aviation (not only in aviation) and is the same no matter where on the globe you happen to be. Obviously if you fly a plane through several time zones you can't have everybody constantly do the math or all the pilots would be as confused as Chuck all the time. Weather information, flight plans, tower information, everything runs of Zulu time in aviation. And quite frankly, if you fly a plane from LA to Frankfurt, who cares what the local time in Idaho is, right?!
The name "Zulu Time" was chosen because a) it sounds cool and b) pilots like to come up with abbreviations and terms that nobody else understands.(The name really derives from Zulu being the word for "Z" in the NATO phonetic alphabet, and Zulu Time is the same as UTC, Coordinated Universal Time)

Disclaimer: This encyclopedia is intended as a reference only. May not be used in actual pilot instruction. Incorporating this material in lesson plans may result in uncontrollable laughter and the student ending up aviationally challenged like Chuck.

Michael Strasser lives and works in California as an accomplished helicopter pilot. After gathering many years of varied experience in aviation as a commercial pilot, aircraft mechanic, and flight instructor, Mike is now the chief pilot for a helicopter company and heavily involved in fighting the nation's wildland fires. You can guess where most of the ideas for Chicken Wings come from.

Stefan Strasser lives and works in Vienna, Austria as an experienced cartoon artist and illustrator. He actually has obtained what one could call a "decent education" (a masters degree in international trade), but rather opted for drawing instead of finding a *real* job. Chicken Wings is now his most important project, but you can find his work in various other magazines and newsletters.